"With this book, Alexandra Barratt completes her translation of all the extant writings attributed to Gertrud of Helfta. Working from digital images of the recently discovered Leipzig Codex MS 827, Barratt provides us with a clear and accessible English translation of the manuscript even before a Latin edition has been published. Scholars of Gertrud will appreciate Barratt's careful and fastidious work with the manuscript. Her translation notes in bold all material that is unique to the Leipzig manuscript, which is not found in the previous translation of Gertrud's *Legatus Divinae Pietatis*, and her introduction highlights new information gained about Getrud and the Helfta community."

— Ella L. Johnson, PhD, St. Ambrose University, Davenport, Iowa

"In *The Memorial of the Abundance of the Divine Sweetness*, Alexandra Barratt, provides an excellent translation of what seems to be an earlier, more intimate, less guarded version of Gertrud the Great's, *The Herald of God's Loving-Kindness,* which Barratt previously translated. Working directly from the only known and recently discovered manuscript of the *Memorial*, she provides a helpful introduction and annotates its sources. To paraphrase Gertrude, those who read this book with intent devotion will surely, by God's grace, find something profitable."

— Fr. Hugh Feiss, OSB

CISTERCIAN FATHERS SERIES: NUMBER EIGHTY-EIGHT

Gertrud the Great of Helfta

The Memorial of the Abundance of the Divine Sweetness

Translated and Introduced by
Alexandra Barratt

from the text in Leipzig,
Universitätsbibliothek MS 827

Cistercian Publications
www.cistercianpublications.org

LITURGICAL PRESS
Collegeville, Minnesota
www.litpress.org

A Cistercian Publications title published by Liturgical Press

Cistercian Publications
Editorial Offices
161 Grosvenor Street
Athens, Ohio 45701
www.cistercianpublications.org

Biblical citations are based on the *Holy Bible: Douay Rheims Version* (Baltimore: John Murphy, 1899, repr. Rockford, Illinois: Tan, 1971), with minimal modernization. All rights reserved.

1	2	3	4	5	6	7	8	9

Library of Congress Cataloging-in-Publication Data

Names: Gertrude, the Great, Saint, 1256–1302, author. | Barratt, Alexandra, translator.
Title: The memorial of the abundance of the divine sweetness / Gertrud the Great of Helfta ; translated and introduced by Alexandra Barratt from the text in Leipzig, Universitätsbibliothek MS 827.
Other titles: Memorialis abundantiae divinae pietatis. English
Description: Collegeville, Minnesota : Cistercian Publications, Liturgical Press, 2022. | Series: Cistercian Fathers series, number eighty-eight | Includes index. | Summary: "A translation of an early fourteenth-century manuscript held at the University of Leipzig, Germany, written by Gertrud the Great of Helfta"—Provided by publisher.
Identifiers: LCCN 2022011907 (print) | LCCN 2022011908 (ebook) | ISBN 9780879071387 (paperback) | ISBN 9780879071394 (epub) | ISBN 9780879071394 (pdf) | ISBN 9780879076276 (pdf)
Subjects: LCSH: Spirituality—Catholic Church. | Spiritual life—Catholic Church. | Mysticism. | BISAC: RELIGION / Monasticism | RELIGION / Christianity / Catholic
Classification: LCC BX2350.65 .G4713 2022 (print) | LCC BX2350.65 (ebook) | DDC 248.4/82—dc23/eng/20220624
LC record available at https://lccn.loc.gov/2022011907
LC ebook record available at https://lccn.loc.gov/2022011908

Contents

Abbreviations

CCCM	Corpus Christianorum, Continuatio Mediaevalis. Turnhout: Brepols.
CCSL	Corpus Christianorum, Series Latina. Turnhout: Brepols.
CF	Cistercian Fathers series.
Conf	Augustine. *Confessions. Sancti Augustini Confessionum Libri XIII.* Ed. Lucas Verheijen. CCSL 27.
Enar in Ps	Augustine. *Enarrationes in Psalmos.* Ed. E. Dekkers. CCSL 38, 39, 40.
Ev	Gregory the Great. *Homiliae XL in Evangelia.* Ed. R. Étaix. CCSL 141.
Hiez	Gregory the Great. *Homilae in Hiezechielem.* Ed. Marcus Adriaen. CCSL 142.
Hom in Ev	Bede. *Homeliarum Evangelii libri II.* Ed. D. Hurst. CCSL 122; *Homilies,* in *The Complete Works of the Venerable Bede.* Vol. 5. Ed. J. A. Giles, 8 vols. London: Whittaker and Co., 1843.
L	Leipzig, Universitätsbibliothek, MS 827.
LDP	Gertrud the Great of Helfta, *Legatus Divinae Pietatis / The Herald of God's Loving-Kindness.*
LSG	Mechtild of Hackeborn, *Liber Specialis Gratiae / Book of Special Grace.*

Mo

Gregory the Great, *Moralia in Iob*. Ed. Marcus Adriaen. CCSL 143, 143A, 143B.

PL

Patrologia Latina. Paris: J.-P. Migne.

SBOp

Sancti Bernardi Opera. Ed. J. Leclercq, H. M. Rochais, C. H. Talbot. Rome: Editiones Cistercienses, 1957–1977.

SC

Bernard of Clairvaux, *Sermons on the Song of Songs*. SBOp 1–2.

SCh

Sources chrétiennes. Paris: Éditions du Cerf.

W

Vienna, Österreichische Nationalbibliothek, Cod. 4224.

Introduction

The essential facts about Gertrud the Great (1256–1302) are well known. She was a German nun at the monastery of Helfta, founded in 1229 and situated in what is today Saxony-Anhalt, Germany.[1] Under Gertrud of Hackeborn, who had become abbess at the age of nineteen in 1251, three of Helfta's members wrote mystical treatises in the late thirteenth century. Mechtild of Hackeborn's spiritual experiences were the source of the *Book of Special Grace* (LSG),[2] recorded and edited by Gertrud the Great and another Helfta nun. Gertrud herself (often confused with the abbess) was the source of the present text, *The Memorial of the Abundance of the Divine Sweetness*, as well as of the much better known version of her revelations, *The Herald of God's Loving-Kindness*, of which she wrote Book Two (largely replicated in *The Memorial*, 2–33) herself, "with her own hand," while a close confidante, now known as "Sister N,"[3] compiled the other four

---

[1] On Helfta and its history, see the documents reprinted in *Revelationes Gertrudianae ac Mechtildianae* II, ed. L. Paquelin (Paris: Oudin, 1877), 714–28; Alexandra Barratt, trans. and annot., *Gertrud the Great of Helfta: The Herald of God's Loving-Kindness: Books One and Two*, CF 35 (Kalamazoo, MI: Cistercian Publications, 1991), 7–8; Alexandra Barratt and Debra L. Stoudt, "Gertrude the Great of Helfta," in *Medieval Holy Women in the Christian Tradition c. 1000–c. 1500*, ed. Alastair Minnis and Rosalynn Voaden (Turnhout: Brepols, 2010), 454–55; Josef Hochenauer, *Kloster Helfta: Raum schaffen für das Licht* (Bamberg: St Otto, 1999).

[2] There is now an English translation of much of this lengthy treatise: *Mechthild of Hackeborn and the Nuns of Helfta: The Book of Special Grace*, Barbara Newman, intro. and trans. (Mahwah, NJ: Paulist, 2017). The translation is selective, and the material has been somewhat rearranged. Translations here from LSG are my own.

[3] See Balázs J. Nemes, "Text Production and Authorship: Gertrude of Helfta's *Legatus divinae pietatis*," in Elizabeth Andersen, Henrike Lähnemann, and Anne Simon, eds., *A Companion to Mysticism and Devotion in Northern Germany in the Late Middle Ages* (Leiden and Boston: Brill, 2014), 116–20; and Almuth Märker and

books. Finally the Beguine Mechtild of Magdebourg composed the seventh and final book of her vernacular treatise, *The Flowing Light of the Godhead*, at Helfta, where she found refuge late in life.

Gertrud's earthly life was externally uneventful but internally intense. She was born on the feast of the Epiphany (January 6) in 1256 and was given to Helfta by her family at the age of four (child oblation was still practised in Benedictine houses, even though the Cistercians had abandoned the practice). Helfta had recently moved from its site in Rodardsdorf to new and better buildings in Eisleben, and no doubt it was raising its profile and increasing its intake. In the monastery the young Gertrud received an excellent medieval education in the trivium (Latin grammar, rhetoric, and dialectic) and possibly in the quadrivium (arithmetic, music, geometry, and astronomy): the abbess was a firm believer in the importance of such learning for the proper understanding of Scripture and, consequently, for the promotion of the religious life. Originally indifferent to the vocation foisted upon her, in 1281 at the age of twenty-five Gertrud underwent a conversion and was thenceforward favored with numerous visions and mystical experiences in which the divine heart of Jesus played a prominent part. Although she never held conventual office (apart from acting as deputy chantress, as emerges in LDP V.1.24),[4] she was renowned for her teaching, her composition of prayers and spiritual florilegia, and her role as spiritual advisor and intermediary with

Balázs J. Nemes, "*Hunc tercium conscripsi cum maximo labore occultandi*: Schwester N von Helfta und ihre 'Sonderausgabe' des 'Legatus divinae pietatis' Gertruds von Helfta in der Leipziger Handschrift Ms 827," in *Beiträge zur Geschichte der deutschen Sprache und Literatur* 137 (2015): 248–96.

[4] References to Books 1 and 2 of *The Herald* are to Barratt, *The Herald, Books One and Two*, references to Book 3 to Alexandra Barratt, trans., *Gertrud the Great of Helfta: The Herald of God's Loving-Kindness: Book Three*, CF 63 (Kalamazoo, MI: Cistercian Publications, 1999); references to Book 4 to Alexandra Barratt, trans., *Gertrud the Great of Helfta: The Herald of God's Loving-Kindness: Book Four*, CF 85 (Collegeville, MN: Cistercian Publications, 2018); and references to Book 5 to Alexandra Barratt, trans., *Gertrud the Great of Helfta: The Herald of God's Loving-Kindness: Book Five*, CF 86 (Collegeville, MN: Cistercian Publications, 2020). References specifically to the Latin *Legatus* (LDP) are to *Le Héraut*, ed. Pierre Doyère and others, SCh 25, 27, 225, and 331 (Paris: Éditions du Cerf, 1968–1986).

the divine. After many years of sickness she died in her mid-forties in 1301 or 1302.[5]

Leipzig, Universitätsbibliothek, MS 827 (L)

This recently discovered manuscript is by far the earliest that contains a text recognizable as a version of LDP. The section containing the Gertrudian texts has been dated to the early years of the thirteenth century, maybe as early as the first decade (Munich, Bayerische Staatsbibliothek, cod. lat. 15332, the closest manuscript in date, which contains the earliest copy of the standard version of the text, was written about a hundred years later). It is still in its late-medieval wooden binding, with a paper title in a sixteenth-century hand that labels it as *Contemplacio anime. Item Revelaciones s. Birgitte*. This erroneous description is the reason that it remained unknown for so long, even though it had been in the university library since its foundation.

L is a quarto manuscript, written on vellum and measuring approximately 24 x 16 cms.[6] It consists of 150 folios written in single columns, in 19 quires of 4, fols. 1–87 containing 21 lines to the page, and fols. 88 to the end 33 lines. The manuscript consists of two distinct parts. Fols. 1[r]–4[v], written by Scribe A in a hand datable to the first quarter of the fourteenth century, preserve a version of the passion of Saint Barbara, beginning *Temporibus Maximiniani imperatoris*. There were various Latin legends of this saint, who had been venerated in the West from an early date:[7] this seems closest to *Bibliotheca Hagiographica Latina* 913a.[8]

---

[5] Our meager information about Gertrud's life is derived from LDP itself. See further Barratt, *The Herald: Books One and Two*, 9–12, and Barratt, *The Herald: Book Three*, 9–11.

[6] For a detailed description, see Almuth Märker, "The Leipzig Codex Ms 827—the earliest transmission of Gertrude of Helfta's Latin *Legatus divinae pietatis*," *Analecta Cisterciensia* 69 (2019): 161–77.

[7] *The Old Norse-Icelandic Legend of Saint Barbara*, ed. Kirsten Wolf, Studies and Texts 134 (Toronto: Pontifical Institute of Mediaeval Studies, 2000), 11.

[8] *Bibliotheca hagiographica Latina antiquae et mediae aetatis, A–J* (Brussels: Society of Bollandists, 1898–1899). For a modern edition, transcribed from the

Fols. 8[r]–148[r] are written in quite different hands. Fols. 8[r]–25[v] contain a hitherto unknown mystical treatise, beginning *Ducam eam in solitudinem et ibi loquar ad cor eius*, composed by Saint Gertrud herself[9] and written down by Scribe B, and, on fols. 25[v]–148[r], the *Memoriale abundantiae divinae suavitatis*. This comprises the Preface on fols. 25[v]–27[v] and 1–189 of the text proper on fols. 27[v]–148[r]. The text appears to be unfinished: only six lines are written at the top of fol. 148[r], corresponding to the conclusion of LDP V.9.7. Scribe B writes up to and including fol. 83[r]; Scribe C takes over on fol. 83[v]. This part of the manuscript is datable to "the first years of the fourteenth century"[10] and is somewhat earlier than the first part.

We can be confident that L was written at the Benedictine monastery of Pegau, about 70 kilometers from Helfta.[11] The same alternating red and blue Lombard "silhouette initials" and other decorations are also found in Leipzig, Universitätsbibliothek, MS 848, the chapter office book of Pegau (and in five other Pegau manuscripts held at Leipzig). MS 848 can be dated on palaeographical and other grounds to "the first third or maybe at the very beginning of the fourteenth century."[12] It also contains corrections similar to those in MS 827, such as the use of "+" with a cross-stroke longer than the vertical and slightly dipping to the left (on, e.g., fol. 47[v]). The chapter book provides some evidence that Pegau was a *Doppelkloster*, or double foundation: the necrology includes some women's names, denominated as *soror nostra, laica, conversa*, or *inclusa* (on, e.g., fol. 1[r]). This might account for the monastery's having made a copy of Gertrud's writings. In addition, one of the related manuscripts, MS 368, contains a vernacular prayer in German.

MS 827 has been very carefully revised and corrected, probably more than once, indicating that it was considered to be of some

---

thirteenth-century manuscript Douai, Bibliothèque Municipale, Codex 838, see *Legend of Saint Barbara*, ed. Kirsten Wolf, 156–60.

   [9] See further below for a detailed justification of this assertion.

   [10] Märker, "The Leipzig Codex Ms 827," 175.

   [11] For a far more thorough discussion of the Pegau provenance, see Märker, "The Leipzig Codex Ms 827."

   [12] Märker, "The Leipzig Codex Ms 827," 175.

importance. We can identify at least four main correctors and some other, more sporadic, contributors. In the first part of the text, that written by Scribe B, a probably contemporary corrector has gone through and indicated in the margin with a cross where a correction was needed; then others (possibly including the original corrector) have made the actual correction. This practice stops once Scribe C takes over, so it is possible that the supervisor of Scribe B's work was identical with Scribe C. This is not the place to discuss the correctors in detail, but one is worthy of mention. Corrector E, who makes maybe half a dozen corrections in a very small hand in scratchy black ink, has glossed the Latin word *uertiginem,* "dizziness," in Middle Low German as *swindel* on fol. 87[v].[13] Middle Low German was one of several languages spoken in the vicinity of Helfta and Pegau.

Ducam eam opens with an impressive four-line capital in red and blue. The text that follows is clearly divided into sections by large one-line initials in alternating red and blue; in the translation below I have used these as a guide to divide it into numbered sections. The Preface to *The Memorial* begins with a two-line initial, blue with red penwork, and a four-line red and blue initial with extensive marginal flourishes marks the opening of *The Memorial* itself. The text is punctuated by two-line red and blue initials, and, again, in the translation below I have interpreted them as chapter divisions. Consequently, I have also introduced chapter numbers in angled brackets (but without titles) for the reader's convenience, the numbered sections within the chapters following as far as practicable those of the SCh edition of LDP.

Between fols. 16[r] and 43[v] there occur a number of notes in the margins, written by Scribe B. Some are comments, others citations from various authorities such as Bernard and Richard of Saint-Victor, designed to support the text. These all occur in parts of the texts written by Gertrud herself.

---

[13] See L 79 below.

Ducam eam in solitudinem: **The Prologue**

The text on fols. 8ʳ–25ᵛ of L is described in the most recent, revised description of the manuscript[14] as *Florilegium und Epilog*. A *florilegium* is, literarily, an anthology or compilation of excerpts from other writings, and in the very first chapter of LDP this kind of literary composition is specifically listed as one of the literary genres practised by Gertrud, along with prayers and spiritual exercises:

> Elucidating and clarifying what lesser minds found obscure, she made compilations [*compilavit*] from the sayings of the saints, gathered as a dove gathers grain, and committed to writing [*conscripsit*] many books filled with all sweetness, for the general profit of all those who wished to read them. (LDP I.1.2)

But this text is more than a compilation. It is true that it begins as such, taking as its starting point a verse from the prophet Hosea, "I will lead her into the wilderness, and there I will speak to her heart."[15] This is then elucidated by a string of quotations, not only from holy Scripture but also from Augustine of Hippo, Gregory the Great, and Bernard of Clairvaux, from both his genuine works and those wrongly attributed to him in the Middle Ages. The first four folios of the text, therefore, consist of this *catena* or chain, skillfully woven together and testifying to the wide reading of the compiler and the comprehensiveness of the Helfta monastic library. (There are just too many quotations, especially from Bernard's *Sermones in Cantica*, to argue that the compiler was herself merely using compilations rather than accessing complete texts.) But from section 3[16] the compiler's own voice emerges more and more strongly, and from section 7 to the end the quotations from the Fathers and other spiritual

---

[14] I am indebted to Dr. Märker for providing a copy of her unpublished description.

[15] Hos 2:14.

[16] As is indicated above, the manuscript does not number the sections of the text. They are, however, quite clearly marked out by the use of colored capital letters, which I have followed to provide a numbering system for the convenience of the reader.

authorities diminish as the compiler gains confidence and develops her own ideas in her own words.

What then is the subject of this text? Read carefully, it emerges as nothing less than a brief treatise on mystical theology. As the opening citation from Scripture suggests, it is concerned with the different ways in which the divine communicates with those whom he has chosen: how he can be said to "speak" with them and "visit" them, how they can be said to "hear" him, "see" him, and, ultimately, experience union with him. It is also an indispensable introduction to the text that follows, as this is an account of Gertrud's own inter-actions with the Lord, in which she hears his words, speaks with him, is visited by him, and sees him and other denizens of heaven. There is therefore a carefully thought-out, theoretical basis for these accounts of her spiritual experiences, which are far from the emotional effusions of an over-enthusiastic nun, as many writers from Eusebius Amort in the eighteenth century onwards have implied.

What Gertrud has to say is not particularly original, if only because originality was not prized in the Middle Ages. Her ideas rely upon and reformulate those of her predecessors: notable among her sources are the *Confessions* of Saint Augustine and the *Sermones in Cantica* of Saint Bernard (sermons 20, 31, 32, 41, 45, 51, 57, 62, 69, 74, 83, and 84 are quoted extensively). Anyone writing on mystical religion in the thirteenth century would probably use the same writers. More surprising, especially in a woman, is the extensive reliance on Richard of Saint-Victor (d. 1173), in particular on his mystical treatise *Of the Instruction of the Inner Man*, here called "Richard on the dream of Nebuchadnezzar," quoted or referenced on at least a dozen occasions. There is also one reference to the better-known *Benjamin Minor*, attributed to "Hugh"; two unattributed quotations from the *Benjamin Major* plus two marginal, possibly scribal, citations; and one quota-tion from Richard's *Liber Exceptionum*, here attributed to Gregory the Great.

This text functions as the prologue to the text that follows: indeed, it is called *prologus* in the preface to *The Memorial of the Abundance of the Divine Sweetness*. So who was its author? Surely Gertrud herself, rather than Sister N, who compiled much of *The Memorial*.

Section 16 relates how the Lord himself approved that text and gave it its name. The account is written in the first person but is otherwise verbally close to passages in LDP, in particular I.Prol. 2, that tell the same story using the third person. There can be no doubt that this is authentically Gertrudian, "written with her own hand" in the same way as LDP II.

The Preface to *The Memorial of the Abundance of the Divine Sweetness*

The preface to *The Memorial* presents a number of frustrating problems. The writer, Sister N, declares that the text that follows is divided into three parts. Any reader can see that Part One consists of 1–35 and contains much of what later becomes LDP II.1–19, though differently arranged and with a different conclusion. Further, Part Two clearly begins with 36. But what is difficult, indeed impossible, to make out is where, if at all, Part Two ends and Part Three begins.[17] If it is true that the text in L is unfinished (see above), it is quite possible that L contains none of this elusive Part Three. All that we know for certain about Part Three is that it was written down by Sister N during the last months of the abbess's life (late 1292 or early 1293); that this was done without Gertrud's knowledge, unlike Part Two, which was written with her cooperation; and that the compiler assumed that Gertrud would never see it. Sister N implies, but does not say so directly, that this third part relied on what she had been told by others who were witnesses to Gertrud's sanctity. This suggests that Part Three was the germ of what later became LDP I, "commendations of her character and testimonies to her grace" (LDP I.Prol. 7). If so, it is arguable that Part Three begins at L 162, as this is the first chapter to make use, indeed extensive use, of material that later appears in LDP I. But the evidence is really too flimsy to be incorporated into the translation. Only the discovery of a new manu-

---

[17] For a far more thorough and extensive discussion of this complex question, see Märker and Nemes, "*Hunc tercium conscripsi.*"

script containing the complete text would settle the question definitively.

A further source of frustration is our inability to know whether, at the time that Sister N put together the text witnessed in L, Gertrud was still alive. Gertrud did not die until 1301 or 1302, but Sister N usually speaks of her in the past tense. However, a cryptic remark at the end of the Preface, in which Sister N entrusts the book "to the divine heart until after her [i.e., Gertrud's] death" (Pref.5), seems to imply that Gertrud was still alive at the time of writing. But if L itself dates to the first years of the fourteenth century, that gives very little time for, at a minimum, the recording at Helfta of L's exemplar (presumably complete) by Sister N (or another nun acting as scribe), the knowledge of that text reaching Pegau, and the subsequent acquisition of a copy for the use of that community.

LDP and Leipzig, Universitätsbibliothek, MS 827

Naturally, the relationship between these two versions demands our attention. It is my contention that L was probably composed before LDP, but the case will not be restated here.[18] No one, however, will disagree that there is a body of material common to LDP and L, some material (roughly about a third) found only in L, and a large amount of material found only LDP. How might we plausibly explain this state of affairs?

Of the shared material, the most striking consists of L 1–33 (that is, almost all of Part One), which corresponds closely to LDP II. But there are subtle differences: L reverses the positions of LDP II.6–10 and LDP II.11–18 and does not contain LDP II.20–24. L's ordering of the chapters seems more logical,[19] but readers can test that hypothesis for themselves. What is harder to fathom is why L does not contain LDP II.20–24. It is true that LDP II.20 and II.23 largely

---

[18] See Alexandra Barratt, "The Chronological Priority of the *Memoriale abundantiae suavitatis divinae* in Leipzig, Universitätsbibliothek, MS 827," *Analecta Cisterciensia* 69 (2019): 198–209 (here 199–202).

[19] See Barratt, "Chronological Priority," 202–5.

summarize what had already been recorded and therefore might be considered superfluous, but 21 and 22 recount important mystical experiences—the beatific vision and "a certain great but secret gift." Various possibilities spring to mind, all of which would suggest that L was largely put together during Gertrud's lifetime. Either Gertrud was yet to experience these visions, or she had not recorded them at the time Sister N was compiling L, or she was unwilling to release them while she was alive.

Pursuing a more general comparison between L and LDP, one notes that L proceeds in roughly chronological order, arranging its accounts of Gertrud's visions and conversations with the Lord mainly in the order in which they were experienced, like a chronicle.[20] It often makes temporal reference to the events of the liturgical year, and we can trace the existence of a series of liturgical cycles and therefore the passage of time. Its organizational principle is thus similar to that of LDP IV, which is arranged around a single cycle of the liturgical year. In contrast, LDP I and V are thematically based: LDP I concerns Gertrud's life and personality, LDP V the deaths of various members of the Helfta community and the events leading up to or foreshadowing Gertrud's own death (though not her death itself). That leaves LDP III, which has no real organizing principle: the compiler has simply gathered in one place other material she considered worthy of note.

LDP's varied principles of arrangement, therefore, are more artful and sophisticated—almost too much so—than those of L, with its "and then . . . and then" approach. But perhaps more important is a detectable difference in tone between the two versions. L is more intimate and unguarded, less "air-brushed" than LDP, which presents a relatively sanitized version of Gertrud and her experiences. LDP has become the sort of text that could be presented with confidence to various male clerics for their approval—as indeed we know was the case from the *Approbationes* (SCh I:104–7) attached to LDP.

This brief text occupies a curious place in LDP and its textual tradition. It is found in only three manuscripts: in Vienna, Österreichische

---

[20] See further Barratt, "Chronological Priority," 205–8.

Nationalbibliotek MS 4224, where it follows LDP III, and in Munich, BSB cod. lat. 15332, where it comes after LDP V, the *Missa*, and the Index—that is, right at the end. Only in Trier (Trèves), Stadtbibliothek MS 1061, which contains LDP I–III, does it appear at the very beginning. Paquelin, Gertrud's first post-medieval editor, based his edition on the Vienna manuscript (he did not know of the Munich manuscript), but he omitted the *Approbationes* from his first volume, containing LDP, instead printing it among a collection of *Documenta* at the end of the second volume, containing LSG (Paquelin II, 724–25). In contrast, the more recent SCh edition chose to place it at the very beginning, as in the Trier manuscript, though it gives no other reason than that this arrangement seemed "preferable" (LDP III:350). This decision endows the *Approbationes* with an importance that it does not altogether deserve, and suggests a deference to male clerical authority not otherwise typical of Helfta.

No one has paid much attention to the *Approbationes*, which lists the names of seven clerics who had approved LDP at the request of the Helfta superiors. They were all Franciscans or Dominicans and are identified as brothers H<enricus> de Mulhausen (Mülhausen, Thuringia); H<enricus> de Wer[i]ungerode (Wernigerode) in Halle; a nameless Franciscan from Burch, living in Halberstadt; Nicholas from Hildesheim, lecturer and later prior of Halberstadt; Theodoricus of Apoldia; Dom Gotfried Rex (i.e., König?), master; and the Dominican Hermannus from Loweia, lecturer in Leipzig. Brother Theodoricus can be identified with the Dominican Dietrich of Apoldia (1228–1302), biographer of Saint Dominic and of Saint Elizabeth of Hungary (the latter was personally known to the co-foundress of Helfta): he spent his entire religious life in Erfurt.[21] He is of particular interest as the *Approbationes* claims that he had "held frequent conversations with" Gertrud, though there is no mention of this in either LDP or L. These authoritative figures are all quite local, coming from or based in religious houses roughly within a one hundred-kilometer radius of Helfta. Two are based in Halberstadt, the cathedral city within whose diocese Helfta was located (and whose canons caused

---

[21] Leipzig, Universistätsbibliothek MS 846, early fourteenth century, contains a collection of his writings. It belonged to the Dominicans of Pirna, near Dresden.

the nuns so much trouble). Although it is usually assumed that Helfta's spiritual directors were Dominican or Franciscan, there are few references elsewhere in the Gertrudian texts to mendicants. There is just one reference to a friar shared by LDP and L (V.25.1/ L 121.1), and two further references in L 79 (not in LDP).

Helfta possibly sought approval from these authority figures as a preemptive strike to forestall the kinds of problems Mechtild of Magdebourg had experienced with her own book of revelations, *The Flowing Light of the Godhead*. She apparently had many detractors: LDP V.7.2 refers discreetly to "sceptics," while, more forthrightly, L mentions "the wicked" and says that the Lord himself castigates "the perverters of good things who attack this book" (L 60). Indeed, the strategies to which Helfta may have resorted in order to ensure clerical approval are well demonstrated by a comparison of the redacted account of Mechtild's own death in LDP V.7 with the probably original version in L 60–62.

LDP's single chapter is about two-thirds the length of L's. While it is true that L is simply more verbose than LDP, the latter has also made substantive changes. It is immediately striking that LDP refers to Mechtild by her initial alone, while L has no problem calling her by her full name. (LDP also occludes her presence altogether in II. Prol., when it describes Gertrud as "standing with her sisters waiting for the Body of the Lord to be carried to a sick nun," while L states that Gertrud "was standing among the members of the community, waiting for the Body of the Lord to be brought when sister M. of blessed memory, who was sick, was about to receive communion before the office" [Preface]).

Other differences are more subtle. The explanation in L 60 of the Lord's reasons for refusing to mark Mechtild's death by "miraculous prodigies," as suggested by Gertrud, is much longer and more convoluted than LDP V.7.1–2. The chapter that follows in L continues to expatiate on the same subject but is completely absent from LDP. Gertrud was again praying

> that, for love of his chosen Mechtild, he would at least condescend
> to exalt her death with signs and prodigies. The Lord answered

her, "She herself will not want this." She replied, "Well, we want it!" The Lord said, "Since you are all still living in the body, you could not have everything that you want." However, she saw the Lord assert this with such great gentleness that from then onwards she used to wonder whether the Lord would agree to the wish of the community in this. (L 61)

Somehow this interchange with the divine is very human. Gertrud is persistent, even pushy, and eternally optimistic; the Lord is brisk but firm, almost brusque. But perhaps this was not the way Helfta wanted the relationship portrayed to the world outside its own walls!

The most telling difference, however, is the presence in L, but not in LDP, of the following sentence:

And when <Gertrud> was praying with these words, "Fortify her, most loving God, with the sacrament of your sweetest Body and Blood," the Lord replied, "She is mingled with my divinity to such an extent that there is no need for her to receive the sacraments, but my unfathomable judgments do not so command." (L 62)

Women mystics often came under suspicion if they dared imply, however obliquely, that because of their personal, mystical, relationship with the divine, the sacraments of the institutional church on earth (and therefore the male clerical establishment) were superfluous. The redacted remark here is carefully nuanced: the Lord says that Mechtild's union with him makes the viaticum unnecessary, but adds that he does not choose to take this to its logical conclusion. But it could still have looked suspect and is absent from LDP.

LDP's image of Gertrud looks as if it has been adapted to the expectations of the male ecclesiastical establishment by smoothing the rough edges of her more extreme behavior that L had presented. LDP's Gertrud is certainly no stranger to self-deprecation and abasement, but in L these features are even more pronounced. Sometimes it is enough for L to remove a single, excessively derogatory, word or phrase: for instance, devotions that Gertrud herself describes as "lukewarm" in LDP II.1.2 were originally also described as "hypocritical and false" in L 1.2; in LDP II.12.1, she admits to having been in a "state of anger," but in L 9 she describes herself as "somewhat bitter"; in LDP II.8.2 she calls herself "unworthy" but in L 27 "most worthless" (*uilissima*). Eager to present herself in an unflattering light, in L 16, she writes about an occasion when "I was blamed for something—undeservedly, as I thought—by one of my superiors, and by your [God's] grace restrained my impatience and chose courtesy (which, alas, is very unusual for me)." This is completely expunged in LDP. In L 34, most of which has evaporated in LDP, she is able through God's grace to "pray sincerely for a dead woman whom I had found a very great burden while she was still alive because of my inappropriate superficiality and other imperfections," and in the process she realizes, "I was less fit for the practice of love because of my excessive failings and numerous negligences." Other examples in L of Gertrud's low opinion of herself are 91 and 171, both entirely absent from LDP, and it is no coincidence that a phrase from 1 Cor 4:13, "the offscouring of all creation," which Gertrud uses of herself, occurs no fewer than three times in L but only once in LDP.

L also presents a Gertrud whose relationship with the divine has its rocky moments. She cannot always rely on her favored status with the Lord, and her supernaturally granted knowledge has limitations over which she has no control. At the end of the three chapters relating the death of Mechtild of Magdebourg discussed above, Gertrud recognizes that, although she was able to perceive part of the Lord's activity in Mechtild's soul, "divine justice . . . had driven her away from the knowledge of those things that the Lord was working in his chosen one because of her unworthiness" (L 62.3). And at the climactic moment when Mechtild dies and is united with the divine for eternity, Gertrud does not shrink from revealing that she deservedly missed it, for quite mundane reasons: "Nor did she consider it inappropriate that she was hindered by outer things at that moment, for she thought herself by her own estimation completely unworthy to participate in spirit in such joyful and secret delights" (L 62.5).

At the other extreme, LDP quietly removes some of Gertrud's more extravagant claims. In L 27, after she has received communion the Lord declares, "Arise from my feet and sit at my side, for by the gift of grace through the assimilative union of the sacrament you are *the figure of my substance.*"[22] This idea, which teeters on the edge of heresy, is expressed more guardedly, and with some important qualifications, in L 23/LDP II.6.2.

Several times L almost identifies Gertrud with the Virgin Mary. In L 49 (not in LDP), in response to her resolution finally to hold a difficult conversation with someone afflicted with "unwise timidity," the Lord greets her with the words of the *Hail, Mary*:

> *Hail, Mary*, that is, bitterness conceived because of me; *full of my grace*, for I *the Lord will be with you*, helping you in all things; *you are blessed among women*,[23] that is, among those who, living only to themselves, seem to show no concern for the salvation of others; *and blessed is the fruit of your womb*,[24] that is, of your mouth.

In L 63 (also not in LDP), which takes place on the feast of the Epiphany, the Lord again greets her in terms often applied to the Virgin, saying, "You are the star of my splendor, receiving light from me, the true sun, to make up for all your shortcomings." In L 97, which takes place at the time of the interdict, Gertrud and the Lord have a conversation about what should happen to the men who have placed Helfta in such a difficult situation. This mainly survives in LDP II.16.3–4, but in L the story ends with Gertrud's implicit desire to imitate the intercessory role of the Virgin: she sought to "soothe the Lord lest . . . he also exercise forceful vengeance against those who had oppressed the community."

LDP is also protective of Gertrud's image in a way that L is not, perhaps because the latter was originally written for the community rather than an outside audience. Sister N quite openly positions herself as a member of the community writing from the community's perspective: for instance, LDP IV.58.1–3 is mainly a discreetly abbreviated version of L 108, but one of the omissions is particularly significant. L describes Gertrud's interpretation of her vision of a

[22] See Heb 1:3.
[23] Luke 1:28.
[24] Luke 1:42.

"divine treasure-house" with jeweled walls: "through the deployment of the gems already mentioned she understood the predestination of all the chosen in the divine heart, **but especially of our community.**" The unabashed use of the possessive adjective binds together the narrator and her audience.[25]

LDP's Gertrud is often sick, but in L her sickness is more prominent than in LDP. Most of L 148 corresponds to LDP IV.48.9–13, with minor variants and expansions, but it opens with some new material that stresses just how sick Gertrud was:

> [S]he had been confined to her bed for more than fourteen days through sickness [and] had spent the night . . . completely without sleep because of her weakness. Finally, with the help of others, she got up at the time of Matins and made her way with difficulty to a place where she could hear the chanting of the choir nuns.

Then towards the end of the chapter L describes her as miraculously "casting aside the stick on which she had earlier relied, which had not been enough unless she was in addition supported by the hands of those who were caring for her," another very human, but undignified, moment. (Gertrud was only 44 when she died, so needing both a stick and the help of others to reach the convent church is a measure of her debility.) But LDP omits not only this episode—perhaps because plaster saints are not usually depicted with mobility aids?—but also the dramatic events that followed. After the newly invigorated Gertrud had eaten breakfast,

> wishing to get up and leave, she fell to the ground as if lifeless, lying there for some time while her strength could not be restored by any physical refreshment. At last she was carried to her little bed, more like someone about to die than to live, and was subsequently confined to bed for some days: she was also unable to lift her head from the pillow.

---

[25] See also the reference to "our relatives" in L 79: again, Sister N is speaking.

There is plenty of touching detail here but not much dignity, and L also goes on to suggest, although obliquely, that these astonishing tergiversations in Gertrud's physical state caused unfavorable comment among some members of the community. Sister N herself addresses the Lord as follows:

> you allow [the soul], although guiltless, to be subject to human judgment. I experienced this on that occasion in that woman [i.e., Gertrud], who . . . did not in the least escape the slander of others. Humbled by this, she was immediately rendered more fit for your gifts.

L's Gertrud sometimes has her own ideas, though these are often given short shrift by the Lord. On occasions she can be persistent. We have already seen this in her efforts to persuade the Lord to perform miracles to mark the death of Mechtild of Magdebourg. But this is not the only time she found the Lord less than cooperative. In the sad episode, completely absent from LDP, of the recalcitrant nun who wanted to choose her own confessor (see further below), after trying to pin down the Lord on which confessor the nun should use, she finally cries out in exasperation, "O Lord God, since it would have been very easy for you to have taught me this with your closing words, why have you drawn it out with such an intricate discussion?" (L 77). And in 78, Gertrud actually argues with the Lord by quoting Saint Bernard at him. The Lord says of the rebel nun,

> "If only she would get up, casting aside the darkness that has collected in her bosom, I would be ready to meet her." [Gertrud] replied, "Does not Bernard, who loved you, say of you, 'When we flee, you pursue us, we turn our back and you meet us face to face'?"

(The Lord charitably refrains from pointing out that Gertrud's quotation, which she uses again in LDP II.3.3, is not found in the authentic works of Bernard.) In another incident (again not in LDP), when the community had serious financial problems, Gertrud reproaches the Lord because of the burden the difficulties place on their administrators.

She suggests a minor modification to his approach but is again rebuffed:

> "Once again, my Lord, you are allowing our administrators to experience anxious sorrows. . . . If you intend to assist our poverty eventually, merciful Lord, at the intervention of your most loving Mother, at least do so more quickly, so that our administrators may be less burdened." The Lord said, "If I lessen the difficulty of their task, I must also lessen their compensatory reward." (L 94)

Gertrud is portrayed as less than the ideal female religious in her aversion to domestic duties in L 40 and 41, which find no place in LDP. L 40 concerns her reluctance when it is her turn to cook for the community. What she felt to be "a huge burden" becomes tolerable only through the continual presence of Christ, who appears in the form of "a delightful young man, inseparable companion, and tireless helper." We are told that she disliked this task because it distracted her from her interior life (one hopes for the community's sake that this dislike did not also distract her from her cooking). So did her tour of duty serving food in the refectory, the subject of the next chapter. She asks for the Lord's help, which is granted, but then worries that she may fall into ecstasy, which would indeed have been awkward. However, together with the remark in LDP III.41.4 that "it is impossible for anyone to touch flour without getting dusty" and with the references to her losing her needle or pencil in the barn among the bales of hay (LDP I.13.4) and dropping balls of wool while spinning (LDP III.32.5), these two chapters suggest that Gertrud was unskilled in the domestic arts.

We do learn from L, however, that Gertrud engaged in scriptural exegesis. L 49 mentions in passing, as not of any great note, that "she had expounded tropologically part of the readings [*hystorie*][26] from the book of Esther." Saint Augustine had taught that Scripture could

---

[26] *historiae* were passages from the historical part of the Hebrew Scriptures read during the night office. In some liturgical uses, a passage from Esther was read in late September. See Andrew Hughes, *Medieval Manuscripts for Mass and Office: A Guide to Their Organization and Terminology* (Toronto: Toronto University Press, 1986), 22, 189, and 356.

be understood in four ways: literally, allegorically, tropologically (that is, morally), and anaogically, and Sister N tosses off the technical term *tropolo[g]yce*—a word so unfamiliar, apparently, that the scribe writes it incorrectly as *tropoloyce*—without comment. But the modern reader wants more information. Although we already knew from LDP I.1.2 that Gertrud "tirelessly ruminated on all the books of the Bible" and gave "constant application to the careful reading . . . of holy Scripture. . . . [e]lucidating and clarifying what lesser minds found obscure," scriptural exegesis, whether written or oral, was not something in which women normally engaged in the Middle Ages. In the twelfth century the canon lawyer Gratian had forbidden women to teach men publicly,[27] and no doubt Gertrud's intended audience for her exegesis were the nuns of Helfta rather than the canons or lay brothers, let alone laymen. However, in around 1220 the English theologian Thomas of Chobham had declared more restrictively that, although abbesses and prioresses might instruct and reprove their own nuns, they were specifically forbidden to expound Scripture by preaching,[28] and in 1245 Gauthier of Château-Thierry, bishop of Paris, had argued that only clerics were allowed to expound and interpret Scripture.[29] So it is no surprise that this reference is removed in LDP.

That Gertrud chose the book of Esther seems inevitable in some ways, though in others it was an unusual choice.[30] The book was not studied extensively during the Middle Ages, partly because the

---

[27] Nicole Bériou, "The Right of Women to Give Religious Instruction in the Thirteenth Century," in Beverly Mayne Kienzle and Pamela J. Walker, eds., *Women Preachers and Prophets through Two Millennia of Christianity* (Berkeley: University of California Press, 1998), 143, n. 18.

[28] *possunt tamen abbatisse et priorisse in capitulis suis moniales suas instruere et vitia reprehendere, sed non licet eis sacram Scripturam predicando exponere* (*Summa de arte praedicandi* III, ed. F. Morenzoni, CCCM 82 [Turnhout: Brepols, 1988], 58), quoted in Bériou, "The Right of Women," 143, n. 17.

[29] Bériou, "The Right of Women," 137–38. See also Ayelet Even-Ezra, "Gauthier de Château-Thierry's Question *On the Office of Preaching,*" *Archives d'Histoire Doctrinale et Littéraire du Moyen-Âge* 81 (2014): 385–462.

[30] Kimberly Vrudny, "Medieval Fascination with the Queen: Esther as the Queen of Heaven and Host of the Messianic Banquet," *ARTS: The Arts in Religious and Theological Studies* 11/2 (1999): 36–43.

Hebrew text (Esther 1:1–10:3) contains no references to God (the Vulgate translates Esther 10:4–16:24 from the Greek). But it was a favorite of Gertrud's and is cited twelve times in LDP and twice in L, quite a total for a rather short book. She clearly identified with the story of Queen Esther, "the woman who shares the king's bed" (LDP III.8.1), an identification supported by the Lord when he says, "You are that lovable Esther, for you are graced in my sight with incredible beauty" (LDP IV.35.5). More commonly Esther was interpreted as a type of the Virgin Mary or of the church, as bride of Christ.

It is intriguing to speculate about what sources Gertrud might have used. Any monastic library would have contained the standard commentaries on Esther by Rabanus Maur (ca. 780–856), *Expositio in Librum Esther*,[31] and the *Historia Libri Esther*, part of the *Historia Scholastica* by Peter Comestor (d. ca. 1178).[32] But perhaps more to Gertrud's taste would have been the three sermons in the *Sermones Centum* wrongly attributed to Hugh of Saint-Victor and actually by Richard of Saint-Victor (d. 1173): as we have seen, she made heavy use of Richard in *Ducam eam in solitudinem* (see above).

It is even more surprising to discover in L 79.4–5 that Gertrud composed sermons. She dictated these, no doubt to another nun, and found the task both distracting and stressful:

> 4. When working at the composition of a sermon [*de scripcione cuiusdam sermonis*], on one day she was too preoccupied with it and had failed to concentrate on her prayer both after Matins and also during Mass. . . .
>
> 5. After this, as a result (so she thought) of the task of dictation [*dictandi*] already mentioned, her head grew weary and, suffering from vertigo, she was chewing cloves for relief. This, too, she offered the Lord for his eternal praise.

Now *sermo* in Medieval Latin does not always mean "sermon" in the sense of a formal speech delivered publicly in a liturgical setting (though this was its most common meaning in the Middle Ages). It can also mean a "talk" or a non-liturgical spiritual discourse, such

---

[31] PL 109:635–70.
[32] PL 198:1489–1506.

as the daily address given by the abbot or abbess to the community, usually on a chapter of the Benedictine Rule.[33] In any case, it was not unknown for medieval women religious to write and deliver sermons: Carolyn Muessig asserts that "women did teach and preach in and outside the cloister,"[34] and Darlene Pryds detects "a small but significant tradition of women who preached without ecclesiastical censure."[35] A hundred years before Gertrud, Hildegard of Bingen (1098–1179) wrote "homilies on the gospels" (*expositiones evangeliarum*) and in her letters preserved other sermons she had composed. But this was exceptional and attributed to her supernatural gift of prophecy.[36] There were a few other exceptions, notably two Italian women roughly contemporary with Gertrud: Rose of Viterbo (1233–1252) and the Benedictine nun Umiltà of Faenza (d. 1310), who "preached in public and in the cloister respectively."[37] Again, immunity from censure was granted because of their prophetic gifts, and their preaching was regarded as miraculous. These were not claims that Gertrud ever made for herself, though they are implicit in Book I of LDP. In general, however, sermon writing by women was outside the norm: once again, we can cite Thomas of Chobham, who declared, "Generally it is true that neither a layman nor a woman can preach publicly, namely [*scilicet*] in the church"[38] and once again the passage does not survive in LDP.

L also offers some surprising pieces of information about Helfta as well as about Gertrud. First, Helfta's church possessed a tower: L 68.2 refers to "those praying in the tower," without further explanation. Perhaps there was a gallery in the tower for the benefit of those

---

[33] Michael Casey, introduction to *Bernard of Clairvaux: Monastic Sermons*, trans. Daniel Griggs, CF 68 (Collegeville, MN: Cistercian Publications, 2016), xiii.

[34] Carolyn Muessig, "Prophecy and Song: Teaching and Preaching by Medieval Women," in Kienzle and Walker, eds., *Women Preachers and Prophets*, 146–58 (here 147).

[35] Darlene Pryds, "Proclaiming Sanctity through Proscribed Acts: The Case of Rose of Viterbo," in Kienzle and Walker, eds., *Women Preachers and Prophets*, 159–72 (158).

[36] Bériou, "The Right of Women," 142, n. 14.

[37] Muessig, "Prophecy and Song," 148.

[38] Pryds, "Proclaiming Sanctity," 162 and 169, n. 22; Thomas of Chobham, *Summa de arte praedicandi* III, ed. Morenzoni, CCCM 82:57.

not able to pray with the community in the choir? And L 153 seems to imply the existence of a number of "stations" within the church marking the progress of Christ's passion: the Upper Room where the Last Supper was celebrated, the Mount of Olives, and the Garden of Gethsemane. From the late fifteenth century such stations are found in German churches, though less is known of the earlier period.

Second, Helfta was not as monolithically female as has often been supposed. Apart from the lay brothers, who emerge from the shadows in LDP V, it seems from L that a college of canons was resident in the monastery. As is clear from L 54.2 (not in LDP), these clerics sang their own liturgy in the convent church, but of course at a different time from the nuns. How many there were we do not know, but there were enough to sing a descant, so we might guess there were at least six. There is also a reference to the clerks' Matins in L 64.1, and to the death of a canon in L 195.1. (One hopes he was not representative of the group, as he had led a sinful life for many years and appears to Gertrud as an ugly black toad, almost beyond hope of redemption.) Both these chapters are largely replicated in LDP, but the specific references to the canons have been carefully expunged.

Why might that be? Possibly it is connected to Helfta's relationship with clerics in general, which seems not to have been altogether happy: the compiler of LDP may have felt that the less said about them, the better. Presumably the role of the canons was to say Mass for the nuns and provide the sacraments of confession and anointing when required, but only too often we are told that no confessor was available when needed. In LDP III.60.1 (not in L) Gertrud wishes to confess some sins that her self-examination has uncovered, but "she could not have a confessor." So she makes her confession to Christ, who points out that he is "high priest and true bishop" and goes on to explain that he can offer her all the seven sacraments better than any priest. The following chapter (LDP III.61.1, not in L), continues the theme of her inability to confess because of her confessor's absence. The same situation is also mentioned in LDP IV.7.4 (not in L) when a group of nuns receive communion on Gertrud's advice "even though they had been hindered by the absence of a confessor." Another time (LDP IV.34.2, not in L) Gertrud bewails to Saint John her lack of "an ample supply of confessors," which she says sometimes causes her to forget some of her sins when she can eventually make her confession.

This may be a rhetorical commonplace—in LSG II.14 Mechtild of Hackeborn wished to confess so she could receive communion, "but not having a confessor, she was greatly saddened"—but it is certainly strange if there was a community of canons living on the premises. Maybe there were only a few of them and they were over-stretched, especially if they had responsibilities towards the local laypeople. Or maybe they were negligent or incompetent. L contains some oblique remarks about their shortcomings as confessors or spiritual directors: in L 45 (not in LDP), Gertrud is unable to make a general confession in preparation for her death because of her confessor's inadequacy, incapacity, or perhaps lack of authorization:

> the desire had come to mind to be absolved before her death by a full confession [*plenam confessionem*], and since she did not have a priest with such a capacity, trusting in God she proposed in prayer that she should confess each and every one of her sins to the Lord. . . .

The idea that the Lord himself will act as her confessor is not unique in the Gertrudian texts, as we have already seen (see p. xxxvi above).

More light is shed by L 77 and 78 (neither in LDP), which tell a sad and disturbing story about a nun who wanted to have a confessor from outside the monastery. She could not abide the confessor to whom she had been assigned, although quite why the nun had such deep-rooted objections to her official confessor is never explained. But as Gertrud initially sympathized with her position, it must have been something more than personal antipathy. Of course, the narrative turns into a story about the need to obey authority, and that superiors should not pander to their subjects, but even the Lord is somewhat equivocal, and it is noticeable that he never endorses the confessor involved.

Unlike most women visionaries, Gertrud was not apparently subject to a particular confessor or spiritual director. Was the rebel nun's official confessor also Gertrud's, who causes her much grief in LDP III.14/L 84–86? Both L and LDP recount the story of this difficult confession, framing it as an example of the Lord's burdening Gertrud to increase her merit or reward, by making something commonplace and routine more difficult than usual for her. Even before she began her self-examination, she found the very thought of the impending confession overwhelming, The Lord, to whom she entrusted it, presented the confession to her as a very hot bath, contrasted with a beautiful garden representing divine grace. Offered the choice (though in the end she got both), she unhesitatingly chose the bath. But in spite of the Lord's assistance, the occasion was fraught, and she could hardly stammer out her confession.

Strangely, LDP does not mention the confessor himself, though it must have been he who was responsible for imposing a penance "of such a nature that it had to be postponed for a while" (perhaps it involved the recitation of an impractically large number of psalms, or maybe the confession had taken so long that it was time for Mass). But this caused Gertrud even more stress, because the sacrament was not completed in time for her to receive communion.

L's version of this story is much fuller. It mainly replicates LDP III.14 but heightens Gertrud's dread as the time of confession draws near. It also offers the telling detail that she found an added trial in the inquisitiveness of the onlookers, probably other nuns or even local parishioners, waiting impatiently to make their own confessions, observing the delay and maybe speculating about the reason. But L also adds two extra chapters that disclose that the whole process of self-examination, confession, and penance was much more protracted than as described in LDP.

The sequence of events is rather unclear, but it seems to be as follows. As we have already seen, in L 84, replicated by LDP III.14, Gertrud prepares for confession, makes her self-examination and her confession, and is given a penance that she cannot complete at that time. Then she attends Mass, apparently on the same day, but cannot receive communion. In L 85 (but not in LDP), she completes her "confession," which here probably means "penance,"[39] presumably

---

[39] See C. Du Cange et al., *Glossarium mediæ et infimæ latinitatis* (Niort: L. Favre, 1883–1887), s. v. *confessio* 5: *Pœnitentia quæ per confessionem injungitur; sed maxime ea quæ in Monasterio exigitur.*

later the same day, with much difficulty and with no further divine help. The whole process seems to have left her traumatized: "afterwards it was very painful for her to accept comfort from anyone by any word or sign, or even speak a word to someone, however necessary." Another Mass follows (the second of the day), at which, "when she was offering the holy Host for the emendation of her sins, it seemed to her that she was leaning her head against Jesus' breast and from it was completely covered with the red hue of a rose in bloom," an experience that LDP does not record, although LDP III.15.1 refers to it.[40]

In L 86 (again not in LDP), considering the penance given her insufficient, Gertrud "requested of her confessor that when he was first to celebrate Mass [presumably on the following day], mindful of her in offering the Host, he should also offer it for emendation of all her sins and compensation for her negligences." This is notable as the only reference in either LDP or L to any communication between Gertrud and her confessor. But the Lord preempts this, telling her at the end of the first Mass on the following day to prepare for spiritual communion. This she receives not during Mass but at the end of Prime:

> he offered her his Body with his blessed right hand, in the form of bread, just as it is taken from the altar, and for taking the chalice, he pressed her face into his lordly breast. After a while, when she raised her head, she saw her face all ruddy, as if sprinkled with blood.

The subsequent chapter (L 87/LDP III.15.1) takes place at high Mass and describes Gertrud's vision at the time of the consecration of the tree of love with shining leaves, laden with flowers and fruit, and of the "gilded clothing" that she receives at the time of the elevation (she seems not to have received communion). Finally, L 88/ LDP III.15.2 describes Gertrud's second vision, on the same day

---

[40] On the significance of this difference between the two versions, see Barratt, "Chronological Priority," 199–200.

during None (the first liturgical office after the conventual high Mass), of the young man who asks her to give him nuts from the tree of love.

The narrative is confusing, but as these five chapters in L contain fifteen of its twenty ocurrences of *confessio(n-)*, while the three chapters in LDP contain eight of its total of sixteen, they are important for any discussion of Gertrud and her relationship with her confessor, on which we have remarkably little information. All was not well, one suspects. There is a marked contrast between the tenor of her sacramental confession—her initial reluctance, her unhappiness before, during, and after, the problems over the length of time it would take and the priest's miscalibration of the penance—and her visionary life: the bath, the garden, the tree and the young man, and, perhaps more important than these somewhat conventional allegories, her experience of leaning her head against the Lord's breast, from which "it was completely covered with the red hue of a rose in bloom" (L 85.3).

Perhaps Gertrud was unenthusiastic about sacramental confession to an earthly priest, regarding it as inferior to her direct relationship with the great high priest, Christ himself. A comment from L 162.7 (removed from LDP I.10.2) might suggest this interpretation. The two versions start out together:

> She had nevertheless decided that it was right for her, spattered as she was with the stains that are an unavoidable part of human existence, to run frequently to the feet of the Lord Jesu to be washed. But, as we said earlier, when she was aware of a more generous influx of divine mercy, she then gave her willing consent to God's good pleasure in all things and gave herself up as an instrument to display all the workings of love in her and with her, to such an extent that she did not hesitate to play with the Lord God of all the world as his equal.

But then L adds,

> And when this happened, she discarded beforehand the thought of her shortcomings and unworthiness, like a person who puts dirty clothes just outside the door or in a corner of the house, with the intention, if the Lord allowed it, of going back and cleansing them

through penitence, but [she did this] only if confident of forgiveness through God's mercy.

So she put her sins aside like a heap of dirty laundry, out of sight, intending to deal with them later through the sacrament of penance. This sounds casual or even dismissive. L immediately follows with another passage (preserved in abbreviated form in LDP 1.10.4) that downplays sacramental confession. It concerns her very unmedieval indifference to sudden death, that is, without the usual preceding sacraments:

> Because of **this** trust, hour by hour **she possessed such great confidence that** she longed for death, **nor did she ever find herself so negligent or weighed down by sin that she feared to die, but always running to God's mercy and loving-kindness, she would confess her guilt. Nor did she hope to postpone her death at any time, but entrusting herself completely to divine providence, she was convinced that,** whatever death she was to die, she would never lack God's mercy, without which she knew she could not be saved by any means, **as much in a** death long foreseen **as** sudden.[41]

A final word in defense of Helfta's confessors. Maybe they found themselves in an invidious position. Canonically only they could provide the sacraments, but when it came to spiritual direction they were left out in the cold, as many members of the community were under the guidance of at least two of the nuns (Mechtild of Hackeborn and Gertrud herself, and possibly also Mechtild of Magdebourg). And the abbess Gertrud, too, was clearly important in the sisters' spiritual lives. This is not in itself surprising: as Sister Marie-Hélène Doffre has kindly pointed out in a private communication:

> in all antique monastic rules, and especially in the Rule of St Benedict, and in the whole monastic tradition up to the present day, spiritual direction and teaching have not been reserved to priests.

---

[41] In this volume all material that is unique to L is printed in boldface.

> In his *Dialogues*, Saint Gregory applies the sentence of the Lord to Peter in Matt 16:19 to Saint Benedict—which can be theologically explained by the two kinds of charisms, ordered and not ordered. And concerning confession, Rhabanus Maur says that mortal sins require confession to a priest, but confession to the abbot is adequate for venial sins.

Perhaps the priests were made to feel that they were there only on sufferance, to be summoned when absolutely necessary but not otherwise given much respect or authority. It sometimes sounds as if Helfta sent for a priest the way others send for a plumber.

Furthermore, Gertrud believed that the Lord had endowed her with a quasi-sacerdotal role that she herself found disconcerting. Both L and LDP mention several times that she gave spiritual advice to some of the nuns. She acted as a teacher who could provide them with access to the divine through her mediation and who offered authentic advice on "doubtful points" (L 166/LDP I.14.2). The only such subject that is ever specified, however, is the question of whether or not people were fit to make their communion. On this matter Gertrud always erred on the side of generosity: in L 166/LDP I.14.2 we are told, "She would advise those who seemed reasonably fit and ready, to approach the Lord's sacrament with confidence, as God is gracious and merciful." But then she develops doubts about the confidence with which she dispenses such advice. Is she acting presumptuously? The Lord reassures her, at greater length in L than in LDP, pointing out that others can have confidence in her judgment because he, "infallible Truth itself," has dwelt in her with his grace for many years. Two chapters later (but not in L) the Lord says to Mechtild of Hackeborn,

> anyone whom she considers worthy to receive communion, my mercy will never consider unworthy. On the contrary, if she encourages someone to receive communion, I shall look on that person with greater love, and in accordance with my divine insight she will give a considered judgment, as to whether they are more or less serious, on the faults of all those who question her. (LDP I.16.1)

Gertrud is also able to judge the seriousness or otherwise of others' sins. In LDP (though not in L), in a summary of her many spiritual blessings, she herself reminds the Lord that

> if anyone . . . [should] uncover . . . some shortcoming for me to see, and then hear from me whether that shortcoming is serious or trivial, you, merciful God, would be willing to judge them more guilty or more innocent according to my words. From that time onwards they would always enjoy relief through your mediating grace in that they would never be so dangerously oppressed by that shortcoming as before. (LDP II.20.2)

This assertion must have passed the scrutiny of the seven friars brought in to approve the LDP, but at this point the modern editors of SCh are quick to disclaim any "sacramental role" being exercised by Gertrud: "Il ne s'agit pas d'un rôle sacramental, mais de grâces de lumière et de persuasion pour mettre au point dans des consciences timorées les problèmes de la culpabilité et du pardon." They make no comment, however, on a passage that relates a momentous visionary experience on the Octave of Easter:

> the Lord breathed on her and gave her too the Holy Spirit, saying, *"Receive the Holy Spirit: whose sins you shall forgive, they are forgiven them."*[42] At this she said, "Lord, how can this be, since this power to bind and loose is given to priests alone?" The Lord replied, "Anyone whose case you have judged to be innocent, discerning through my Spirit, will certainly be reckoned guiltless in my sight, and anyone whose case you have determined to be guilty shall appear answerable in my sight: for I shall speak through your mouth." (LDP IV.32.1; see also I.16.1; not in L)

The Lord's words here could be interpreted as meaning that although Gertrud does not possess the priestly power to absolve sins, nonetheless by speaking on the Lord's behalf she is able to declare whether or not a sin has been forgiven. While this reading would avoid her

---

[42] John 20:22-23.

making any claim to priestly status, it does seem to render earthly priests unnecessary, at least on occasion.

Finally, even more startling, a passage unique to L, at the conclusion of its account of Gertrud's painful confession, suggests that she herself can make an oblation at Mass in exactly the same way as the priest:

> she perceived the Lord saying to her, "Prepare for spiritual communion, for you too are about to receive communion and to make an offering in the way that you desire the priest to offer on your behalf." (L 86)

Conclusion

The Memorial of the Abundance of the Divine Sweetness is indeed full of surprises. From it Gertrud emerges as less conventionally saintly but more interesting. Was she a "black swan," or would she seem less unusual if we knew more about other religious women of the time? She is certainly a misunderstood saint. Not only was she regularly confused with the abbess of the same name, and was almost always represented in art with a crozier, although she never held a position of authority; not only is she best known in the popular mind for a prayer said miraculously to release souls from purgatory, though the prayer is in fact spurious. She is also inextricably associated with devotion to the Sacred Heart. Gertrud does indeed refer frequently to the divine (never the sacred) heart of Jesus, as symbolizing his humanity and loving-kindness, and this heart figures prominently in her visionary experiences. But she never promotes a cult as such or particular private prayers, nor does she demand the establishment of a feast or other liturgical innovations.

A Brief Note on the Texts

We do not as yet have a published Latin edition of the two Gertrudian texts translated here, although Sources Chrétiennes plans a dual language (French and English) edition, edited and translated by Sister

Marie-Hélène Deloffre, OSB. The present translation has been made from the translator's own transcription of L, from digital images kindly provided by the University of Leipzig. The translator would like to thank Sister Marie-Hélène Deloffre, OSB, and Dr. Elena Tealdi, who have also transcribed the texts and shared the results of their work. Final decisions, however, about the readings adopted here are my own.

All material that is unique to L in the translation is printed in bold. Material shared by L and LDP is reproduced from my earlier translation of the five books of *The Herald of God's Loving-Kindness*. Minor changes have, however, been made without notice to correct egregious errors or to accommodate second thoughts.

<PROLOGUE: I WILL LEAD HER INTO THE WILDERNESS>

1. *I will lead her into the wilderness, and there I will speak to her heart.*[1] It is written in Hosea, *I will lead her.* Augustine says, "The soul that God's loving-kindness regards (that is, chooses), humility lays low, penitence leads back, righteousness leads forth, obedience leads together, perseverance leads through, devotion leads in, purity anoints, and charity unites."[2]

Into the wilderness. Bernard says, "The wilderness of the heart is where the faithful soul takes its rest, in a place that is deep within it, where, the gates of all the senses having been closed, it may join with its beloved the more securely and intimately in a most chaste embrace, and there it is the better for it since it does not know where it is; it feels safer since it has lost itself in this way."[3]

In John we read, *We will come to him, and we will make our abode with him.*[4] Bernard says, "How great the grace of intimacy between the soul and the Word, do you think, that would arise out of that encounter? How great the confidence that follows from that intimacy?"[5] Augustine says, "O, how exalted are you on high, and the humble of heart are your dwelling places."[6]

---

[1] Hos 2:14. See also LDP IV.23.8, and LDP V.1.

[2] Ps-Augustine, *Liber de Spiritu et Anima* 36 (PL 40:1177).

[3] Ives, *Epistle to Severinus on Charity*, IV.35, ed. G. Dumeige (Paris: J. Vrin, 1955), 81, 83; Richard of Saint-Victor, *De gradibus charitatis* (PL 196:1206C).

[4] John 14:23, also quoted in LDP II.3.2, lines 4–6, and see LDP II.2.1, line 10.

[5] Bernard, SC 69.7 (SBOp 2:206); *Sermons on the Song of Songs*, trans. Kilian Walsh, CF 40 (Kalamazoo, MI: Cistercian Publications, 1980), 34. The CF translation of the SC, in CF 4, 7, 31, 40 (Kalamazoo, MI: Cistercian Publications, 1971, 1976, 1979, 1980) is used throughout, adapted where necessary.

[6] Ps 29:11; Augustine, Conf XI.31 (41).

Again, Augustine says, "Led by you, I have entered into my inmost being,[7] and this I was able do because you *became my helper.*"[8] Wisdom says, *My delights were to be with the children of men.*[9] Thence he[10] presents himself to the chosen soul as a garden of delights. The Song of Songs says, *My beloved is gone down into his garden, to the bed of aromatical spices.*[11] The bed is high ground sown with aromatical spices, marked out *with equal sides.*[12] In this way let the mind chosen by God be <called> *ground* through fruitfulness, *high* through chastity, *sown* through the sweetness of virtues, *marked out with equal sides* through the loveliness of composure, tilled by the frequent digging of self-examination, and watered by the waters of grace! (Gregory says, "*Running waters*[13] are the alternations of breathing. For the Holy Spirit flows in to justify us; he flows out to humble us. He comes in so that we may grow in virtue, and he goes away lest we should glory in our virtue through abundant grace. Christ is the source; the rivers are the gifts of grace."[14])

But this is not enough, for the Lord also asks for a little bed of repose in his dwelling-place. Bernard says, "The calm and clear conscience of those who have subjected the flesh to the spirit"[15] is the bed of the soul, in which she rests with Christ her bridegroom.[16] Let our bed therefore be of ebony, that is, cool with chastity;[17] let it be of cedar, that is, strengthened by truth; let it abound with flowers, that is, flourish with the spirit of joy; let it be aromatic; that is, smell

---

[7] See also LDP II.23.5, lines 22–25.

[8] Augustine, Conf VII.10 (16).

[9] Prov 8:31, frequently quoted in LDP.

[10] *Ipse*, though *sapientia* is grammatically feminine: Wisdom is traditionally identified with the Second Person of the Trinity.

[11] See also LDP II.1.1.

[12] Ezek 43:16.

[13] Ps 1:3.

[14] Richard of Saint-Victor, *Liber Exceptionum*, Secunda Pars, Lib. X, Cap. VI, ed. Jean Châtillon (Paris: J. Vrin, 1958), 388, lines 8–15.

[15] See Bernard, *Sermo de Diversis* 112.1 (SBOp 6:390).

[16] Alanus de Insulis, *Summa de Arte Praedicatoria* (PL 210:139).

[17] *caritate* L.

sweetly with a variety of graces; let it be *of gold*,[18] that is, shine with the brightness of wisdom; let it be *of silver*,[19] that is, gleam with purity; let it be elevated, that is, hanging in a spiritual sense on a hunger for heaven.

Gregory says, "The hearts of those in whom the soul is invisibly united with the bridegroom through love, so that it burns with desire for him and now desires none of those things that are in the world, are nothing other than the bedchambers in Holy Church."[20] Hence it is not called a bed, but a little bed, for the narrower it is, the closer the union of those who repose in it. Hugo[21] says, "God is united to the soul more joyfully in a conscience made narrow by reason,[22] for, according to Augustine, God is closer to the soul than it is to itself."[23] Augustine says, "Who will grant me this, that you may come to my soul and thus make it drunk, that I may forget all my sins?"[24] And again: "I have invited you into my soul, which you are preparing to receive you, out of the desire that you breathe into it."[25]

2. Bernard says,

> Just as God once came, visible in the flesh, to work salvation in the midst of the world, so today he comes, invisible in the spirit, for the salvation of the souls of each and every one. It is not *a great way*[26] that is set before you, but you must go as far as compunction of heart and confession of the mouth.[27] It is not with the steps of

---

[18] Esth 1:6.

[19] Esth 1:6.

[20] Gregory, Hiez 2.3.162–65 (CCSL 142:242).

[21] This quotation not identified.

[22] *in stricta racionabiliter consciencia* MS.

[23] See Quodlibet Anonyme IX, 19, *La Littérature Quodlibetique de 1260 a 1320,* I, ed. P. Glorieux (Tournai: Le Saulchoir Kain, 1925), 343, which also attributes this to Augustine.

[24] Augustine, Conf I.5 (5).

[25] Augustine, Conf XIII.1 (1).

[26] 1 Kgs 19:7.

[27] Bernard, *Sermo in Adventu Domini* 1.10 (PL 183:40).

the feet that God is sought but with desire.[28] Therefore the Lord comes to the soul with love and desire to show mercy, he quickens his pace in his eagerness to help, he draws near by assuming our lowliness, he is here with gifts in his hands, he provides for the understanding with illumination, he speaks, teaching persuasively about God's kingdom. Such is the coming of the bridegroom! The riches of salvation come with him.[29]

Furthermore, "she who loves *watches and waits*.[30] Blessed is she whom the Lord *shall find watching*"[31] and alert at every single moment,

so that *when he comes and knocks*, she *will open* the door *to him immediately*.[32] As one bound in duty to speak, one who may not remain silent, I am saying whatever I know on this subject from my own or from others' experience. If I were instructed, inwardly by the Spirit or outwardly by some person, on how righteousness must be protected and justice must be preserved, or if the discourse spoke loudly of humility, patience, and brotherly love, or the need to strive for holiness and peace and purity of heart, or if some suggestion had been made about similar things, it would indicate to me that the visitation of the Lord of hosts to my soul is at hand.[33] But if the discourse is welcome and heard with desire, then not only is the bridegroom coming, but we have to believe that he is speeding, that is, coming with desire. For his desire gives rise to yours, and because you are eager to receive his word, he himself hastens to enter.[34]

But now if you experience *the word as exceedingly refined*[35] and are filled with compunction, be sure that he is near you. If however you are not only filled with compunction but are also totally con-

---

[28] Bernard, SC 84.1 (SBOp 2:303).
[29] Bernard, SC 57.1 (SBOp 2:119).
[30] See Prov 8:34.
[31] Luke 12:37; Bernard, SC 57.1 (SBOp 2:119).
[32] See Luke 12:36; Bernard, SC 57.3 (SBOp 2:120).
[33] Bernard, SC 57.5 (SBOp 2:122).
[34] Bernard, SC 57.6 (SBOp 2:123).
[35] See Ps 118:140.

verted to the Lord, *vowing and determining to keep the judgments of his justice,*[36] then you know that he is present. For you read two things about him, both that fire goes before him, and that he is himself fire. They differ, however, because the fire that goes before has heat but no love; it boils up but does not boil dry. But the fire that is God does indeed devour, but it does not debase; it burns pleasantly and lays waste felicitously. For it is a *coal that lays waste*[37] but a fire that rages against vices, so that it may produce a place for healing unction in the soul. Recognize therefore that the Lord is present in the power that transforms you, and in the love that sets you aglow, for *the right hand of the Lord has itself wrought this strength.*[38]

Let us say therefore that the Word of God, God the bridegroom of the soul, both comes to the soul and leaves it again *according as he will,*[39] only that we experience these things by the soul's sensitivity, not the movement of the Word. That is: when it [i.e., the soul] senses grace, it acknowledges his presence; when it does not sense it, it mourns its absence and again seeks its presence.[40]

I confess that the Word has come to me, too—*I speak foolishly*[41]—and has come many times. And although he has quite often come to me, I have sometimes not been conscious of the moment of his coming; I perceived his presence, I remember that he had been with me; sometimes I had a presentiment that he would come, but I was never conscious of his going. For where he comes from to visit my soul, and where he goes when I lose him again, and by what means he enters and leaves, I admit that I do not know even now.[42] So you ask, although *his ways are altogether unsearchable*[43] how I knew he was present?[44]

---

[36] See Ps 118:106.
[37] See Ps 119:4; also LDP II.7.2.
[38] See Ps 117:15; Bernard, SC 57.7 (SBOp 2:124).
[39] 1 Cor 12:11.
[40] Bernard, SC 74.2 (SBOp 2:240).
[41] 2 Cor 11:21.
[42] Bernard, SC 74.5 (SBOp 2:242).
[43] Rom 11:33; see also LDP II.1.1 and III.22.1.
[44] Heb 4:12; Bernard, SC 74.6 (SBOp 2:243).

He is *living and effectual, and more piercing than any two-edged sword; and reaching unto the division of the soul and the spirit,*[45] and again when the soul decides to speak, much less can the Word lie hidden, not merely because he is present everywhere, but rather because, without his inspiration, the soul will lack the devotion that urges speech.[46] And so truly the speech of God is an infusion of grace, and the soul's is wonder and thanksgiving.[47]

Bernard again: "And so, even in this body we can often enjoy the happiness of the bridegroom's presence, but it is a happiness that is never complete because the joy of the visitation is followed by the pain of his departure."[48]

3. Now such a visitation[49] "does not lie in the will of the one who receives it, but in the grace of the one who bestows it; that is, since *the Holy Spirit breathes where he will,*[50] he breathes when, how, and on whom he will.[51] But equally it is the human task to prepare the heart, freeing it from extraneous affections, the reason or understanding from preoccupations, the memory from distractions or practical affairs, and sometimes from essential activities, so that in God's good time, and at the hour he pleases, when it has heard the voice of the Spirit, it will immediately run to it and work together with it for good."[52]

---

[45] See also LDP I.1.3.

[46] Bernard, SC 45.7 (SBOp 2:54).

[47] Bernard, SC 45.8 (SBOp 2:55).

[48] Bernard, SC 32.2 (SBOp 1:227).

[49] *visitatio* L: see also LDP I.Prol.6 and 7, chapter heading of LDP II.6, and LDP II.22.1.

[50] John 3:8.

[51] See also LDP I.1.3.

[52] William of Saint-Thierry, *Un Traité de la vie solitaire: Epistola ad fratres de Monte Dei*, ed. M.-M. Davy, 2 vols. (Paris, 1940), §251 (see also PL 184:347BC). In the Middle Ages this treatise was generally accepted as the work of Bernard of Clairvaux. For an English translation, see *William of St Thierry: The Golden Epistle*, trans. Theodore Berkeley, intro. by J. M. Déchanet, CF 12 (Kalamazoo, MI: Cistercian Publications, 1980).

I said too little[53] when I said that it does not lie in the will, since it is also rightly deserved,[54] according to the words of the Apostle: *Whom he predestinated, them he also called. And whom he called, them he also justified,*[55] for he finds no one <already> justified. "Although the Lord wishes for a *glorious* bride, *not having spot or wrinkle, or any such thing,*[56] yet he does not seek such a one. For where would she be found? Rather, he himself makes one like that, such a one as he presents to himself."[57] Augustine says,

> I attribute it to your grace that you melted away my sins like ice; I also attribute to your grace all the evil that I have not committed. I declare that they have all been set aside, both the evil that I committed of my own accord and what, under your guidance, I did not commit.[58] You drove away from me those fruitless joys, and you took their place, you who are sweeter than all pleasure, though not to flesh and blood, brighter than all light, but hidden deeper than any secret, higher than every honor, but not to those who are high in their own estimations.[59]

4. This visitation is altogether divided into three kinds. First, then, he appears to the devout souls as present, *beautiful above the sons of men,*[60] of a lovely virgin the lovelier son, appearing or working beside them, or caressing them in some other courteous companionship, or at the altar, or in some other physical location. And although

---

[53] From this point the compiler strikes out on her own.

[54] *non inmerito* L: see also LDP I.5.1, LDP I.12.1, LDP IV.38.7, and L 117.2 below.

[55] Rom 8:30; see LDP I.Prol.3.

[56] See Eph 5:27.

[57] Bernard, *Sermo in Nativitate S. Ioannis Baptistae* 11 (SBOp 5:183–84). For an English translation, see *Bernard of Clairvaux: Sermons for the Summer Season*, trans. Beverly Mayne Kienzle, CF 53 (Kalamazoo, MI: Cistercian Publications, 1991), 95–96. It is noticeable that a few lines later, Bernard quotes Hos 2:11: our text opens by quoting Hos 2:7.

[58] Augustine, Conf II.7 (15).

[59] Augustine, Conf IX.1 (1).

[60] Ps 44:3.

this kind is very sweet, nonetheless it does not greatly affect the soul spiritually, but we can apply to it what Bernard says about the love of the heart,[61] that he himself says is, as it were, the lowest grade of love. About this he says, "There stands before the person who is praying the sacred image of the God-man, either being born or suckling or teaching or advising or dying or rising again or ascending into heaven."[62] And later: "The measure of this devotion is that its sweetness completely fills the heart, completely frees it from the love of all sensual pleasures: this is truly what it is to love with your whole heart."[63]

But the second kind is when the devout soul seems "raised aloft on the wings of desire,"[64] up to the throne of the King of Glory, more lovely than the countenances of angels,[65] so that "it may feed on divine mysteries at the refreshing table of the citizens of heaven in pastures beside abundant waters,"[66] and may enjoy God for delight even if not for intimate companionship. But this kind is not very different from the first; since God deigns to manifest his presence everywhere, we can never complain of the absence of true delight, except in that <first> kind, and let this corroboration be added, that the lover's devotion is accustomed to meditate continually on heavenly things, according to that verse, *Our conversation is in heaven,*[67] and hence it has there found for itself a more gracious intimacy. Of these two <kinds> Bernard says, "Thus that man is devout, he chants, he reads, in all his deeds as careful and circumspect as if God were there before his eyes, as is indeed the case; he prays as if caught up and presented before the face of majesty on his lofty throne."[68]

There is a third kind, of which Bernard also says, "It is divine contemplation, different from the others in that it takes place inwardly," since it is not through corporeal images, but "God himself

---

[61] That is, "carnal love."
[62] Bernard, SC 20.6 (SBOp 1:118).
[63] Bernard, SC 20.7 (SBOp 1:119).
[64] Bernard, SC 32.2 (SBOp 1:227).
[65] See LDP IV.35.1 and LDP V.7.4.
[66] Ps-Augustine, *Liber Meditationum* 37 (PL 40:933).
[67] Phil 3:20; Bernard, SC 27.8 (SBOp 1:187).
[68] Ps-Augustine, *Manuale*, cap. 19 (PL 40:959).

is pleased to visit *the soul that seeks him,*[69] provided it is committed to seeking him with all its desire and love."[70] For it is not content unless it welcomes him down from heaven by a special privilege into its inmost heart, into its deepest love; it wants to have the one it desires present, not in bodily form but by inward infusion, not by appearing externally but by laying hold of it within. It is beyond question that the vision is all the more delightful the more inward it is and not external. It is the Word, who penetrates without sound, who is effective though not pronounced, who wins the affections without striking on the ears. His face is not the recipient but the giver of form, not affecting the eyes of the body but rejoicing the face of the heart, pleasing not by its outward appearance but by its gift of love.[71]

This is truly the visitation *through the bowels of the mercy of our God <in which> the Orient from on high <has visited us>,*[72] concerning which those words of the psalm can worthily be said with thanksgiving: *You have visited the earth, and have plentifully watered it; you have many ways enriched it.*[73] For truly this visitation, sweetest and most joyful above all things sweet and joyful, can by no means be received without its fruit being plentifully enriched. For the soul is both inflamed and softened[74] to be conformed to God in charity, in whose *image and likeness*[75] it finds itself made lovely. Thence Bernard says,

> Such conformity weds the soul to the Word, since it is like it by nature, and no less shows itself like it in the exercise of the will, loving as it is loved. Therefore, if it loves perfectly, the marriage has taken place. What more joyful than this conformity, what more desirable than the charity by whose operation, O soul, not satisfied with human teaching, you approach the Word with confidence,

---

[69] Lam 3:25.

[70] Bernard, SC 31.4 (SBOp 1:221).

[71] Bernard, SC 31.6 (SBOp 1:223); also quoted in LDP II.21.1.

[72] See Luke 1:78.

[73] Ps 64:10.

[74] See also LDP II.7.1 and II.8.4.

[75] Gen 1:26.

reliant on yourself, clinging to the Word with constancy. Do you linger with the Word as a familiar friend, refer to him in every matter with an intellectual grasp proportionate to the boldness of your desire? Truly this is a spiritual contract, a holy marriage. No, it is more than a contract; it is an embrace. Plainly an embrace, where it wills, and does not will, the same thing, and makes of two, one spirit.[76]

5. "It is one thing for the soul to go in with God, another for it to go out to him."[77] For to enter is "to linger alone with the Alone, to forget all outer things and to delight in his sweetness with supreme intimacy."[78] But to go out to him is to be led out of oneself and raised up to the sublimities of contemplation, "so that it may have within itself," to God's likeness, "that by which it may be admonished either to stay with God or to return if it has strayed. For it does not stray by walking on its feet, but it strays in its affections, or rather defections, and degenerates. Indeed, its return is the conversion of the affections to God, as it must be conformed to him in charity."[79] For the love of God gives intimacy, "intimacy gives boldness, boldness gives a foretaste, a foretaste gives hunger.[80] It is carried away by prayers, drawn on by longings; it forgets its deserts, closes its eyes to the majesty <of the bridegroom> and opens them to the pleasure <he brings>, *setting <him> in safety and dealing confidently in his regard.*"[81]

6. *And there I will speak to her heart.*[82] Augustine says, "My soul, do not deafen the ears of your heart. Listen! The Word himself calls

---

[76] Bernard, SC 83.3 (SBOp 2:299).

[77] Richard of Saint-Victor, *Benjamin Major*, IV.16 (PL 196:154B).

[78] Richard of Saint-Victor, *Benjamin Major*, IV.16 (PL 196:154C).

[79] Bernard, SC 83.2 (SBOp 2:299).

[80] Bernard, SC 74.3 (SBOp 2:241).

[81] See Ps 11:6; Bernard, SC 74.4 (SBOp 2:242).

[82] Hos 2:14.

you to return, and there is the place of rest that cannot be disturbed, where love does not withhold itself unless it has itself first been withheld."[83] Again, "I wandered away and I remembered you, and I heard your voice calling after me to return, and I could hardly hear it because of the uproar of my sins! Well! now I return hot and thirsty, panting for your fountain."[84] And again Augustine says, "The ears of my heart are here before you, Lord. Open them and *say to my soul, I am your salvation.*"[85] "I shall run after that voice, and I shall seize you!"[86]

I shall speak to her heart.[87] Bernard says, "O the sweet discourse of God in the soul and with the soul! It is formed without the tongue and without the sound of words, and is sensed without the ear and in silence; only he who speaks and is spoken to hears it, every outsider is excluded. But those words are flowing from a heavenly source, watering and moistening what is dried up before the multitudinous desires of love, whose talk is about loved ones, dispelling distaste from the heart and weariness from the body."[88]

Gregory says, "Holy souls speak with God through their desires that are indeed not at odds with God, not that they pay no attention to future events, but they cling to him the more ardently; they receive from him what they ask from him, because they see that he wants to do it, and if they did not ask, they would be at odds with his will. God answers them because of their inner conviction."[89]

Bernard says, "God is a spirit, and the soul is a spirit, and they possess their own mode of speech with which they speak to each other and make known their presence. The speech of the Word is the favor of his condescension; that of the soul, the fervor of devotion: if it does not have that, it is like a speechless infant, and it cannot in

---

[83] See Augustine, Conf IV, 11 (16).

[84] Augustine, Conf XII, 10 (10).

[85] Ps 34:3.

[86] Augustine, Conf I, 5 (5).

[87] Hos 2:14.

[88] Ives, *Epistle to Severinus on Charity*, IV.37; and Richard of Saint-Victor, *De gradibus charitatis* IV (PL 196:1206D–7A).

[89] See (distantly) Gregory, Mo 2.VII.5 (CCSL 143:66).

any way hold converse with the Word. Therefore when the Word wishes to speak to my soul and moves its tongue, the soul cannot but hear, for *the word of God is living and effectual, and more piercing than any two-edged sword.*[90] And again, when the soul decides to speak, much less can the Word hide from it, not merely because it is present everywhere but rather because without his inspiration the soul would lack the devotion that urges speech."[91]

Therefore for God, to hear is to perceive our desires, but for us, to speak to God is to pant with manifest desires.[92] And so the soul must speak with God ardently and forcefully. Gregory says, "It is not our words but our desires that act as more forceful voices in God's most holy ears."[93] Next, it must speak trustingly, which is why the Lord himself says, *All things whatsoever you shall ask when you pray, believe that you shall receive, and they shall* be done *to you.*[94] Next, silently. Isidore says, "The prayer of the heart is not the prayer of the lips, for God does not attend to the words of the person interceding, but he looks into the heart of the person praying, and if the heart prays silently and the voice is mute, even though it is hidden from human beings, it is not hidden from God, who is present [to the conscience]."[95] Next, frequently, Bernard says, "If you are in your bed, or somewhere else, be constant in prayer, and that place is a temple! You must pray frequently, and when the body is bowed, the mind must be raised up to God."[96] Next, perseveringly. Gregory says, "Holy desires increase through delay, but if they diminish through delay, they are not desires!"[97] Next, humbly and reverently. When Abraham began to speak with the Lord, he acknowledged that he was *dust and ashes.*[98] And Isaiah lamented that he was *a man of*

[90] Heb 4:12; see above, n. 44, and LDP I.1.3.
[91] Bernard, SC 45.7 (SBOp 2:54).
[92] See Gregory, Mo 35.III.4 (CCSL 143B:1776).
[93] Gregory, Mo 22.XVII.43 (CCSL 143A:1122).
[94] Mark 11:24.
[95] Isidore of Seville, *Sententiarum* 3.7.4 (PL 83:672).
[96] Ps-Bernard, *Meditationes* 7 (PL 184:676).
[97] Gregory, Ev 25.2.58–60 (CCSL 141:207).
[98] Gen 18:27.

unclean lips.[99] Similarly, Jeremiah confessed that he could not speak,[100] and "all those who are strong in virtues, when they see the more lofty things of God, become weak and feeble in their own estimation."[101]

Therefore, faithful soul, speak with the Lord your God, but with desire, with prayer, and with love. And so God speaks with the soul, but by teaching. The soul speaks with God, but by praying. Isidore says, "Anyone who wishes constantly to be with God should pray or read without ceasing. For when we pray, we are speaking with God himself, but when we read, God speaks with us."[102] The psalm says, *I will hear what the Lord God will speak in me.*[103]

7. Three ways of hearing God in the soul can be distinguished. The first way, then, is when the soul desires something: turning it over in its mind, it takes refuge in prayer, striving to beg for [it] from God. Thence it comes about that the faithful soul takes consolation from this when it receives a divinely inspired reply. But you should know that there can never be complete certainty in such matters, since human understanding is sometimes contaminated with preconception, and thence an answer sometimes seems to be formed according to the preconceived opinion of the understanding. Thence Bernard says, "Sometimes the thoughts of our own mind are very like the words of Truth speaking within us, and no one can easily differentiate between what springs from his own heart and what he hears [from without],[104] unless, enlightened by the Holy Spirit, he receives that special gift that the Apostle calls *discernment of spirits*."[105]

---

[99] Isa 6:5.
[100] See Jer 1:6, also LDP I.Prol.3, lines 11–12.
[101] Gregory, Hiez 1.8.377–79 (CCSL 142:111).
[102] Isidore of Seville, *Sententiarum* 3.8.2 (PL 83:679).
[103] Ps 84:9.
[104] Bernard, SC 32.5 (SBOp 1:220).
[105] 1 Cor 12:10; Bernard, SC 32.6 (SBOp 1:230).

The second way is when grace is infused from sudden inspiration, enlightening the intellect either to understand Scripture or to comprehend holy mysteries. The first of these, says Bernard, is given for our own satisfaction and the second for the instruction of our neighbors.[106] This is what Bernard calls "the eye of the bridegroom," that is, the gaze of God on the soul, and even if this is received without any great taste for devotion, as if in an impulse, nonetheless the more it is known to be uncontaminated by previous human consideration, the more it can be trusted. Hence Bernard says, "Let the enemies of grace know that without grace the human heart has no power to think what is good, but *our sufficiency is from God.*"[107]

Then the third way is when, according to Job, *my ears by stealth as it were received the veins of its* divine *whisper,*[108] *the voice as it were of a gentle wind.*[109] For it does not make a great noise, but it drips the honeyed speech of God with sweetness and gentleness as if from the golden vessel of divinity into a silver one, that is, into the soul, purified by the fire of love and the re-echoing devotion of thanksgiving, while gently and kindly making known to the soul his will or the delightfulness of his unbounded love. Melted by this, the soul flows back into God[110] so that, if one may say so, from the gold and silver vessels, that is, the one that pours and the one that receives, there comes into existence a wonderful electrum[111] through unanimity of wills.

Thence Bernard writes to the brothers of Mont Dieu, "To be one spirit with God is perfection of the will, when not only does the soul now will what God wills, but in this way it is not only affected but perfected in its affections so that it cannot will other than what God wills. To will what God wills is now to be like God, but to be unable to will unless God wills is to be what God is, for whom it is the same

---

[106] Bernard, SC 57.8 (SBOp 2:124).

[107] 2 Cor 3:5; Bernard, SC 32.7 (SBOp 2:230).

[108] Job 4:12.

[109] Job 4:16, see also LDP I.16.3.

[110] See LDP V.27.7.

[111] An amber-colored alloy made from gold and silver; see also LDP I.3.4, LDP III.10.2, and LDP IV.6.6.

thing to will and to be able."[112] And this is what is said in John: *We shall see him as he is*, because *we shall be like to him.*[113]

In the Song of Songs it says, *My soul melted when he spoke.*[114] Augustine says, "I heard, and sucked out a drop of sweetness from your truth."[115] Here the soul receives such tried and true certainty that it is completely impossible to doubt it in any way. Hence Augustine says, "I heard, as God is heard in the heart, and at once I had no cause to doubt; I would have more easily doubted that I was alive than that it was not the truth."[116]

But one should note what was said about the first way, that one cannot always be certain of it. Hence we should make this distinction: when a reply that a person takes to be from God is such that someone can be induced to do something good, or avoid something evil, then we can be certain that it is from God, at least if the authority of holy Scripture agrees. But when the reply relates to a matter in which there is only encouragement of human weakness or longing of one's own will, then it should be entrusted to God as uncertain. But in all things we must trust in the goodness of God, who by no means allows someone who trusts in him to be deceived, especially when they seek nothing for themselves but purely for God's praise alone. Augustine says, "Throw yourself on God, O man; he is not so cruel as to draw back from you and let you fall!"[117]

8. There are numerous results from this conversation of God with the soul. First, then, it makes the soul chaste. For it speaks with chaste eloquence, since it teaches chastity with chaste mouth and leads to chaste love. Second, God's speech is life-giving, for it gives life to the soul and preserves the life that it has given it. In this way when

---

[112] See William of Saint-Thierry, *Epistola ad fratres de Monte Dei* (PL 184:348AB).

[113] See 1 John 3:2.

[114] Song 5:6.

[115] Augustine, Conf XIII.30 (45).

[116] Augustine, Conf VII.10 (16).

[117] Augustine, Conf VIII.11 (27).

the word of God is received, understood, and grasped, it grows in the soul, and so its life, too, grows. Third, it makes the soul fertile in virtues, in gifts of grace, and in rewards. Fourth, it inflames, ignites, and liquefies. Furthermore, what is liquified must be purged and heated for purity, in case it contains *dross*,[118] by that very love that is a *consuming fire*,[119] purifying it from the straw of ignorance and the delinquencies of youth, and rendering the soul, once completely purified, worthy of marriage with God, *not having spot or wrinkle*.[120]

Fifth, it flows with honey and sweetens the soul, and as a result enlightens it. Jonathan *dipped* the rod *in a honey-comb* [. . . *and his eyes were enlightened*].[121] *Jonathan* means "the dove coming"; the dove-like soul is the bridegroom's beloved, illuminated by the Holy Spirit; raised up on wings of contemplation, it comes to the source of the outflow of honey-sweet divinity,[122] which is the Holy Spirit that surpasses all sweet things. When the soul has tasted its honeyed sweetness,[123] it will be enlightened, at any rate in the eyes of its understanding.

Sixth, the words of God are beautiful and make the soul beautiful. Thence is said: *Nephthali, a hart let loose, and giving words of beauty*.[124] Jesus is called a hart for his swiftness, because *he has rejoiced as a giant to run the way*.[125] He is said to be *let loose* because *the Word was made flesh, and dwelt among us*.[126] He is *giving words of beauty* because, ever thinking sweetly of us in the presence of the Father, he corrects all our shortcomings. And he himself says: *Now you are clean by reason of the word, which I have spoken to you*.[127]

---

[118] See Isa 1:25; see also LDP II.3.2 and II.7.2.

[119] Deut 4:24; see also LDP II.7.2, II.17.1, and V.4.6.

[120] Eph 5:23-27.

[121] 1 Sam 14:27.

[122] See LDP II.6.1.

[123] See LDP 1V.48.3.

[124] Gen 49:21.

[125] Ps 18:6; see also L 109 below.

[126] John 1:14.

[127] John 15:3.

9. It is written in John, *I will manifest myself to him.*[128] Bernard says, "Perish the thought, brothers, that any of you should be so lacking in perception as to think that one who sees in the Spirit sees nothing."[129] Richard says, "We are certain of this: that many people receive the light of revelatory grace in the time of their prayer, and that many progress towards the same grace from the strength of their devotion."[130] Augustine says, "I entered into my inmost being, and saw with the eye of my soul, such as it was, the unchanging light [casting its rays] over my mind, which was not the everyday light visible to all flesh and blood."[131] Bernard says, "I do not think, brothers, no, I do not think this vision is to be lightly esteemed or that it is common to all, even though it cannot match that vision that is to come."[132] Again, Bernard says:

> The Lord often appears to those who are fervent under more than one form.[133] It is essential that the enjoyment of God's presence be varied in proportion to the various desires of the soul, and that the infused experience of supernal sweetness delight the palate of the soul, desiring diverse things, in different ways.[134] For *God is a spirit,*[135] and covets the beauty of that soul that he observes *walking in the spirit*[136] and not fulfilling the desires of the flesh, especially if he has seen that it burns with love for himself.[137] Therefore if there is a *man of desires,*[138] *having a desire to be dissolved*

---

[128] John 14:21.
[129] See Bernard, SC 70.2 (SBOp 2:208).
[130] Richard of Saint-Victor, *De eruditione hominis interioris* 2.11 (PL 196:1310).
[131] See Augustine, Conf VII.10 (16).
[132] Bernard, SC 45.6 (SBOp 2:53).
[133] Bernard, SC 31.1 (SBOp 1:219).
[134] Bernard, SC 31.7 (SBOp 1:223).
[135] John 8:34.
[136] Gal 5:16.
[137] Bernard, SC 31.6 (SBOp 1:223).
[138] Dan 9:23.

and to be with Christ,[139] let him desire vigorously, thirst ardently, meditate unflaggingly: straightway he will meet God.[140]

Nor will he be there for every soul, but only for the one who is proved to be a worthy bride by intense devotion and vehement desire and sweet affection, on whom God, who is about to approach for visitation, bestows beauty. If someone is found who has not yet been raised to this state but is pierced by the memory of his shortcomings, he needs a physician, not a bridegroom, to anoint his wounded conscience with the oil of his mercy.[141]

Again:

For those who have grown weary of studying spiritual doctrine and have become lukewarm and grumble about the tasks enjoined on them, if the compassionate Lord draws near to them on the way they are traveling and begins to talk to them, so that *their heart is burning within them,*[142] does he not take away distaste from the mind and weariness from the body?[143]

Again:

It seems to me that he appears in the guise of a mighty father of a family[144] or a sovereign ruler to those who, climbing up *to a deep heart,*[145] and restless and curious because of greater liberty of spirit and purity of conscience, dare to penetrate deeper mysteries and to strive for what is more perfect, not only of the senses but also of the virtues. For because of the grandeur of their faith these are considered worthy of experiencing all fullness, and in all the treasure houses of wisdom there is nothing from which the *God of all knowledge*[146] would think of turning these people away.

---

[139] Phil 1:23; see also LDP III.30.31 and V.23.1.

[140] Bernard, SC 32.2 (SBOp 1:227).

[141] Bernard, SC 32.3 (SBOp 1:228).

[142] See Luke 24:32.

[143] Bernard, SC 32.4 (SBOp 1:228).

[144] For the image of God as *paterfamilias*, see LDP II.18.1, III.54.1, IV.48.6, and IV.55.2.

[145] Ps 63:7.

[146] 1 Sam 2:3.

For they undertake great deeds, and what they undertake they achieve, for great faith deserves great rewards.[147]

Therefore to great spirits like this the bridegroom comes in his greatness, and he *will do great things for them,*[148] *sending forth his light and his truth, and conducting and bringing them unto his holy hill, and into his tabernacles.*[149] *Their eyes shall see the king in his beauty*[150] going before into *the beautiful places of the wilderness,*[151] to *the flowers of roses*[152] and *lilies of the valley,*[153] to the gardens where delights abound and streams run from the fountains, to the delights of the wine cellars, to the sweet smells of spices, and last of all to the privacy of the bed chamber.[154]

Augustine says on this verse from Exodus, *Man shall not see me and live,*[155] "The divine nature cannot be seen by human sight, but is seen by that sight that renders those who now see with it not human but superhuman."[156] Gregory says, "Eternal brightness can be seen with the penetrating eye of contemplation by those living in this flesh and growing in inestimable virtue; nonetheless no one will see him and live, for anyone who sees wisdom, which is God, dies utterly to this world, to avoid being hindered by love for it."[157]

10. This manifestation, too, can be divided into three kinds, of which the first is that which we read happened very often to the fathers, and is also understood to happen to certain chosen ones even

---

[147] Bernard, SC 32.8 (SBOp 1:231).

[148] See Ps 125:2-3.

[149] See Ps 42:3.

[150] See Isa 33:17.

[151] Ps 64:13.

[152] See Sir 50:8.

[153] See Song 2:1.

[154] Bernard, SC 32.9 (SBOp 1:232).

[155] Exod 33:20.

[156] Augustine, *De Trinitate* I.6.11, in *De Trinitate Libri XV*, ed. W. J. Mountain and F. Glorie, CCSL 50 (Turnhout: Brepols, 1968).

[157] Gregory, Mo 18.LIV.89 (CCSL 143A:952).

now: that is, it "takes place exteriorly, and consists of images, either splendid apparitions or the spoken word."[158] This kind is sufficiently well-known.

The second kind is the same one that was divided into two in the kinds of visitation described earlier: that is, when something is seen in the spirit through mental images,[159] and things incorporeal are known through mystical understanding. For instance, one sees spiritual beings adorned with gold and precious stones, and one understands through those adornments the rewards of virtues; or one sees buildings or gardens with flowers or trees, and one understands the delights of eternity, and so on.[160] Bernard says of this <kind of> image that angelic spirits accompany it so that those things that God provides in the understanding may be the more comprehensible and can be communicated to the instruction of one's neighbors.[161] Hence the Apostle says, *We see now through a glass, in a dark manner.*[162] Thus it is necessary that this revelation should be supported by the witness of holy Scripture. Hence Hugh says that, according to the word of Jesus Christ, *in the mouth of two or three witnesses every word may stand.*[163] He himself, too, turns to the authority of Scripture to confirm the truth of his revelation, not only figuratively but also openly.[164]

Next, the third kind is when the experience of the divine rushes into the inmost recesses of the soul, and pours inwardly the quintessence of wisdom from the secrets of the divine treasuries.[165] Thence it is said of Paul, "You have beheld things *which it is not granted man*

---

[158] Bernard, SC 31.4 (SBOp 1:221).

[159] *per ymaginaciones* L: see LDP I.Prol.6 and IV.12.3.

[160] Many of Gertrud's visions are of this type. See also the quotation from "Master Hugh . . . *On the Inner Man*" (more correctly, Richard of Saint-Victor, *Benjamin Minor*, 25 [PL 196:10–11]) in LDP I.1.4.

[161] A paraphrase of Bernard, SC 41.4 (SBOp 2:31); later in this text (para. 10 below), as also in LDP IV.26.2, the passage is quoted more closely.

[162] 1 Cor 13:12.

[163] Matt 18:16; see LDP I.2.2.

[164] Richard of Saint-Victor, *Benjamin Minor* 81 (PL 196:57). See also LDP I. Prol.8.

[165] *de occultis diuinorum thesaurorum suorum* L: see LDP II.16.6.

to utter."[166] Bernard says, "Think that in this the Lord was consoling his [i.e., Paul's] love, concerned about such things, and said, 'Why do you worry that human hearing cannot grasp your thought? *Let your voice sound in my ears*';[167] that is, if you cannot reveal what you perceive to mortals, nevertheless be consoled because your voice can delight the ears of God."[168] "The psalmist says, *The remainders of the thought shall keep holiday to you.*"[169] Bernard says, "Whatever the faithful soul is able to learn from the mystery of wisdom by an eager and inquiring mind, it imparts by zealous preaching for the salvation of the people; the 'remainder,' which the ordinary people cannot grasp, is employed in praising God with festive jubilation."[170]

Now, concerning both of those <kinds of> outer revelations, Bernard says, "When the spirit is ravished out of itself and granted a vision of God that suddenly shines into the mind with the swiftness of a lightning flash, immediately images of earthly things fill the imagination, either as an aid to understanding or to temper the intensity of the divine light. So well adapted are they to the divinely illumined senses, that in their shadow the utterly pure and brilliant radiance of the truth is rendered more bearable to the mind and more capable of being communicated to others. My opinion is that they are formed in us by the inspirations of the holy angels,"[171] which is their function.[172] Thence "we feel that the being of God in its pure state is perceived without any shadow of corporeal substances. The elegance of the imagery that so worthily clothes and reveals it I attribute to angelic skill.[173] The things we speak of are divine, and they remain absolutely unknown except to those who have experienced them.[174] Angels not only provide this to the chosen inwardly, but outwardly

---

[166] 2 Cor 12:4.

[167] Cant 2:14.

[168] Bernard, SC 62.3 (SBOp 2:156).

[169] Ps 75:11; Bernard, SC 62.3 (SBOp 2:157).

[170] Bernard, SC 62.3 (SBOp 2:157).

[171] Bernard, SC 41.3 (SBOp 2:30).

[172] Also quoted in LDP IV.26.2, with the same additional comment.

[173] Bernard, SC 41.4 (SBOp 2:31).

[174] Bernard, SC 41.3 (SBOp 2:30).

they also provide elegance of diction, so that these things may be understood more easily and pleasurably by the audience."[175]

Concerning this kind of grace one must know that, in the first state, when God begins to give his chosen one[176] a foretaste through grace, after the divine visitation has been received there is a very great temptation, in accordance with human weakness, to rush back to outer reality. Those things that at the time of the visitation were received through the understanding as completely certain come to be doubted, to the extent that she is also weighed down by sorrow, as if deceived in such things. But this should not disturb the faithful soul, for it is under the control of the divine goodness, which cares more for the soul than any mother has ever cared for her only child.[177] Moreover, the wisdom of God is unsearchable:[178] it best knows what grace, or rather what thought, advances progress or discourages failure at each and every moment. For just as the sight of someone who passes rapidly from great and prolonged darkness into the brightness of the sun[179] is struck by excessive light, so when the soul is first drawn to intimacy with the divine, if it were not made humble, it could sometimes fall into the wilderness from some disposition arising from human weakness.

And so, when the most faithful lover[180] sees that the grace of intimacy[181] is appropriate for that person, he breathes it in; but he overshadows her with some trouble when he knows that is more useful, just as someone holding a light in his hands would illuminate or obscure[182] what is opposite, as he chose. Amid these changes, therefore, let the faithful soul cling to the words of the wise man: *In the day of evils, be not unmindful of good things*, and *In the day of good things, be not unmindful of evils*.[183] That is, although grace has

---

175 Bernard, SC 41.4 (SBOp 2:31).

176 *electe sue* L, i.e., feminine gender.

177 LDP contains many images of God as mother, e.g., III.63.2 and III.83.1.

178 *inscrutabilis . . . sapientia* L: there are 16 examples of this phrase in LDP.

179 See LDP I.10.1.

180 See LDP V.10.4.

181 See LDP III.74.1 and IV.40.1.

182 See LDP III.18.8.

183 See Sir 11:27.

smiled[184] upon her, let the soul be bashful with chaste and filial fear, lest she misuse it. Nor should we be unaware that the ancient enemy, who hates this grace in every way, may attack it, either raising it up by pride or throwing it down by lack of faith. But since anyone may learn from various scriptural witnesses,[185] if unction itself is their teacher, to oppose pride with humility, and since I have found that very many people, cast down through lack of faith and consequently through ingratitude, have lost this gift, from that follows what Bernard says: "Ingratitude is a scorching wind, drying up the source of mercy, the flowing waters of grace."[186]

And so when, after you have received a salutary visitation, the suggestion is made in your heart that it was not from God, since you are a woman unworthy[187] of such a gift, reply that you were worthy to have the Son of God die for you, and that you often deserve to share in his body and blood, and similar much greater things, if only because of God's freely given loving-kindness. Therefore by the same loving-kindness, when he foresees your lack of faith to be so great that he could not attract you in any other way, he forestalls you with such gifts, as if you were a hireling. Thence if you were proved ungrateful and negligent, God's righteous judgment would find you guilty of a rather serious offence, and so you should strive with all your might to show yourself worthy of such visitations. Therefore by the exertions of such efforts, it will always *work together* with you *for good*,[188] or rather, for the best, even if, perish the thought, it had originated from some misleading spirit.

11. Richard on the dream of Nebuchadnezzar bears witness concerning such revelations when he says,

---

[184] See LDP III.30.21 and IV.15.1 (MS W).

[185] See LDP I.1.2.

[186] Bernard, SC 51.6 (SBOp 2:87).

[187] *indigna* L, i.e., feminine gender.

[188] See Rom 8:28 and LDP I.10.1, III.9.3, and V.1.5.

Some people receive a divine revelation in their prayer, others in their meditation, and others often during their speech. The first group can never ascend to lofty things except through inward compunction and after emendation of heart. But the second group also abound in divine revelations while they meditate. The third group have become so proficient that they are so familiar with the light of divine revelation that many things previously unknown to them are revealed in the midst of speech. They can at any time discourse subtly about subtle matters, and whatever they are asked, they can almost always answer satisfactorily without any premeditation, and, as they wish and as they choose, they can at almost any time effortlessly supply answers on anything someone wants discussed, asserted, or defended.[189]

And so in the same treatise he says on this verse, *except the gods, whose conversation is not with men,*[190] "By the gods you can understand people divinely inspired, whose conversation now is not with other human beings, that is, those wise in human affairs, because now they could truly say, *Our conversation is in heaven.*[191] For many things that are beyond human investigation are known from divine inspiration."[192] But there are other things that we discern from divine revelation, and others again that we understand from the liveliness of the reason that is innate in us.[193] For just as in the latter steadiness falters and does not achieve complete and confident certainty," so in the former, [that is,] what is known by certain revelation in God's light, those things are believed with such great confidence and certainty that no uncertainty can assault the soul on these matters.[194]

12. But you should know that the grandeur of revelations sometimes elevates to pride heedless minds, placed among those wonderful sights, so much so that they pursue the breeze of empty fame."[195] God's righteous judgment allows such ones to fall into sin or to fail, that they may cease to be proud. For when they fall

---

[189] Cf. Richard, *De eruditione* 1.16 (PL 196:1255C–57A). See also LDP I.17.3.

[190] Dan 2:11.

[191] Phil 3:20.

[192] Richard, *De eruditione* 1.6 (PL 196:1241A).

[193] Cf. Richard, *De eruditione* 1.41 (PL 196:1296AD).

[194] Richard, *De eruditione* 1.35 (PL 196:1290CD).

[195] Cf. Richard, *De eruditione* 1.40 (PL 196:1294D).

into sin, they are confounded, and thence they are filled with re-morse, and being remorseful they are purified, and being purified they are enlightened. But the enlightened will again become proud, and in their pride they lose once more the light that they had received. They alternate frequently between falling and rising again, and some repeat these changes for long periods. But some, alas, finally come to the worst possible end while persisting in their heedlessness. Whence we can be sure, concerning these, that they received spiritual grace not so much for their own benefit as for that of others.[196]

As the experienced recognize, those who deserve to be made divinely joyful by frequent revelations are completely accustomed to receive the light of illuminating grace in the time of their prayer, and thus to penetrate the profundities of divine mysteries.[197] [But] one vision, as of eternal joys, makes the contemplative joyful; but another, as of divine Judgment, terrifies. These are usually thoroughly terrifying, not at the time that they are seen in ecstasy but rather when they are recalled to the memory, that is, when the mind judges itself with scrupulous examination, lest perhaps it should deserve a similar fate. The grace by which we perceive our own deserts in meditation is one thing; another is that by which we recognize God's judgments in contemplation. Often, however, one and the same person receives both graces simultaneously, though unable to make use of both at one and the same time.[198] But sometimes one first brings back something from the light of contemplation that one later gets to know more fully through meditation.

Whatever reliance is placed on human effort concerning divine secrets is in vain, and however long one seeks in this way, the labor is futile.[199] What can be safely understood will only be given by the divine loving-kindness, if someone seeks with faith and from true devotion, to that person who, having received this grace, relies not on their own strength but on God's loving-kindness alone.[200] For that saying is very true: *he will give it to whomsoever it shall*

---

[196] Richard, *De eruditione* 2.10 (PL 196:1309A).
[197] Richard, *De eruditione* 2.10 (PL 196:1309B).
[198] Richard, *De eruditione* 2.2–3 (PL 196:1300B–1301C).
[199] Richard, *De eruditione* 2.6 (PL 196:1304D).
[200] Richard, *De eruditione* 2.36 (PL 196:1333AC).

> *please him.*[201] *So then it is not of him that wills, nor of him that runs, but of God who shows mercy.*[202]

Richard ends here.

13. If one uses this grace properly, a person can sometimes eventually achieve union with God again, not as if one had him present[203] but rather as if one found oneself inwardly united to him. Nor is there any need to search out God's will by prayers or meditations, but rather God quite often makes himself known to that person's attention, when indicating the good pleasure of the divine will with a certain "light of confidence";[204] the soul's attention, as it were, penetrates the divine heart, which is united to the soul as if it were that soul's own.

Then that blessed soul retains whatever it receives, both during conversation or other external business, in such a light with greater confidence than that with which it earlier retained answers that were undoubtedly from God, which it had obtained from time to time by devout and lengthy prayers. That grace is a thousand times greater than the one that it had possessed earlier when God seemed to speak with it, for just as a bridegroom makes his will known to his new bride in one thing at a time, so God too in the early days instructs such souls and attracts them by his answers. But when from frequent companionship and growth of love she becomes *one heart and one soul*[205] with her bridegroom, she knows his will in all things from habit;[206] in this way after numerous spiritual exercises the soul receives this grace that I have described as a wedding gift from God, that is, so that it may be set up as an oracle[207] so that not only may it know God's good pleasure in all that must be done, but also the various people who inquire through it may be instructed the more

---

[201] Dan 4:14.

[202] Rom 9:16; Richard *De eruditione*, 2.31 (PL 196:1329A).

[203] See LDP II.3.4 and II.17.1.

[204] Augustine, Conf VIII.12 (29).

[205] Acts 4:32.

[206] See LDP I.17.2.

[207] See LDP V.1.9.

fully without delay in that timely conversation, when he pours into it through the light of confidence, as was said,[208] the knowledge of his response in each and every matter. And this, I think, is what Richard posits as the highest kind when describing the three kinds of revelations. In this state the chosen soul *adheres to God*[209] with such complete faithfulness and is united with his will so that, if by a single word or the least thought it could achieve all things in heaven or on earth that can be considered desirable,[210] it would hold them as valueless, or rather would choose to be annihilated in preference to willing in any way that anything should be done, in any creature, that would not be most praiseworthy to God. It is not surprising if the most kindly Jesus then promises it power over all his goods, even while it is in some way still a pilgrim in the flesh, since he proves it faithful, because it never expends his goods unless it pleases and glorifies him.

14. Although blessed Bernard says that discretion of spirits is difficult,[211] nonetheless it is possible to determine to a certain extent whether it is from God's spirit or the opposite. For when inspiration is from God's spirit, <the soul> can never again cast itself down through humility so that desperation ensues, but always the more it distrusts itself, the more it trusts in God. Conversely, it can never be so greatly elevated in the loftiness of grace that it would fail always to abase itself through humility. But when it is tempted by a spirit of deception, it is easily cast down through elevation, or depressed through humiliation,[212] and this can be held to be a reliable indication of the different spirits.

---

[208] See above, p. 26, and n. 204.

[209] See Ps 72:28 and below, L 109, where this verse is quoted in full. See also LDP III.29.1, IV.8.1, IV.10.1, IV.38.2, and V.25.2.

[210] See LDP II.8.2 and III.26.2.

[211] See Bernard, SC 32.6 and above, para. 7.

[212] See LDP I.3.3 and I.4.3.

15. Led by holy Scripture, I have written these things according to what I could discover, to the praise of our sweetest lover[213] and for the profit of souls,[214] desiring that if anyone has learned something from personal experience or from writings that is clearer or more useful about similar things, they should not refuse to make it known, just as they are obliged to serve the praise of God and the edification of their neighbors. If anyone reads those things that follow[215] with intent devotion,[216] not to satisfy their curiosity or to scrutinize my simplicity, but to increase edification and arouse devotion, let them be sure that they will find something profitable, God's most kindly clemency[217] working with them, for it was certainly not his will that this should be committed to writing[218] in vain. But let the readers receive whatsoever is offered at any time in the knowledge that God's most faithful providence has preordained it for them, and if they do not feel the benefit immediately, let them hope that they will in the future. For, alas! I have never used any of those gifts with a zeal so diligent that I could believe I had been given anything for myself alone.[219]

16. For on one occasion when at the time of prayer I was recalling the wonderful condescension of God's gifts towards me, unworthy as I am, and was entrusting to his loving-kindness for protection his share in those things that I had laid out to increase his praise, both those already written and those yet to be written,[220] I received this response from his kindliness: "No one can take from me the memorial of *the*

---

[213] See LDP IV.2.5 and V.4.3.

[214] See below, L 109.

[215] That is, the rest of the Leipzig manuscript.

[216] See LDP III.29.2.

[217] See LDP V.13.1.

[218] See LDP II.5.5.

[219] See LDP II.5.5.

[220] See LDP II.24.1.

abundance of my divine *sweetness.*"[221] By these words I understood that the Lord wanted this little book to be entitled *A memorial of the abundance of the divine sweetness,*[222] because the divine sweetness, unable to restrain itself, has superabounded and overflowed through my inmost being to the lowest depths of my worthlessness, that by this a greater confidence in more powerful rewards may be granted those *abiding*[223] more closely with <him>. And the Lord added, "If anyone[224] wishes to read this book with devout intention of spiritual progress, I shall myself draw him[225] to myself so much so that he will read it as if my own hands were holding the book and I myself shall keep him company at the task. As when two people are reading the same book, each is aware of the other's breath, so shall I, wholly his,[226] draw in the breath of his longings. By this my loving-kindness *shall be moved upon him,*[227] and moreover I shall breathe into him the breath of my divinity, which, through the Holy Spirit, will create him anew within."[228]

[221] See Ps 144:7.
[222] See LDP I.Prol.2.
[223] See Song 1:12.
[224] *quaecumque* L, i.e., feminine gender.
[225] *illum* L, i.e., masculine gender.
[226] See LDP III.17.4.
[227] Gen 43:30.
[228] See LDP I.Prol. 2.

The Memorial of the Abundance
of the Divine Sweetness

<Preface **Not in LDP**>[1]

1. Let this book be called *The Memorial of the Abundance of the Divine Sweetness*, because, as is made clear at the end of the Prologue,[2] this was the name bestowed upon it by the author himself, who gives being to all creatures.

2. Now this book is divided into three parts, the very first part of which she who was worthy to receive these things from the giver of all graces wrote down with her own hands, after the eighth year[3] of her reception of grace, on the holy day of Maundy Thursday. She was standing among the members of the community, waiting for the Body of the Lord to be brought, when sister M. of blessed memory, who was sick,[4] was about to receive communion before the Office. <Gertrud> was driven to praise God by such vehement fervor of the Holy Spirit that she immediately snatched up stylus and tablet and, standing in that place, wrote just as the divine unction flowed into her, without any

---

[1] As was explained at the end of the Introduction, all material that is unique to L in this translation is printed in bold. Material shared by L and LDP is reproduced from my earlier translation of the five books of *The Herald of God's Loving-Kindness*. Some minor changes and corrections, however, have been made without notice.

[2] Note that this does not mean the end of what is often known as the Prologue but is here called the Preface. The story of the divine naming of the book, corresponding to the third-person account in LDP I.Prol.2, comes at the end of *I will lead her into the wilderness*, on L, fol. 25ʳ (see above, pp. 28–29).

[3] That is, early in the ninth year of Gertrud's conversion, i.e., 1289; see LDP I. Prol.1, lines 9–10, and II.Prol.1, lines 1–2.

[4] This is probably Mechtild of Magdebourg: the date of her death is usually given as 1282, but there is some reason to believe that she lived on into the 1290s. Evidence from L would put her death just before the interdict, ca. 1293 or 1294.

premeditation. And thus throughout that week, receiving communion every day, she remained as if in an ecstasy in her inmost being, and she wrote the following[5] in the Lord's presence, he himself ordering and, as it were, inspiring it.

3. Later, on the feast of the Lord's Nativity,[6] when she was [moved] by similar devotion and fervor of spirit, the Lord persuaded her that she should choose someone to whom to reveal her secrets, to the advantage of divine praise. Since this was completely contrary to her own will, but nonetheless she could not gainsay the divine will, she labored so hard in this struggle, beyond her body's strength, that she was sick for very many weeks. her strength failing. Then since she judged it right to consent to the divine will rather than to her own, one day in Lent[7] God provided an opportunity, since I was the only one with her, unworthy though I was. She revealed some things to me, speaking so obscurely and her limbs trembling so wretchedly that everyone who was watching would clearly understand how much she was acting against her own, human, will if she made known any of these things.

4. Then, again by divine disposition, having been instructed about these things at greater length with the passage of time, I had secretly begun to write certain things in a document with the intention that I would more willingly have chosen all burdens that a person could ever suffer rather than ever to have revealed my secret to the world. By the Lord's providence, as I hope, at whose command all is governed and disposed, it so happened that these things came to the attention of our spiritual superiors. This was as completely against my will as against hers, for truly we would both have rather chosen death than to have agreed to this happening voluntarily. She herself gave clear proof of this,

---

[5] That is, L 1–6.

[6] That is, in the winter of 1289. LDP II.6 takes place on the feast of the Nativity of the first year but makes no mention of the events recounted here, though possibly LDP III.1 refers to them.

[7] In 1290, presumably.

for at that very moment, while someone was making this known to her—that some writings about her had been made known—she was seized by so severe a fever that for some time afterwards she was confined to her bed. How far I am guilty, I leave to the One who alone *tries the loins and the heart.*[8] Then, however, compelled beyond measure against her own will, out of obedience she allowed me to write the little book that follows, but in such a way that I had to disguise[9] very many things that I was writing, lest I should place an unbearable burden on her, and also that I had to omit very many of the things she said.

5. As for the third little book—that is to say, the last five gatherings[10]—I wrote it down on the following occasion. When Abbess Gertrud of sweetest memory, dearest and most faithful both to God and men, was laboring under such sickness[11] that I despaired of any further assistance from her (even though I had not made much progress[12] with it in this matter), judging it unworthy to bring to an end a book so exquisite and dear to me, which was being rendered the more credible by the clear witness of very many people,[13] I wrote down this third [book] as well,[14] taking very great care to keep it secret. Yet I did so with a certain amount of confidence, because I knew that that person [Gertrud], who should certainly not see it, had firmly decided that, after the death of the aforementioned Abbess G. of venerable memory, she would never take this book back into her own hands, but rather would

---

[8] Jer 11:20.

[9] *occultare* L.

[10] Not, of course, the last five quires of L itself. She may mean the last five quires of her original copy, or she may be qualifying "the third little book"—on this occasion she wrote not all of it, but just the last five quires.

[11] That is, during the five months in 1292 between the abbess's stroke and her death, which took place sometime after 12 November (feast of Saint Leafwine): see LDP V.1.12.

[12] She might have already written L 35–50 (fourteen folios in L, so a fairly modest amount).

[13] The phrasing suggests that "this third" part was the germ of LDP I, for which Sister N uses the structuring device of the three witnesses in LDP I.2.2–I.5.1.

[14] *et hunc tercium* L.

entrust it to God in the care of that person [i.e., Sister N] to whom the oft-mentioned faithful abbess our mother had entrusted it, giving it with her own hands. I too agreed with her, lest on some occasion she should be distressed rather than [brought to][15] every kind of secret consolation that can be had in that book. Nonetheless it seems to me so magnificently sweet that I would not exchange it for any good thing except only for God's praise and that person's salvation, knowing that it is written: Praise the good fortune of the sailor, but only when he has arrived in port.[16] Thence I entrust it to the divine heart until after her death, desiring and hoping that God will render to its preserver, if she has preserved it with complete fidelity, such reward as he would be willing to give if she had endured as many heavy toils for fidelity to God's name as there are letters written in this book! Amen.

[15] *abdito* L, conjecturally emended to *addita*.
[16] Maximus Taurinensis, *Hom. de sanctis*, 78 (PL 57:419AB), but in the Middle Ages variously attributed to Saints Ambrose, Augustine, Jerome, or Bernard.

<CHAPTER ONE = LDP II.1>

1. May the deep of uncreated Wisdom call to the deep of wonderful **Power**, to praise and exalt such breath-taking Goodness, **by which** the overflowing abundance of your mercy flowed down through the lowest parts to the valley of my wretchedness!

I was twenty-five years old. It was the Monday (a Monday most beneficial for me) before the feast of the Purification of Mary, **your** most chaste mother, which fell on January 27 that year, at the longed-for time after Compline, as dusk began. You, O God, Truth shining brighter than every light yet more inward than every hidden secret, had resolved to temper the thick mist of my darkness. You began gently and easily, **out of the love of your fatherly goodness,** by calming that **severe mental** storm that **your wise providence (as I hope) had** stirred up in my heart for **almost all** the past month. By that **storm**, I believe, you were attempting to pull down the tower of vanity and worldliness into which my pride had grown, even though I bore—alas, an empty boast—the name and habit of the religious life. All this you did to find a way to show me your salvation.

2. At the hour already mentioned, then, I was standing in the middle of the dormitory. On meeting an elder sister, according to the custom of our Order I bowed my head. As I raised it I saw standing beside me a young man. He was lovely and refined, and looked about sixteen; his appearance was such as my youth would have found pleasing at that time. With kindly face and gentle words he said to me, "Your salvation will come quickly; why are you consumed by sadness? Do you have no counselor? for sorrow **will overwhelm** you."[1]

---

[1] *Jerusalem, cito veniet salus tua; quare moerore consumeris? Numquid consiliarius non est tibi quia innovabit te dolor? Salvabo te et liberabo te, noli timere*; response for the second Sunday in Advent.

While he said this, although I knew I was physically in the place mentioned, it seemed to me that I was in choir, in the corner where I used to make my lukewarm **and, I fear, hypocritical and forced** devotions, and it was there that I heard the following words, that is, "I shall free you and I shall deliver you: do not fear."[2] At these words I saw a tender, finely wrought hand holding my right hand as if confirming what had been said with a promise. He added, "You have licked the dust with my enemies, and you have sucked honey among thorns; return to me at last, and I shall make you drunk with the rushing river of my pleasure!"

While he spoke, I looked and saw that between us (to his right and to my left) there was a hedge of such endless length that I could not see where it ended in front or behind me. On its top **it**[3] seemed to bristle with such a great mass of thorns[4] that I would never be able to cross it to join the young man. While I stood hesitating because of it, both burning with desire and almost fainting, he himself seized me swiftly and effortlessly **by the shoulders**, lifted me up, and set me beside him **and let me go**. But then I recognized on that **royal** hand, from which I had received the promise already mentioned, the glorious gems of those wounds that canceled the debts of all **sins**.

I praise, adore, bless, and offer thanks (as far as I can) to your wise mercy and merciful wisdom. For you, my creator and redeemer, were trying in this way to make my stiff neck submit to your easy yoke, by concocting **most temperately** a drink suitable for my sickness. For from that time forward, calmed by a new joy of the spirit, I began to go forth in the **vehemence**[5] of your balm, so that I too **declared** the yoke easy and the burden light that a little before I had reckoned unbearable.

---

[2] See previous note.

[3] "Our sins have divided us from our God" added in the margin; see Isa 59:2.

[4] See Hos 2:6.

[5] *in sua violencia* L, where LDP reads *in suaveolentia* ("in the delightful perfume"), an obviously superior reading. Possibly L's reading is a scribal error, though the manuscript has usually been carefully corrected.

<CHAPTER TWO = LDP II.2>

1. Hail, my salvation and the light of my soul. May all that is encompassed by the path of heaven, the circle of the earth, and the deep abyss give you thanks for the extraordinary grace with which you led **me** to experience and ponder the innermost recesses of my heart. These had been of as little concern to me before, if I may say so, as the soles of my feet! But then I became **troubled and** aware of the many things in my heart that would be offensive to your most chaste purity, and of all the other things so disordered and chaotic that **they** could offer no resting place to you who wished to dwell there. But no more than all my worthlessness did this drive you away, my **sweetest** Jesus, **for you honored** me frequently with your visible presence on those days when I came to the life-giving food of your Body and Blood. Though I could see you no more clearly than one sees things at dawn, nonetheless with kindly condescension you induced my soul to exert itself, that it might be united with you more closely.

2. I planned to work at achieving this on the feast of the Annunciation, when you betrothed our human nature to yourself in the Virgin's womb. But you who say "Here I am!" before you are summoned anticipated that day by forestalling me, unworthy as I was,[1] in the blessings of sweetness. On the vigil of that feast, because it was a Sunday, chapter took place after Lauds. I cannot find the words to describe how you, **my God,** the Orient from on high, then visited me through the depths of your loving-kindness and sweetness. Giver of

---

[1] "The Lord, by coming to the unworthy mind, shows it to be worthy by uniting it with himself" added in the margin (Gregory the Great, Mo 18.XXXIX.63).

gifts,[2] give me this gift: may I henceforward offer on the altar of my heart a sacrifice of joy, that by my supplication I may win for myself and all those whom you have chosen the privilege of enjoying **more** often that sweet union and unifying sweetness, which was quite unknown to me before that hour![3] For acknowledging the nature of my life, both before and since, I declare in utter sincerity that it was a grace given freely and undeservedly. From that time forth you endowed me with a clearer light of knowledge, in which the sweet love of your loveliness always attracted me more greatly than the harsh punishment I deserved ever castigated me.

I do not remember, however, having ever enjoyed **at that time** such fulfillment except on the days when you invited me to taste the delights of your royal table. Whether your wise providence ordered this, or my **indolent** neglect brought it about, is not clear to me.

---

[2] Cf. *Veni, dator munerum* from the sequence "Veni, sancte spiritus." See also L 6/LDP II.5.

[3] "Where sin abounded, grace did more abound" (Rom 5:20) added in the margin.

<CHAPTER THREE = LDP II.3.1–3>

1. This is how you dealt with me, this was how you aroused my soul on a certain day[1] between Easter and Ascension. I had gone into the courtyard before Prime and was sitting beside the fishpond absorbed by the pleasantness of the place. The crystalline water flowing through, the fresh green trees standing around, the freedom of the birds, especially of the doves, wheeling in flight, all gave me pleasure: but most of all the secret peace of a secluded place of rest.[2] I began to turn over in my mind what I would like to add to this that would make my pleasure in that resting-place seem complete. This was my request: that I might have there a lover—**faithful,** affectionate, able, and companionable—to relieve the solitude.

I trust, my God, that it was you—you who produce pleasures beyond price—who had anticipated me and guided the beginning of this meditation, and it was you, too, who drew its conclusion to yourself in such a way. You **put into my mind** that if I poured back like **flowing** water the flowing streams of your graces with constant and proper thanksgiving, I would grow in a zeal for virtue like the trees and would blossom with a fresh flowering of good works. Moreover, if I looked down on the things of earth and, in free flight like the doves, sought the things of heaven, and if my outer self with its bodily senses were held aloof from hustle and bustle, **with my mind's inmost**

---

[1] This was 4 May, the feast of Saint Gothard: see L 53.

[2] "Spiritually, water signifies thanksgiving; the trees, the vigorous growth of good works; the doves' flight, contemplation of heavenly things; the secluded seat, the peace of devotion" added in the margin.

devotion I would be completely at your disposal; my heart would offer you a dwelling-place **most joyful above all loveliness**.

2. Since my mind had been busy all day long with these thoughts, in the evening when I knelt in prayer, about to sleep, there suddenly came into my mind this verse of the gospel:[3] *If anyone loves me, he will keep my word and my Father will love him, and we will come to him and will make our abode with him.*[4] Meanwhile my heart of clay realized that you had indeed come and were there present. Oh, how I wish—how many thousand times do I wish—that I could pour over my head all the sea that turned into blood, to **purify** the cistern of my utter worthlessness in which you, the ultimate manifestation of a worth beyond human thought, chose to live! Or, would that my heart might be given me for an hour, drawn out of my body, to be assayed piece by piece by white-hot coals! Its dross melted away, it might offer, if not a worthy home, at least one not so unworthy of you.

For this was how you, my God, showed yourself to me from that time, sometimes more soothing, sometimes more severe, according to whether I was amending or neglecting my life. Although, to tell the truth, if the most painstaking amendment that I ever, even for a moment, achieved had lasted all my life, it could not by any means have merited even the single most severe appearance that I ever experienced after numerous faults and, alas, grave sins. For your great sweetness made you often pretend to be more concerned than angry with what I had done. It seems to me that you showed greater strength of patience in so calmly bearing such great faults of mine than when in the time of your mortal life you bore with Judas the betrayer.[5]

---

[3] "Bernard. You err if you expect to find apart from yourself a place of rest, the privacy of solitude, unclouded light, the abode of peace" added in margin (Bernard of Clairvaux, SC 52.5 [CF 31:54 (adapted); SBOp 2:93]).

[4] John 14:23.

[5] "Augustine. There are many things that take away the sweetness of the divine presence, but they do not take away the presence of God, as in those who are not careful of frivolous and idle words, who say the hours without attention or are idly occupied elsewhere and the like. Isidore. Sometimes God does not withdraw his gifts from sinners so that the human mind may rise up to the hope of divine favor" added in the margin. The first sentence is not found in Augustine; the final sentence is, however, from Isidore, *Sententiae*, 2.5.1.

3. For although I wavered mentally **in any place whatsoever** and enjoyed certain dangerous pleasures, when I returned to my heart—after hours and even after days, alas, and after weeks, I fear to my great sorrow—I always found you there. The result is that I could never complain that you withdrew from me for even the blink of an eye from the hour mentioned to the present day, now that the ninth year has passed. The only exception was on one occasion, eleven days before the feast of Saint John the Baptist: this happened, so it seems to me, as a result of a worldly conversation on a Thursday, and lasted until the Monday, which was the vigil of the feast,[6] in the course of the Mass "Fear not, Zacharias." Your gentle humility, and the wonderful goodness of your wonderful divine love, saw me in such a state of abandoned madness that I did not care that I had lost such a treasure. I cannot recall having mourned its loss or having the least wish for its return. I wonder now what madness had taken my mind prisoner, unless it was perhaps your intention to allow me to have personal experience of what Bernard says: "As we flee, you pursue us; we turn our backs, and you run to meet us face to face. But no embarrassment or scorn can turn you aside or stop you from acting unwearyingly to **lead** us to that which eye has not seen, not ear heard, and that has not risen into the heart of man."[7] **And just** as I was undeserving in the first place, so you deigned to bestow the joy of your saving presence on me who had done more than simply fail to preserve it, for it is worse to re-lapse than to lapse; and it has continued to this day. For this be praise and thanksgiving to you—that thanksgiving that, going gently forth from uncreated Love and incomprehensible to all created being, flows back to you.

---

[6] The vigil of the feast of Saint John the Baptist (June 23) fell on a Monday in 1281.

[7] Not found, but also quoted by Gertrud, speaking to the Lord, in L 78.

<CHAPTER FOUR = LDP II.3.4>

1. Again, for preserving so great a gift I offer you that most excellent prayer[1] that, as your bloody sweat testifies, the pain of strait necessity made strong, the innocence of pure simplicity made devout, and the love of white-hot divinity made potent. By the power of that same most perfect prayer **of yours, may you perfect it so** completely in union with yourself and draw me to yourself in my inmost being. Then whenever it happens that I must devote myself to external works for practical purposes, may I be given to them on loan, as special cases: then when they have been perfectly completed to your praise, may I return at once to you in my inmost being, as the general rule, just as the tumultuous rush of water flows back to the depths when whatever barred the way has been removed. For the rest, may you often find me as intent on you as you show yourself present to me. By this may you **conduct** me to as great perfection as ever your justice permitted a soul to achieve while burdened by the weight of flesh and so resistant to your mercy **in every way**. As it breathes its last within your most strait embrace and most potent kiss, may my soul find itself, without **a moment's** delay, there where you live and are glorious, unbounded, and **undivided** in flourishing eternity with the Father and the Holy Spirit, true God throughout unending ages. **Amen.**

[1] "Here is meant the prayer that the Son prayed in his agony" added in the margin.

< CHAPTER FIVE = LDP II.4 >

1. In the early stages of these events, in the winter of the first or second year,[1] I think, I found in a **little** book a short prayer that went as follows:

> Lord Jesus Christ, son of the living God, grant that I may aspire to you with all my heart, with abundant desire, with thirsting soul. Grant that I may respire in you, who are most sweet and most delightful. Grant that my whole spirit and all my inner being may unceasingly pant after you who are true blessedness. Most merciful Lord, write your wounds in my heart with your precious blood, that I may read in them your suffering and your love alike. Then may the mindfulness of your wounds remain with me unceasingly in the recesses of my heart, that sorrow for your **passion** may be aroused in me and the **love** of your affection may be kindled in me. Grant also that all creation may become worthless, **so** that you alone may impart sweetness to my heart.[2]

2. I was in complete agreement with the sentiments this little prayer expressed, and I was eager to repeat it **the more attentively** when you, **most kindly**, who never despise the **prayers** of the humble, came to me ready to offer the fulfillment of that little prayer. A short while later during that same winter, I was sitting in the refectory at supper after Vespers beside a certain person to whom I had revealed **to a certain extent** the secrets of my experiences. I add this

---

[1] That is, late 1281 or early 1282.

[2] The earliest example of a popular prayer found in a very large number of fourteenth- and fifteenth-century manuscripts.

here for the benefit of the reader, for I often felt the fervor of my devotion increased by such an interchange. Whether it was your Spirit, **my** Lord God, or human affection that prompted this, **I do not know**. I have however heard from someone skilled in such matters that such a secret should **always** be more profitably revealed to someone who is not only a close friend by reason of faithful goodness but also superior by reason of the respect due to greater age. But since **this is unclear to me**, as I said before, I entrust the matter to you who keep most faithful watch over me, whose Spirit, which is sweeter than honey, maintains the whole strength of heaven. But if this did indeed come about from human affection, so much the more **profoundly worthy** is it that I should plunge into the depths of gratitude, as you deigned the more worthily to unite the gold of your inestimable worth to the clay of my worthlessness, so that the jewels of your graces might in this way find a place in me.

3. At the time I mentioned, when my mind was occupied with this subject with great devotion, I became aware that what I had just sought in the prayer I mentioned had been conferred on me, as if by divine intervention, utterly unworthy as I was. That is, inwardly in my heart, as if in physical places, I realized that the Spirit had impressed **one by one** the **lamentable** and adorable imprint of your most holy wounds. By those wounds you healed my soul and gave me the cup of the nectar of love to drink.

But my unworthiness had still not exhausted the depths of your loving-kindness, or prevented me from **also** receiving this unforgettable gift from the **overflow** of your most generous munificence: **as often as** I concentrated on paying a daily visit, in spirit, to the tokens so lovingly imprinted, greeting them with five verses from [the psalm] *Bless, my soul*,[3] I never had grounds to complain that I had been cheated of a special blessing!

4. For at the first verse, "Bless, my soul," I received the blessing of being able to lay down the rust of sin and the worthlessness of worldly sensuality at the wounds of your blessed feet. Then at the second verse, "Bless, and forget not," I received the blessing of wash-

---

[3] Ps 102:2.

ing away every spot of carnal evanescent pleasure in the fountain of love whence flowed blood and water for me. At the third verse, "He who is propitiated," I received the blessing of building my nest in the wound of your left hand for repose of spirit, while hastening there like the dove making its nest in the rock. Then at the fourth verse, "Who redeems," I draw near to the right hand, and all that I lack in perfection of virtue is there deposited for me to claim as my own.[4] When I am suitably adorned with these, at the fifth verse, "Who fills with good things," may I who am now purified from all infamy of sin, and with my lack of merit made good, deserve to **delight** in your chaste embraces with your most sweet and **joyful** presence. I am for my own part unworthy, but made worthy enough through you.

5. I declare that together with **this** were granted the requests made in that prayer, that I might read in those wounds your sorrow and **your** love alike. But to my great sorrow, though I cannot accuse you of having withdrawn this privilege from me, I mourn having shortly lost it through my own ingratitude and carelessness. But your great mercy and limitless loving-kindness turning a blind eye, **you have preserved** to this very day that first, greater gift,[5] totally undeserved, without any merit on my part. For this be honor and power, **glory, praise, and rejoicing.**

---

[4] "It seemed to her that as often as she fled to the stigmata of the holy wounds she perceived through her understanding with what love the Lord bore them for human salvation and with what sorrow he endured them, but in a little while she lost this gift, although by God's grace she retained the marks of the most holy wounds" added in the margin.

[5] That is, the spiritual stigmata.

<CHAPTER SIX = LDP II.5>

1. The seventh year after this, before Advent,[1] as you, source of all good, had ordained, I had laid a certain person under an obligation to slip these words on my behalf into her daily prayer before the crucifix. She was to say, "By your heart that was wounded through and through, Lord, pierce her heart with the shafts of your love, so much so that it may be unable to possess anything that is of this earth, but may be possessed by the unique power of your divinity." It was these prayers, I believe, that spurred you into action during Mass on the Sunday when *Rejoice in the Lord*[2] is sung.

Out of the overflowing generosity of your goodness and by the permission of your sweetly flowing mercy I was **on the way** to receive the sacrament of your most holy Body and Blood when you infused me with an earnest longing that compelled me to break out and say, "Lord, I admit that, as far as my merits go, I am not worthy to receive the least of your gifts. But **with** the merits and earnest longing of all those present I beseech your loving-kindness to pierce my heart with the arrow of your love." Soon I became aware that the force of these words had reached your divine heart, as much because of an inflow of inner grace as because of the manifestation of an unmistakable sign on an image of your crucifixion.

2. For when after **the reception of** the life-giving sacrament I had returned to my place in choir, it seemed to me as if something like a ray of the sun came out from the right-hand side of the crucified

---

[1] That is, probably sometime in November 1288: in that year Advent began on November 28.

[2] Third Sunday in Advent.

Christ painted on the page, that is, from the wound in the side. It had a sharp point like an arrow and, astonishingly, it stretched forward and, lingering thus for a **moment**, it gently elicited my love. But my longing was not thus satisfied until the following Wednesday when, after Mass, the faithful honor the generous gift of your incarnation and annunciation, which all must adore. I too, although less worthily, was concentrating on this devotion. Suddenly you were there unexpectedly, opening a wound in my heart with these words: "May there be a swelling of all your emotions here; that is, may the sum total of your delight, hope, joy, and your other emotions be fixed firmly in my love."

3. I immediately remembered that I had sometimes heard that wounds should be washed, anointed, and bound up, but at that time you had not yet taught me, once and for all, how to **provide** this. But after a while you revealed it more fully to me, by means of another person[3] who to your praise, I believe, has attuned her inner ear much more reliably and more sensitively than I have, I am afraid, to catch the continual flow of your loving whispers. Her advice to me was that while worshiping with constant devotion the love of your heart when you were hanging on the cross, I should draw water of devotion, to wash away every offence, from the moisture of **generosity** produced by the burning heat of a love so indescribable. From the liquid of loving-kindness **poured out** by the sweetness of a love so incalculable, I should take the salve of thanksgiving, sovereign remedy against all adversity, and from the potent power of charity, perfected by the strength of a love so incomprehensible, I should find the binding of righteousness, so that I might direct all my thoughts, words, and deeds, given strength by love, toward you, and in this way cling inseparably to you.

4. May the power of that love whose *fullness dwells in him*[4] who *is sitting* at *your right hand,*[5] **having** become *bone of my bones and*

---

[3] Probably Mechtild of Hackeborn.
[4] Col 1:19.
[5] See Col 3:1.

flesh of my flesh,[6] make up for whatever I have distorted as a result of my malice and wickedness in this account! For **just as** it is through him, in the **unity** of the Holy Spirit, that you have given us this capacity, with nobility of compassion, humility, and reverence, **so** through him I offer you my lamentation for my far too numerous offences against your divinely noble goodness, which I have assaulted in so many ways, in thought, word, and deed, but **more** especially in that I made such faithless, careless, and disrespectful use of the gifts of yours I have mentioned. For if you had handed over to me a hempen thread in your memory, I should rightly have treated it with more conscientious respect.

5. My God, you who know my secrets, you know that this is the reason that compels me,[7] reluctantly or rather against my will, to commit these experiences to writing: for I consider that I have profited from them **as if hardly at all because** I am unable to believe that they have been given to me for myself alone, since your eternal wisdom cannot be set aside by anyone. Therefore, giver of gifts, you who have given me gifts so free and undeserved, give the reader of these words too the gift that the heart of your friend may at least feel pity for you, in that your passion for souls has for so long confined a jewel worthy of a king to the muddy bilge-water of my heart! **In prayer and adoration**, may [the reader] exalt your mercy and say with heart and mouth [the antiphons] *Te Deum patrem, Ex quo omnia, Te iure laudant, Tibi decus, Benedictio et claritas.*[8]

6. **Since I have not plumbed the depths of your plan concerning the salvation of the human race,**[9] **I hope that these [words] will**

---

[6] Gen 2:23.

[7] "The secrets of God's gifts are entrusted to writing so that it may be fruitful for all who read it, for when someone reads how courteously the divine mercy condescends to an unworthy person, they trust to the same goodness of God in similar things, that God will be [the same] to them and thence they may grow in devotion through gratitude" added in the margin.

[8] Liturgical texts for the feast of the Holy Trinity.

[9] See "For in this too she recognized the admirable plan of the divine loving-kindness concerning the salvation of the human race" (LDP III.30.28).

not come to the attention of any of those[10] who have known the corruption of my life; although just as heaven is raised above the earth, so is the exterior life above the inner condition, which is known to you, my Lord, lest perhaps those, who have not learned how to distinguish the precious from the worthless, in holding it worthless might trample underfoot gold with mud!

---

[10] *illorum* L, i.e., masculine gender, so possibly a reference to her confessors or spiritual directors.

<CHAPTER SEVEN = LDP II.11.1>

1. How often during this time did you communicate the sense of your saving presence to me! *In* what an immense *blessing of sweetness have you* consistently *gone before*[1] my **depravity**, especially during the first three years,[2] but more especially whenever I was permitted to share in your blessed Body and Blood. Since I can **by no means** *answer one for a thousand*,[3] I trust in that everlasting, immense, and unchanging goodness by which, O **brightest,** ever-tranquil Trinity, all that is owing is paid to you in full out of your own resources, by them and in them. Flinging myself, like a tiny speck of dust, on this mercy, through him who sits at your right hand while sharing my nature, I offer you the thanks that you have made possible through him, in the Holy Spirit, for all your benefits, and especially I thank you for having **taught** me, stupid as I am, by means of a clear demonstration, in what way I was corrupting the purity of your gifts.

[1] See Ps 20:4.
[2] That is, 1281–1284.
[3] Job 9:3.

<CHAPTER EIGHT = LDP II.11.2–4>

1. For **one day**, when I was attending Mass and about to receive communion, and was aware that you were there in supernatural condescension, you used this analogy to teach me how you were asking me for a refreshing drink, like a thirsty man. When I complained that I did not have one and had proved conclusively that I could not squeeze out even a single drop **to offer you,** it seemed to me as if your hands offered me a golden cup. When I had taken it, my heart dissolved in sweetness, and out of it burst a flood of fervent tears. While this was happening, there sat **on my left** a creature loathsome **in appearance,** who was surreptitiously putting something poisonous and bitter into my hand and forcing me, secretly but earnestly, to poison **and make bitter** the wine in the cup with it. There soon followed an immense outbreak of vainglory,[1] so that I was permitted to understand clearly what deception the ancient Adversary uses in his fight against us, out of envy for your gifts.

2. But thanks be to your faithfulness, my God, and to your protective care, true and single Divinity, single and threefold Truth, threefold and single Deity, *who will not suffer* us *to be tempted above that which* we *are able.*[2] For **however much** you grant the enemy the power to tempt us, to test our progress, if you see that we are trustingly relying on your help, you take upon yourself the struggle planned for us. You do this so much so that, reserving the fight for yourself, out of your most abundant generosity you credit us with

---

[1] "A[ugustine]. The devil by his secret attack is trying to infect the grace of devotion with the poison of vainglory" added in the margin.

[2] 1 Cor 10:13.

the victory as long as we cling to you with the **consent** of our will. And what is outstanding among your gifts is that, to increase our merit, your grace preserves the freedom of our will. You do not allow the Adversary to take it away, nor do you have the desire to do so.

3. Another time, however, you taught me by another image that in any matter in which someone gives way too easily to our Adversary, the door is opened for a more powerful assault by him, since the beauty of your justice demands that you sometimes hide the power of your mercy in areas that our own neglect has made more vulnerable. And so the more prompt our resistance to any evil whatsoever, the more effective, profitable, and potentially successful it is.

<CHAPTER NINE = LDP II.12>

1. I thank you, just as I did earlier, for another similar analogy that was no less welcome and useful **to me**. By it you showed me how your kindly patience bears with our inadequacies so that, when we have remedied them, you may be able to raise us to a state of blessedness.

2. For one evening I had been in a **somewhat bitter** state of anger; the next morning there was a chance to pray before sunrise. You appeared to me in the form of a vagrant, so that I might judge from your appearance that you were completely forlorn, bereft of possessions and power.[1] Then my conscience, guilty because of its recent lapse, gnawed at me, and lamenting, I began to ponder how outrageous it was to **disrespect** you, the source of perfect purity and peace, with the stings of the vices that disturb me. I judged it to be more proper, or rather I had made up my mind that it was preferable, for you to take your departure rather than to be present at that very moment when I had failed to repel the Adversary, who was driving me into actions so contrary to you.

At this I received the following reply:[2] "If a sick man has, with difficulty, made his way outside with others' help to enjoy the splendid sunshine that he likes so much, what consolation can he have when a sudden storm blows up, except the hope of a return of the

---

[1] "Bernard. Love divine prevails even with God, so that you might know that it was the fullness of love that was outpoured" added in the margin (Bernard of Clairvaux, SC 64.10; CF 31:177 (adapted); SBOp 2:171).

[2] "What is done against a friend in his presence could greatly disturb him" added in the margin.

earlier fair weather?[3] In the same way I, laid low by my love for you, choose to make my home with you amid all the squalls of your faults, setting my course for the calm of repentance and the harbor of humility."

3. Since the power of speech cannot expound how you have distinguished me more abundantly in this revelation **for three days continuously**, I pray that my heart's love may go forward, and that out of the abyss of humiliation into which the condescension of your love drew me more powerfully, it may teach me to direct the effect of my thanksgiving toward the affect of your loving-kindness.[4]

---

[3] "If a righteous man falls, he will arise the stronger" added in the margin. See Prov 24:16 and Innocent III (PL 217:941).

[4] *Gratitudinis effectum . . . pietatis affectum* L.

<CHAPTER TEN = LDP II.13>

1. Once more I give thanks to your loving-kindness, most kindly God, for in yet another way you intervened to arouse me from my inertia. Although you had initiated it through an intermediary, you brought it to fruition in person, acting both mercifully and courteously. The intermediary was explaining to me that, according to the gospel, when you were born on earth shepherds were the first to find you.[1] She added that you had passed this message to her, that if I really wished to find you, I **ought to** keep watch over my senses, just as the shepherds kept watch over their flocks. I did not welcome this advice and considered it completely inapplicable to me since I knew you had not dealt with me as if I were serving you as a hired shepherd serves his master. This thought preoccupied me from morning until night, and I became depressed. After Compline, when I retreated to my place of prayer, you assuaged my sorrow by means of this guiding thought: if a bride is sometimes busy procuring food for her bridegroom's falcons,[2] this does not mean that she is completely deprived of his embraces. Similarly if I worked at the custody of my affections and senses for your sake, I would not for that reason be deprived of the sweetness of your grace. For this purpose you gave me the spirit

---

[1] "Bede. Everyone who is thought to live a secluded life holds the office of shepherd and feeds the spiritual flock of his affections" added in the margin (Bede, Hom in Ev 45, 348).

[2] "Bernard. No names as sweet as bridegroom and bride have been found by which the sweet emotions of the Word and the soul for each other might be expressed" added in the margin (Bernard of Clairvaux, SC 7.2 [CF 39:4; SBOp 1:31]).

of fear[3] under the form of a green staff with which, without leaving your close embraces even a little, I could feel my way through all the border lands of uncharted territory, where human affections have a habit of **wandering**. You also added that **at whatever time** anything should slip in that threatened to lead any of my affections astray, whether to the right, as joy and hope, or to the left, as fear, sorrow, or anger, I would instantly drive back that affection with the staff of your fear, and, by **restraining** my senses, I would cook that affection in the heat of my heart and serve it up, like a tender newborn lamb, as a feast for you! How often when at the instigation of evil I had in word or deed allowed some gift I have formerly offered up to you,[4] when there was an opportunity to escape through euphoria or depression, I have seen myself snatching that gift away from you (as if I were pulling out your teeth) and offering it to your enemy. In the midst of all this you would seem to look at me with such kindly serenity, as if you, being completely incapable of deceit yourself, thought that I was doing this as a gesture of affection. Hence you have so often led me out of such a state to so great a sweetness of loving agitation that I do not believe you could ever by terrifying me with threats induce me to long so much to correct and keep careful watch over myself.

---

[3] "The fear of the Lord drives out sin and makes one depart from all evil" (Sir 1:27) added in the margin.

[4] "Whatever is offered up to the Lord in the first flush of enthusiasm can be more welcome than what is offered later when [that enthusiasm] grows cold in the heart and is partly wasted on human sensual pleasure, as when one thinks at greater length, or speaks, or is otherwise occupied with something that influences the mind with anger or hope or joy and the like" added in the margin; source unknown.

<CHAPTER ELEVEN = LDP II.14>

1. Once, before Lent, on the Sunday when at Mass the introit is *Esto mihi **in Deum protectorem**[1] **and so on,**[2] you granted me the grace of understanding that, abused and harassed by all and sundry, you were asking me through the words of that introit for a dwelling-place to rest in. For the next three days, whenever I returned to my heart I saw you in the likeness of a sick man reclining on my breast. During those **three** days I did not find any meal **that** I could serve you that was more gladly received than my being constant in prayer, silence, and other **sufferings** offered in reparation for those leading worldly lives.[3]

[1] Ps 70:3, introit for the Sunday before the beginning of Lent: see also L 27, 48, and 51.

[2] "Bernard. Whatever the eye of love, which now is only looking for recompense, gazes upon, is completely safe, for some day it will see fully," added in the margin (Ps-Richard of Saint-Victor, *De gradibus charitatis*, 3 [PL 196:1204A]).

[3] Gertrud is always particularly conscious of the spiritual dangers of excessive indulgence during the pre-Lenten (carnival) period.

<CHAPTER TWELVE = LDP II.15.1–2, line 6>

1. Similarly, as the grace of your loving-kindness illuminates my understanding, you have revealed to me many times how the soul, as long as it remains in the body of human weakness, is in darkness like someone who stands in the middle of a confining room. From every side, around, above, and below, he is assaulted by the haze the room gives off, just as a boiling pan gives off steam. On the other hand, when the body happens to be afflicted by some suffering, in relation to the suffering organ the soul receives something like a breath of fresh air shot through and through with sunlight, and is granted light in this supernatural way. And the more all-embracing or the more serious the suffering, the purer the enlightenment of the soul. But, more particularly, affliction or the disciplining of the heart in humility, patience, and the like tint the soul with a dazzling white-ness insofar as these practices touch it more closely, effectively, and intimately. But it becomes especially calm and radiant from works of charity.

2. Thanks be to you, lover of men and women, for so often draw-ing me towards patience in this way. But alas! a thousand times alas! that I have given you my consent so little and so rarely—or rather, not at all as I should have done. Lord, you know **my own** sorrow, confusion, and dejection **and that of** my spirit over this, and the desire of my heart that I should make up for my shortcomings toward you in some other way.

<CHAPTER THIRTEEN = LDP II.15.2, line 6–end>

1. Again, when on one occasion I was about to receive communion at Mass, you had bestowed your riches rather **freely,**[1] and I sought to discover what I could do in my turn to repay you for a fraction at least of your condescension. You, most wise of teachers, put before me the words of the apostle: *I wished myself to be an anathema from Christ, for my brethren.*[2] At that moment, when thanks to your prompting I had known that my heart was the dwelling-place of my soul, you then showed me that my soul also had a dwelling-place in the head; afterwards, I declare that I realized this from the evidence of Scripture, although I had not known it before. You explained to me that it is a great deed if the soul gives up the sweetness of the heart's fulfillment for your sake, keeps vigil in governing its bodily senses, and labors over works of charity for the salvation of its neighbors as well.

[1] "The fruit of the heart is that hundredfold of which we read in the gospel, *He shall receive a hundredfold* [Matt 19:29]. He who for God's sake alone has renounced [something] receives a hundredfold, a thousand times greater, from God's overflowing generosity" added in the margin at the head of the chapter. Source unknown.

[2] Rom 9:3.

<CHAPTER FOURTEEN = LDP II.16.1>

1. On the day of your most holy Nativity, I took you from the manger as a **delicate boy** *wrapped in swaddling clothes.*[1] You were imprinted on my innermost heart, so that I might gather together from all the bitter humiliations of childhood's need *a bundle of myrrh,* **abiding** *between my breasts,*[2] and thence might press and drink from the cluster of grapes of divine sweetness in the depths of my being. Although I reckoned I could never receive any gift greater than this, you, who so often follow up on what has gone before with an even nobler gift, condescended to embroider on the theme of the overflowing abundance of your saving grace in the following way.

[1] Luke 2:8.
[2] Song 1:12-13.

<CHAPTER FIFTEEN = LDP II.16.2>

1. The next year, on the same day, during the Mass *Dominus dixit*,[1] I took you from the lap of your Virgin Mother in the shape of a most tender and delicate little child.[2] While I was carrying you on my bosom, it seemed to me that the compassion I had shown someone in trouble before Christmas by offering special prayers was at work here too. But I have to say that even though I had that gift, to my sorrow I was not as ardent in my devotion as I should have been. I do not know whether it was your justice or my carelessness that was responsible for this lack of ardor. It was my hope, however, that your justice, with the help of your mercy, had so disposed things that on the one hand my worthlessness **is** made known the more clearly to me, and on the other that I might be filled with fear that my carelessness was to blame, in that I was too sluggish in removing myself from vain **activities**. Whatever the reason, *answer for me*,[3] O Lord my God; however, as I was collecting myself somewhat to fondle you with loving caresses, I realized that I had made little progress until I recited prayers for sinners, souls in purgatory, and those otherwise troubled. I was soon aware of the result of these prayers, especially when one evening I decided to pray with all departed souls in mind. Up until then I had made an intention for my parents with the collect, "God, you have commanded us to honor our father and

---

[1] Ps 2:7; introit for Midnight Mass at Christmas.

[2] "It seemed to her that this gift was granted because of mercy and compassion" added in the margin.

[3] Isa 38:14.

mother,"[4] so by extension I made an intention for those dear to you with the collect, "Almighty and everlasting God, to whom never without hope."[5] It seemed to me that you took greater pleasure in this. Moreover you seemed to take a sweet delight in it when, putting all my efforts into singing, I fixed my intention on you at every single note, just like someone who carefully keeps her eye on the book because she is singing without the thorough knowledge that comes from long experience. How many things I neglected in these matters, and in others I knew to be done for your praise, I confess to you, most kindly Father, in the bitterness of the passion of your guiltless son Jesus Christ, in whom you testified that you took greatest pleasure when you said, *"This is my beloved son, in whom I am well pleased."*[6] Through him I **request** amendment of life, so that through him all that I have failed to do may be **fully** made good.

[4] Collect for a Requiem Mass.
[5] Prayer for the dead.
[6] Matt 17:5.

<CHAPTER SIXTEEN **Not in LDP**>

1. But to praise you I shall make no secret of this: since I possessed the gift already described like someone who while struggling to carry a little child in their arms can take less pleasure in its childish beauty, this was the way you used to render patience, which is so pleasing to you, the more pleasing to me, too. For on one occasion during this time, when I was blamed for something—undeservedly, as I thought—by one of my superiors and by your grace restrained my impatience and chose courtesy (which, alas, is very unusual for me), you promptly granted me that virtue, which you had preceded by your inspiration,[1] together with the reward that in addition to the gift described earlier I was given sweet satisfaction, like someone who, sitting comfortably with a little child whom she is holding on her lap, is able to delight now in one game and now in another.

---

[1] See LDP I.11.1; Gertrud "accept[ed] those gifts only because he who offered them precedes by his inspiration those whom he calls."

<CHAPTER SEVENTEEN = LDP II.16.3>

1. Then on the day of the most holy Purification, when we celebrate that procession in which you chose to be **conducted** into the temple with the other sacrificial victims as our salvation and redemption, in the course of the antiphon *Cum inducerent*, your Virgin Mother asked me with **a serene countenance** to give her back the dear little child of her womb, as if I had not looked after you as well as she wished—you who are the honor and the joy of her spotless **motherhood**. Remembering that because she found favor in your sight she had been given to sinners as their reconciliation and to all people in despair as their hope, I burst out and said, "O Mother of loving-kindness, **was not** the fount of mercy given you as your son for this purpose, that you might win it for all those in need of **mercy**, and that your boundless love might cover the *multitude of our sins*[1] and shortcomings?"

At this, the expression of that kindly lady became calm and merciful, and she showed that although she had seemed severe since my wickedness demanded it, her inmost being was nonetheless brimful of **loving-kindness**, and that she was suffused through and through with the sweetness of divine love. Soon her face grew radiant, while, at my feeble words, the **pretence of severity** vanished and a tranquil sweetness, her innate characteristic, shone forth. May your mother's generous loving-kindness, in the presence of your mercy, act as **glorious** intercessor for all my shortcomings!

[1] 1 Pet 4:8.

<CHAPTER EIGHTEEN = LDP II.16.4–5>

1. Finally it became clearer than daylight that you could not contain the overflowing abundance of your sweetness when the next year, on the same **most sacred** feast, you **gave** me a gift more welcome than the one I have mentioned but not unlike it. It was just as if my attentive devotion had earned it from you the year before, although in all justice I had earned not another gift but rather a fitting punishment for having lost the earlier one! For while they were reading the gospel *She brought forth her first-born son,*[1] with her **delicate** hands your spotless mother proffered me you, the child of her virginity, a lovable baby struggling with all his might to be embraced by me. I (though to my sorrow most undeserving) took you, a fragile little child, who clung to me with your little arms, whence I became aware of such life-giving refreshment **out of** the breath of the sweetly flowing spirit coming from **your** blessed mouth that my soul should, in all justice, bless you, my Lord God, from that moment forward, and *let all that is within me bless* your *holy name.*[2]

2. And while your blessed mother was busy wrapping you in a child's swaddling clothes, I was asking to be wrapped in them with you, lest you should be separated from me by even so much as a piece of cloth, **however thin**! For your embraces and kisses far surpass draughts of honey. Thus I saw you wrapped in the **white** linen of innocence, and bound by the golden bands of love; if I wished to be wrapped and bound in them with you, I was obliged above all to work wholeheartedly at purity of heart and works of charity.

[1] Luke 2:7.
[2] Ps 102:1.

< CHAPTER NINETEEN = LDP II.16.6 >

1. Thanks be to you, who made the stars and dressed the bright heavens and all the varied flowers of spring! Though *you had no need of **our** goods*,[1] yet with my instruction in mind you **implored** me after this, on the feast of the Purification, to dress you, little child that you were, before you were taken to the Temple. You persuaded me, out of the secret treasury of divine inspiration, to carry out this task in the following way. With all my might I was struggling to praise the spotless innocence of your most pure human nature with such complete and faithful devotion that, if I could have had in my own person all glory **due to your most worthy innocence**, I would have freely made it over (as would be right and proper), so that I might make you yet more praiseworthy in your innocence. As a result of such an intention on my part, I saw you dressed in white garments like a little child—you whose omnipotence *calls those things that are not, as those that are.*[2] While with similar devotion I contemplated the depth of your humility, I saw you also wearing a green tunic, to symbolize the fact that your grace, which has burst into flower, is always alive and vital, and never dries up in the valley of humility. Next, when I recollected in the same way as before the motive **of your love** that spurred you on in all that you did, you were wrapped around with a purple cloak to show that love is a truly regal garment, without which no one may enter the kingdom of heaven. But while I praised, as far as I could, the same virtues in your glorious mother, I saw her too dressed in the same way. And since this blessed Virgin,

[1] See Ps 15:2.
[2] Rom 4:17. See also L 190.

the rose that blossoms without a thorn, the white lily without spot, abounds—abounds to overflowing—with the flowers of every variety of virtue, we pray that she may act as our eternal mediator, that through her our poverty may be transformed into riches.

<CHAPTER TWENTY = LDP II.17>

1. One day,[1] when I had washed my hands and was about to go to eat, I was standing around with the other members of the community and noticed the brilliance of the sun shining with all its strength. This gave me pause for thought, and I said to myself, "If the Lord who created that sun and at whose beauty it is said that the sun itself and the moon are filled with wonder, the Lord who is also **called** *a consuming fire*,[2] was really and truly with me as he so often presents himself to me, how could it possibly be that I could lead my life among human beings with such a chilly heart, and so **humanly weak**, or rather, so full of evil?" All at once you, whose words, always sweet, were at that moment even sweeter as being more necessary to my wavering heart, put these words into my mind: "How could my almighty power receive its due of praise if it were not possible for me, wherever I might be, to remain within myself so as not to appear or be perceived beyond what is most appropriate for the place, the time, and the individual? For from the beginning of the creation of heaven and earth, throughout the labor of redemption, I have made greater use of kindly wisdom than of majestic **power**. This kindly wisdom shines forth with greatest power in my forbearance towards those who are less than perfect, going so far as to lead them, through their free will, to the path of perfection."

---

[1] "B[ernard]. If God never fails the righteous as their reward, he is however very often absent as their consolation. For he is present but hidden while that sweetness, present but concealed, does not touch the perception of the heart" added in the margin (Ps-Richard of Saint-Victor, *De gradibus charitatis*, 2 [PL 193:1199B], reading *abest* for L's *adest*). This is the last marginal note of this type in the manuscript.

[2] Deut 4:24; Heb 12:29.

<CHAPTER TWENTY-ONE = LDP II.18>

1. One feast day, while I noticed that a number of **people**[1] were going up for communion who had entrusted themselves to my prayers, I was myself held back by physical weakness—or rather driven away, I am afraid, at divine instigation by my unworthiness—and I called to mind **God's** many blessings on me. I began to fear that the wind of vainglory might be able to dry up the floods of divine grace, and I longed to be imbued with insight **by your generosity,** which would fortify me for the future. Then your fatherly loving-kindness taught me that I should judge your affection for me to be like that of the father of a family, who takes a real joy in the graceful poise of his numerous children, on whom a vast crowd of relatives and neighbors congratulate him. Among them he has a little child who has not yet achieved the poise of the rest, but in his fatherly love he feels sorry for it, clasps it to his bosom more often, and spoils it more than the others with kind words and little presents. You also added that if I genuinely considered myself to be less perfect than others, the torrential flood of your honey-sweet divine nature would never cease to flow into my soul.

2. I give thanks to you, my most loving God, lover of men and women, through that reciprocal movement of thanksgiving to and fro within the Trinity, ever to be worshiped and adored, for this and for many other salutary demonstrations that you, the best of teachers, have used on many occasions to instruct my foolishness. In the bitterness of the passion of Jesus Christ I move my plea, offering up to you his sufferings and tears for all my acts of negligence that have stifled your sweetly flowing Spirit within me. In union with that most

---

[1] *qui* L, i.e., masculine or common gender, as opposed to LDP *quae*, feminine.

potent prayer of that same beloved Son in the power of the Holy Spirit, I ask you to amend all my sins and make up all my inadequacies. May you condescend to grant me this, through that love that restrained you when the only son of your fatherly delight was counted among criminals.

<CHAPTER TWENTY-TWO = LDP II.6.1 >

1. O unattainable height of marvelous power! O depth of the abyss of inscrutable wisdom! O **immeasurable** breadth of desirable love! How strongly swelled the ambrosial torrents of your honey-sweet divinity when they flooded me so fruitfully, worm of utter worthlessness that I am, squirming in the gravel of my sins of omission and commission! The outcome was that, to my great pleasure, even in my wandering exile I was allowed, in proportion to my ability, to experience again the foretaste of the most pleasing delights and sweetest pleasures, by which anyone who clings to God becomes *one spirit*[1] with him. The boundless nature of his blessedness, spread abroad so abundantly, permitted me, just a speck of dust, to have the audacity to lap up some of its droplets, in the way I shall describe.

[1] 1 Cor 6:17.

<CHAPTER TWENTY-THREE = LDP II.6.2>

1. On that most holy of nights, when by the sweetening **and melted** dew of **deity** the heavens rained down honey[1] on the whole world, my soul, drenched like Gideon's fleece with dew on the threshing-floor of the convent, was intent by meditation, and through the practice of certain devotions, on being present and offering help at that heavenly birth, at which the Virgin brought forth her son, true God and true man, like a **star sending forth** a ray of light. As in a moment of revelation my soul **realized** that, in place of its heart so to speak, it had been offered and had received a tender little boy. In him there lay hidden a gift **supremely perfect** and truly most excellent. When my soul cradled him within itself it suddenly seemed to be completely changed into the same color as him—if that can be called a color that cannot be **likened to** anything visible. Then my soul perceived the meaning that defies explication **of that sweetly flowing sentence** full of wonder, *God* will be *all in all*.[2] It felt that it held within itself the beloved, installed in the heart, and it rejoiced that it was not without the welcome presence of most enjoyable caresses. Offered the honeyed draughts of the following, divinely inspired words, it drank them in with a thirst that could not be satisfied: "Just as I bear *the figure of the substance*[3] of God the Father in regard to my divine nature, so you bear the figure of my substance in regard to my human nature; for you receive in your deified soul the emanations of my divine nature, just as the air receives the sun's rays. Penetrated to the very marrow by this unifying force, you will become fit for a more intimate union with me."

[1] Second response for Christmas.
[2] See 1 Cor 15:28.
[3] Heb 1:3.

1. O noble balm of the divine, sending out **little** streams of loving-kindness on every side, **verdant** and flowering in eternity, but to be spread everywhere when time shall come to an end! O true power of the invincible hand of the Most High, when a vessel so fragile and cast into ignominy for its own sin contained the immanence[1] of **so supremely worthy** a liquid! O proof most clear of the abundance of God's loving-kindness! It did not shrink from me, wandering so far into the pathless wastes of sin, but rather made known to me, as far as I was capable of it, the sweetness of that most blessed union!

[1] LDP reads *ad immanationem*, "immanence," a word that occurs nowhere else in LDP. L reads *ad inmacionem*, corrected in a different hand to *adempcionem*, but neither makes sense in context.

<CHAPTER TWENTY-FIVE = LDP II.7.1>

1. Then, on the feast of the Purification, I was lying in bed after a serious illness. At sunrise I was silently mourning and lamenting that, held back by physical weakness, I was to be deprived of the divine visitation that had quite often given me strength on such a day. But then I was given consolation by the mediatrix of the mediator of God and man: "Just as you do not remember having suffered a more bitter pang of sickness in your body, so you should know that you have never received a more noble gift from my Son, which your preceding physical sickness has strengthened **and sanctified** your spirit to receive as it should be received." These words lifted a load from my heart. When it was time for the procession, after I had received the life-giving sacrament and was intent on God and myself, I realized that my soul, like wax carefully softened in the fire, lay on the Lord's breast, as if about to be impressed with a seal. Suddenly it seemed **to me** to be seized and partially drawn into **the place** where the fullness of the divine dwells bodily, and it was sealed with the indelible mark of the bright and ever-tranquil Trinity.

<CHAPTER TWENTY-SIX = LDP II.7.2>

1. O devastating glowing coal, my God, you who contain and radiate **from yourself** living heat! You exercised your inextinguishable power on the damp and slimy **place of** my soul, first drying up in it the flood of worldly pleasures and afterwards softening the rigidity of its attachment to its own ideas, a position in which it had long been completely fixed. O truly devouring fire, you who wield your power against vice so that you may gently reveal yourself to the soul when the time comes to anoint it! In you and **not in any** other do we receive this strength, so that we may have the power to be re-formed into the image and likeness of our original state. O powerful furnace, in the lovely vision of true peace, by whose operation dross is transformed into refined and choice gold when the soul, wearied by deceit, at long last blazes with an inner and insatiable desire to track down what belongs to it, and which it may receive from you alone, very Truth!

<CHAPTER TWENTY-SEVEN = LDP II.8.1–4>

1. After this, on *Esto mihi* Sunday, you stirred me up during **Matins** and increased my longing for those more excellent gifts that you intended to confer on me. You did this in particular by means of two texts whose greater power I **felt deeply** in my soul, that is, the first responsory, "Blessing, I shall bless you," and the **eleventh**, "For I shall give these lands to you and your seed." At these words you touched your most blessed breast with your adorable hand and showed me the lands that your unrestrained generosity promised me.

2. O that blessed land that is a source of blessing and beatification, beatifying **with abundance**! Field of delights, the smallest particle of your soil could satisfy and more than satisfy the hunger of all those whom you have chosen, in every single thing that the human heart could imagine as desirable, lovable, delightful, lovely, and delicious! While **during Mass** I was concentrating on those things on which one should concentrate (if not as much as I should, at least as much as I could) there appeared the goodness and humanity of God our Savior! (This was not the result of deeds of righteousness, as if I, **most worthless**, could possibly have deserved it, but in virtue of his own **inestimable** mercy.) It was strengthening me by adoption and rebirth, and fitting me, most unworthy beyond the bounds of worthlessness, for something that should rightly strike us dumb and make us tremble but that we must worship and adore: a more potent union with yourself, transcending heaven and transcending human thought.

3. But to **what merit** of mine, to what decision of yours, my God, are we to attribute the fact that your love, heedless of its own riches but **supremely** rich in condescension—a precipitate love, I say, which does not wait for a judicious decision and cannot be **moderated** by

human reason—that this love, my sweetest God, made you take leave of your senses (dare I say it?) as if you were drunk? In your madness you united two such total opposites. Or, to phrase it with greater dignity, the innate, natural loveliness of your goodness, utterly permeated with the sweetness of love, making you not merely a lover but wholly Love itself, whose more natural flow you directed toward the salvation of humanity, persuaded you to summon the farthest-flung, most miserable specimen of the human race—one devoid of all gifts of grace and fortune, of despicable life and conduct—from the far reaches of her complete worthlessness to keep company with royal—no, divine—grandeur, so that every creature living on earth might grow in confidence **in the divine loving-kindness**. What I hope and desire for every Christian is that, because of the honor due to my Lord, no one may be found who is worse than I am when it comes to distorting God's gifts and scandalizing neighbors.

4. But **just as** *the invisible things of* God can be expressed to the understanding *by the things that are made,*[1] as I described it earlier, the Lord made his appearance in that part of his blessed breast in which he had, at Candlemas, received my soul like **melted** wax.[2] It was covered with little beads of sweat breaking out on it, as if the substance of that wax, shown to me earlier, had melted and liquefied because of the excessive heat **lying hidden** within. But the divine treasure chest, by some supernatural but indescribable, or rather unthinkable, power, **absorbed** these apparent beads of moisture, so that the overwhelming force that love there possessed was fully revealed where so great and impenetrable a secret **is** unlocked.

[1] Rom 1:20.
[2] See L 25.

<CHAPTER TWENTY-EIGHT = LDP II.8.5>

1. O eternal **solace**, safe dwelling, place containing all pleasure, heavenly garden of everlasting delights, flowing **stream** of pleasure beyond price, coaxing forth the blossoming springtime of all kinds of loveliness, soothing with sweet sound, or rather with the sweetly **affecting** melody of spiritual music, bringing refreshment with perfumed **breathing** of life-giving scents, intoxicating with the melting sweetness of inner savors, bringing transformation with the wonderful caresses of **close** embraces! O thrice fortunate, four times blest, and, if I may say so, a hundred times holy are you who, prompted and guided by grace, have deserved to approach this place *innocent in hands and clean of heart*[1] and with pure lips.

What sights, what sounds, what scents, what delicious savors, what sensations! But why does my stumbling tongue attempt to stammer them out? For though I am allowed to enter, thanks to the goodness of God (though still along the paths of my sins of omission and commission), I am as it were encased in a thick shell and am unable to catch at anything as it really is. For even if the combined abilities of human beings and angels could be concentrated into a single moment of worthy knowledge, it would not be adequate fully to express even **one** word by which one could in the least degree worthily aspire to the sublimity of such great excellence.

[1] Ps 23:4.

<CHAPTER TWENTY-NINE = LDP II.9.1>

1. Quite soon afterwards, toward the middle of Lent, while I was confined to bed suffering once more from serious **weakness**, I was lying alone one morning as the other sisters were busy with other concerns. The Lord, who does not know how to abandon **his own** when abandoned by human comforts, was there present, proving the truth of the **prophet's** words, *"I am with him in tribulation."*[1] For from his left side, as if from the depths of his blessed heart, he **was extending** a liquid stream of the purity and strength of crystal. As it went forth it covered that adorable breast like a collar; it seemed **the brighter** with gold and rosy pink, flickering between the two colors. While this was happening the Lord added, "The sickness that causes you distress at present has sanctified your soul with the result that whenever, for my sake, you lower yourself to thoughts, words, and deeds that are not concerned with me, you will never go further from me than is shown you in this stream. Moreover, just as it shines with gold and rosy pink through the purity of crystal, so the co-working **of the love** of my golden divine nature and the perfect patience of my rosy human nature, suffusing and permeating all that you intend, will be pleasing **to me**."

[1] Ps 23:4.

<CHAPTER THIRTY = LDP II.9.2–3>

1. O the grandeur of that **tiny** speck of dust, which the chief jewel of the nobility of heaven **lifts up** from the dusty chaff to place at his side! O the perfection of that tiny flower, which the sun's ray itself coaxes out of the swamps as if to make it shine out brightly! O the **blessed** happiness of that fortunate and blessed soul, which the lord of majesty considers worthy of so great a state! Although he is all-powerful in creating, nonetheless he created the soul—a soul, I mean, made lovely in his own image and likeness but still as far from him as the creation is from the Creator! And so a hundred times blessed is she who is granted the grace of continuing in such state—a state **in** which, I am afraid, I have never **stood fast** even for a moment. But I earnestly wish that the mercy of God will grant me the gift of such a grace by the merits of those whom, I hope, he has preserved in such a state for some length of time.

O gift that is above every gift, to be satisfied so abundantly in the store-room by the sweet scents of the divine! and in the wine-cellar, hutch of pleasure, to become so overflowingly drunk on the wine of love, even to be drowned, so that one is not suffered to take the slightest step toward those distant lands where the power of such fragrance is likely to grow faint! Not only that: **wherever it is necessary to go** under the guidance of love, what a gift it is to carry with one the lingering aftertaste of such total satisfaction that one may be able to offer sweet odors from the divine richness of **opulent delight**! I have complete confidence, Lord God, that out of your **triumphant** omnipotence you have the power to grant this gift to those whom you have chosen. And I do not doubt that you wished to grant it to me out of your loving goodness. As to how you could grant it to me in spite of my unworthiness, I am totally unable to penetrate your unsearchable wisdom. But now I glorify and magnify your wise and kindly omnipotence. I praise and adore your omnipotent and kindly wisdom. I give blessings and thanks to your omnipotent and wise kindliness, my God, for no matter what you could ever have bestowed on me, I have always received incalculably more than I deserve from your generosity.

<CHAPTER THIRTY-ONE = LDP II.10>

1. As I considered it so inappropriate to write down **what is re-corded above**,[1] I could not come to any agreement with my conscience on the subject, and I had put off a decision until the feast of the Exaltation of the Holy Cross. On that day it was my firm intention to concentrate on other matters during Mass, but the Lord guided my understanding **to** these words: "You may know for certain that you will never leave the prison of the flesh until you pay out that final penny that until now you have held back." I was meditating on the fact that I had written down what he had **just** mentioned—or even if not through writings, I had nonetheless made restitution through my words, with my neighbors' profit in mind. But the Lord put in my way the verse that I had heard read at Lauds that very night: "If the Lord had given nothing but oral teaching to those who were present, there would only have been sayings, not writings **as well**; but now they have in addition been written down, for the salvation of many." The Lord added, "Do not cross me! It is my wish to have in your writings irrefutable evidence of my divine loving-kindness for these last days, when I plan to bestow blessings on many."

2. Overwhelmed by this, I began to ponder how difficult or even impossible it would be for me to find expressions or words **with which to make public** his many, **many,** sayings without shocking human understanding. The Lord, aware of my faint heart, seemed to drench my soul with a most generous shower of rain. Its heavy fall beat down on me, miserable scrap of humanity that I am, a delicate

---

[1] That is, L 7–30 (or possibly the whole of Part One).

and tender little shoot, and flattened me to the ground. I could absorb nothing of any use except some profoundly significant words that I could not grasp with my human understanding. Completely overwhelmed by this, I asked what could come of these words? Your usual loving-kindness, my God, gently lightened this burden, and **you** refreshed my soul with these words: "Since you found the rushing flood of those torrents of no use, I **am** now **drawing** you to my divine heart so that I may **thence** flow gently and sweetly into you, rhythmically, and proportioned to your capacity."

3. This promise I declare was absolutely true, because of its complete fulfillment, O Lord God. Every day for four days continuously, early in the morning at the most suitable time, you inspired me with a part of the discourse recorded above, so clearly and so gently that, without any mental effort, I was able to write without any previous thought, just as if I had learned it by heart long ago. You did this, however, with such restraint that when I had written down a suitable section, with **every effort of my mind** I could not run to earth one more of those phrases that on the next day would spring to mind in such effortless abundance. Throughout, you somehow controlled and bridled my impetuosity, just as Scripture teaches[2] that no one should be so wedded to action as not to show any desire for contemplation. Being always consumed with a passion for my salvation, while **you grant** me leisure to rejoice in the lovely embraces of Rachel, you do not however allow me to lose the glorious fecundity of Leah.

[2] See Luke 10:41-42.

<CHAPTER THIRTY-TWO = LDP II.19.1>

1. I give thanks to your kindly mercy and merciful kindness, most loving Lord, for the proof you have revealed of your most generous loving-kindness. By this you settled my unstable and wavering **soul** when, as was my custom, I begged with incessant longing to be released from the prison of this wretched flesh. It was not my purpose to avoid experiencing further wretchedness, but that your goodness might be released from that debt of grace that you are obliged to pay me in full, a debt in which the powerful love of your own divine nature entangled you, for the sake of the salvation of my soul. Not that you, who are divine Omnipotence and eternal Wisdom, could be constrained by necessity to give anything against your will. No, it is rather that out of the overflowing generosity of your loving-kindness you were making payment to a woman who was totally undeserving and gave you no thanks.

For you, splendor and *crown* of heavenly *glory*,[1] seemed to come down from the imperial throne of your majestic state in a most sweet and gentle downward flight. Throughout the length and breadth of heaven this journey shed what appeared to be streams of a most sweet liquid, to which every single one of the saints gladly bent down and, as if **having been given to drink** the nectar of that torrential flood with joyful pleasure, burst into a song praising God, delightful to hear. Amidst this I heard these words: "Consider how sweetly this praise penetrates the ears of my divine majesty, and reaches the molten core of my loving Heart. No more are you to long so persistently

[1] 1 Thess 2:19.

to be released because you do not wish, while living in the flesh, to be the recipient of a gift of freely given loving-kindness such as I lavish on you. For the more unworthy the one to whom I condescend, the greater the reverence with which I am rightly glorified."

<CHAPTER THIRTY-THREE = LDP II.19.2>

1. Since I had been granted this experience at the moment when I was approaching your life-giving sacrament, I was therefore, quite properly, concentrating on it. You then granted me, in addition to the revelation I have just described, this moment of understanding: everyone ought to approach the most sacred sharing of your Body and Blood in this way and with this intention, that for love of **your love**[1] **and glory they should disregard, if possible, the possibility of receiving** great condemnation in that sacrament, **so that** the divine loving-kindness **might** shine out the more, in that God did not disdain to give himself in communion to someone so unworthy. When I brought forward the objection that those who abstain from communion because of their own unworthiness abstain with the intention of not bringing dishonor on so **great** a sacrament by their presumption, I received your blessed answer to this as follows: "No one could ever come to communion irreverently who relied on an intention such as that." For this be praise and glory to you for ever and ever! **Amen.**

---

[1] See Augustine, Conf 2:1.

<CHAPTER THIRTY-FOUR **Not in LDP**;
LDP III.72.3, lines 2–8>

1. I also give thanks to your compassion, most merciful God, not only for another useful demonstration[1] but for an even more useful gift that your loving-kindness, my God, condescended to grant me, worst of the wicked. For I can produce nothing but thorns and bitter prickles, but you added this rose: that I might pray sincerely for a dead woman whom I had found a very great burden while she was still alive because of my inappropriate superficiality and other imperfections. For by your grace I was striving to win this from your loving-kindness: that for every burden she had inflicted on me you would condescend to repay her with some alleviation, if she were in purgatory, or with increase of joys, if she had already escaped. And when I asked if you would allow any prayer for her, I received this response from the overflow of your loving-kindness: "Sometimes my loving compassion would be able to gently soothe the blows inflicted by the severity of my righteousness." And since at that time I realized that I was less fit for the practice of love because of my excessive failings and numerous negligences, because I had received this from you as a gift as well, in the spirit of humility I threw myself before the wounds of your most holy feet, intending to plead both for my own salvation and for that of the dead soul previously mentioned.

2. There and then my weakness was strengthened by this insight: "For just as it is impossible for someone's foot to be pierced

---

[1] *documento* L; see LDP II.18.2.

without their own heart suffering with it, in the same way it is utterly impossible for my fatherly loving-kindness not to look with compassion on one who, although realizing that burdened by their own aberrations they need the healing power of divine forgiveness, is guided by the affection of charity and does not fail to make supplication for the salvation of their neighbors." **For this, too, may the kingdom and the glory be yours!**

<CHAPTER THIRTY-FIVE **Not in LDP**>

1. On one occasion around the time of Terce, while praying attentively before the image of the Crucified she saw little streams of the most holy blood and water flowing out of the wound in the side of that same image. She perceived that he was saying to her, "Look! I am giving you what flows from my heart with such headlong force as a drink. If, however, I have made you fit to enter that opening by setting aside your vanity and worldliness,[1] you will rejoice to find far more gracious things within."

[1] See LDP II.1.1.

<CHAPTER THIRTY-SIX **Not in LDP**>

1. Again, on one occasion while she was intent on prayer after holy communion, she saw the Queen of Heaven sitting beside her son in imperial glory; approaching her kneeling, she greeted her like this:

> **Hail, mother of loving-kindness and noble resting-place of the whole Trinity. Hail, hail, made beautiful both from the reverence of the bright and ever-tranquil Trinity and from its manifestation in the incarnation of your most loving son, sweetest bridegroom of my soul, Lord Jesus Christ, and from the grace bestowed on his human nature and on all of us in him, and to you, his most blessed mother, and on all of us in you. Praise him ever on our behalf, give thanks, bless, and entreat him, on behalf of all those in heaven, on earth and in hell, all that are, were, and will be, throughout all ages.**

Then while she was uttering these words, that is, "Praise, give thanks, bless, and entreat," she saw the Queen of virgins, rose without thorn,[1] rising up from her royal throne and, kneeling before her son, stretching out her hands and inclining her head at each one of the four phrases described. Her son said to her, "Lady mother, on whose behalf do you make such supplication?" Then she said, "Dear son, your bride entrusts herself to me." The Lord said, "Stand aside, mother, so that I may look upon her." For it seemed that the Mother of Mercy, standing between the

---

[1] See also LDP V.4.10.

Lord and <Gertrud>, was casting a shadow. And when the Lord's mother stood aside, the King of Glory himself bent down most courteously and clasped that person already mentioned to his bosom. Caressing her with wonderfully soothing words and delightful embraces, he kindly commended his gracious working in her, among other things exalting her desires and emotions with these words: *How beautiful are your steps in shoes, O prince's daughter!*[2]

[2] Song 7:1.

<CHAPTER THIRTY-SEVEN **Not in LDP**>

1. Another time, when she had received communion, as was quite often her practice she threw herself at the Lord's feet, intending to kiss his wounds. The Lord kindly raised her up and said, "Arise from my feet and sit at my side, for by the gift of grace through the assimilative union of the sacrament you are *the figure of my substance.*"[1] **And when she saw herself sitting there, striving for the embraces of her beloved, she said, "Since it befits a virginal mouth to kiss you alone, vigorous bridegroom of virginal purity, and a spotless breast to embrace you, I now remember with dejection of spirit that my heart, alas, has been so often distracted by human affections that I am deservedly judged unworthy of your most chaste and delightful embraces." Then the Lord sent forth from the loving wound of his pierced breast flowing streams, as it were, with which he washed her and rendered her** *whiter than snow,*[2] **showing that he was not only able but also prepared to reform all our deformities.**

---

[1] See Heb 1:3. The same idea is expressed somewhat more guardedly in LDP II.6.2.

[2] See Lam 4:7.

<CHAPTER THIRTY-EIGHT = LDP III.1 >

1. **Similarly**, when she had understood **through** a spiritual revelation that some misfortune was threatening that would increase her merit, and consequently shrank from it through human weakness, the kind and loving Lord, coming down to the level of her faint-heartedness, appointed his merciful Mother, the glorious empress of heaven, as her kindly guardian. As a result, whenever she was weighed down by some excessive trouble beyond her powers, she might always have confident recourse to the Mother of Mercy, through whose intervention she knew she would receive relief.

2. After a short time had elapsed, she was greatly weighed down because someone devoted to God compelled her to disclose **what** the Lord had conferred on her as a special gift at the preceding feast. For various reasons she considered it very difficult to do this at that time. If, however, she refused altogether, she was afraid of going against God's will. She ran to the comforter of the desolate, longing to learn from her what was the better course of action in this situation. She received this reply from her, "Pay out what you have, for my son has riches enough to repay whatever you pay out in his praise." But since she had hedged around her secret with so many barriers of her own devising that only with the greatest difficulty could she bring herself to disclose it, for that very reason she flung herself at the feet of the Lord, that he might make known to her what would better please him and provide her with the will to carry it out. Hence by his kindness she merited to be assured by such an answer: "Give *my money into the bank, that at my coming, I might exact it with interest.*"[1] In this way she learned that those promptings that she thought

[1] Luke 19:23.

rational and sent her by the Holy Spirit had in fact sprung from a human root, her own personal opinion. Hence from that time forward she began to relax the rigor of her intention[2]—rightly so, for as Solomon bears witness, *The glory of kings* is *to conceal the word*; but *the glory of God* is *to search out the speech.*[3]

[2] See LDP III.Prol.
[3] See Prov 25:2.

<CHAPTER THIRTY-NINE = LDP III.2>

1. While she was offering up to the Lord in a little prayer all the suffering that weighed upon her both in body and in spirit, and all the pleasure of which she was deprived both in the spirit and in the flesh, the Lord appeared wearing on both hands, like ornaments in the shape of jeweled rings, those two offerings that she had made him: that is, pleasure and suffering. When she had perceived this, she repeated the previous prayer again and again. A little later, while she was reciting the same prayer, she **felt deeply** that the Lord Jesus was anointing her **right** eye with the ring on his left hand, which she understood to represent physical suffering. Then that same eye, which the Lord seemed to have touched in spirit, became physically painful, so much so that afterwards it never recovered its former health.

2. From this she understood that just as a ring is a sign of betrothal, so misfortune, both physical and spiritual, is a most certain sign of divine election and is, so to speak, the soul's betrothal to God, so much so that everyone who is weighed down may truly, indeed confidently, say this: "My Lord Jesus Christ has plighted his troth to me with his ring."[1] And if, amidst one's troubles, one possesses this gift—that is, to be able to raise up the mind to God in praise and gratitude—in consequence one can **proceed** with delight and say this: "And he has adorned me as his bride with a crown."[2] For in time of trouble gratitude is the most splendid crown of glory, precious *above gold and the topaz.*[3]

---

[1] Antiphon for the feast of Saint Agnes.
[2] As above.
[3] Ps 118:127.

<CHAPTER FORTY **Not in LDP**>

1. One Sunday, when she was intent on prayer after holy communion, the time had come when she had to busy herself about the duties imposed on her, that is, the cooking of the food to be served. She was thinking that it was a huge burden because she had to turn from the inner to the outer. Well! She saw a young man[1] standing by her, of vigorous appearance with a beautiful face and elegantly dressed, who took her by the hand and gently said, *Come, my beloved, let us go forth into the field.*[2] Rising up, she followed him in the body, and thus throughout that day that delightful young man, inseparable companion and tireless helper, was present in all that she did. O truly, as Bernard says, a kind "companion, who by the spell of his words and manners, persuades everyone, as if in a sweet-smelling cloud arising from the ointments, to follow him,"[3] "joining up and lightening the hardships of the journey for the whole company by his fascinating conversation, so that when he has parted from them they ask concerning Jesus, '*Was not our heart burning within us?*'"[4] To him with the Father and the Holy Spirit be praise and glory for ever and ever!

---

[1] This image of Christ as a young man is persistent in the Gertrudian texts: see also LDP II.1.2/L 1; LDP III.65.3/L 47; LDP III.15.2/L 88; L 48, 109 and 187 below (none in LDP); LDP IV.9.4; and LDP IV.23.2 (neither is in L).

[2] Song 7:11.

[3] Bernard, SC 31.7 (CF 7:130; SBOp 1:224).

[4] Luke 24:32; Bernard, SC 31.7 (CF 7:130 [adapted]; SBOp 1:224). The Prologue *Ducam eam* quotes extensively from SC 31.

<CHAPTER FORTY-ONE **Not in LDP**>

1. Some years after this, while she was giving thanks to God during the Mass, *The Lord became <my protector>*,[1] **for the courteous gift just described, speaking earnestly, she added, "O my Lord, you who were with me so courteously at that time, it would indeed be welcome if now too I might experience your help during the week that I am to serve in the refectory." The Lord replied, "I shall minister with you." Then she said, "Therefore, most kindly Lord, gird yourself with your royal belt, for it is written of you, *Girding himself he* ministered *unto them*."**[2] **The Lord replied, "I shall gird you with my belt**[3] **and encircle you with [my]**[4] **girdle, that you will carry out all your duties to the praise of God the Father in the power of your union with me, and I shall compensate for all your negligences and shortcomings by making amends to the Father on your behalf." Then she said, "Lord, if you were with me with such obvious courtesy while I was serving, how could I ever prevent myself from being betrayed by outward ecstasy?" The Lord replied, "Do you not remember that I have sometimes indicated to you that my divine omnipotence has this great power: that wherever I was, I could restrain myself so that I am not experienced any more than would be most suitable and**

---

[1] Ps 17:19; introit for the second Sunday after Trinity.

[2] See Luke 12:37.

[3] *baltheus* L, but possibly more like the *subcinctorium*, a kind of liturgical apron worn by bishops up to the thirteenth century.

[4] *tuo* L.

expedient, according to the place, the time, and the individual?"[5] "Lord," she asked, "when the week of my serving is over, with what reverence or gratitude shall I return your belt?" The Lord replied, "No, you will give it back not when that week is over but on the day of your death, for in the meantime you will remain girded with it in every task that you are performing for the divine praise, and especially in the one that I welcome above others." Then she asked the Lord that he should confer some special gifts on her during this time of service as an indication of his almighty presence. This she rejoiced to have so clearly obtained on that very day through Jesus the Son of God.

[5] Cf. LDP I.1.3; LDP I.21.4; LDP II.17.1/L 20 above.

1. On the feast of Saint Martin,[1] **while they were chanting** the response *Saint Martin <foresaw> his death*,[2] burning with desire she **burst out, saying**, "O Lord, when will you do the same for me?"[3] The Lord **gently** replied, "I intend to take you away from this life very soon." **Greatly consoled, she was** inflamed with **such great fervor of spirit**[4] **that** she longed **with vehement desire** *to be dissolved and to be with Christ*,[5] even though she had not previously been **the least** concerned **about leaving the body. The heat of this desire did not cool, but she was growing more and more unwell, thirsting to be dissolved more quickly, according to the answer that she had received from the Lord. For that reason the Lord, in his accustomed fashion, delighting to increase a desire that he had already prompted by pursuing it, appeared to her on the day of his most holy incarnation. He opened up the loving wound of his blessed side, and from the heat of its love something like a powerful vapor appeared, moving outwards but not going very far. It retreated and collapsed into itself, as if continually moving out and back. At that sight she inwardly acquired a wonderfully**

---

[1] November 11.

[2] *Beatus Martinus obitum suum longe ante praescivit dixitque fratribus dissolutionem sui corporis imminere quia indicavit se iam resolvi*, "Saint Martin foresaw his death long in advance and told his brothers that the dissolution of his body was at hand, for he indicated that he was now being released."

[3] That is, inform her as to her death (see previous note).

[4] A frequent phrase in the Gertrudian texts.

[5] Phil 1:23.

sweet sense of readiness and, feeling herself somehow allured by that vision, was delightfully affected. During these <experiences> she perceived a voice saying, "You are being summoned." Hesitating, she replied, "Summoned to what, Lord?" He replied, "Soon you will come to me." Then she said, "My Lord, are the continual bodily pains that I often feel, especially in my sides, harbingers of my death?" The Lord replied, "Yes." And with this he vanished.

1. Then on Palm Sunday, when during Prime the Lord was trying to place a heavy cross on her, and she complained of her inability to carry it, the Lord changed its position in as many ways as the adversities under which she afterwards labored. As he placed that cross now on her shoulders, now on her arms, now on her hands, now between the two of them, it seemed as if, taking pity on her weakness, he was leaving to her own choice which she judged the easier to bear. For if at that time she had possessed the insight that she received a year later, she could have foreseen that by the display of the imposition of this cross she had been fortified to endure the various sicknesses and troubles under which she began to labor within the following month. Some of these seemed hindrances, but others seemed to advance her enjoyment of the divine, according to the preparatory warnings that she had been given through the imposition of the cross described above.

<CHAPTER FORTY-FOUR = LDP V.23.1, lines 8–17>

1. Also on the Wednesday after Easter, while still holding in her mouth **the Body of the Lord** she had taken, she was divinely greeted in this way: "Come, my chosen one, and I shall establish my throne in you."[1] From these words she **plainly perceived** that the time had **come** of which on the feast of Saint Martin the previous year she had heard it said, "I intend to take you away very soon," and so on. The Lord added, "However long you live on after today, strive to live not for yourself, but **take care to** augment my praise according to your desire in all things."

[1] Antiphon for the Common of Virgins.

1. After those events just described, burning with greater desire, she spent her time in augmenting the Lord's praise in many ways, as instructed by divine grace, and preparing herself for death in every possible way. More particularly on those days when she intended to receive communion, she begged and beseeched the Lord to be released with such great desires and strenuous prayers that often, as if forced, the Lord seemed to yield to her voice, had not something frequently intervened because of which she herself decided that her death should be deferred, for instance, when she thought of some good intention that she wished to carry out in the flesh. On one occasion in particular, however, inflamed by greater desire, she was praying with both abundant tears and insistent prayers that her will should be carried out. Sweetly soothing her with varied consolations, although now no caresses could console[1] her importunity, the Lord gently addressed her and said, "Why are you disturbed, beloved? What more could I add as a sign of my love for you? Look, I am already offering you my body as food and my blood as drink."

2. Hearing this, as if having no further objection that she could raise, she fell silent for a while and, giving thanks for such great blessings, devoutly approached the life-giving sacraments. But when she had taken communion and returned to her seat, she suddenly reverted to the very same thing and became importunate in praying to the Lord for the usual reason. The Lord said

---

[1] *consulere* L.

to her gently, "Do you still wish to make the amends that you undertook for your sins?" She replied, "Yes, Lord." He said, "Then be patient, and if when it is completed I have not acquiesced to your desires, then you can complain!" She replied, "I know, Lord, that you will never take me away unless I have said to you from the innermost depths of all the parts of my body that my soul thirsts for you." And she recited this verse three hundred and fifty times, in accordance with the number of the parts of the human body, as devoutly as she could, as if on behalf of all her members: *My soul* thirsts *after you, Lord*, living fountain; *O when shall I come and appear before* your desirable *face*,[2] most kindly Jesu? The Lord accepted this with kindly approval.

3. The reason for the amends mentioned earlier was this: the desire had come to mind to be absolved before her death by a full confession,[3] and since she did not have a priest with such a capacity,[4] trusting in God, she proposed in prayer that she should confess each and every one of her sins to the Lord with that contrition that he condescended to grant her, and that she should do penance for any sin with whatever psalm she found on opening the psalter. This she did. Therefore since her death was unexpectedly postponed for so long after the Lord's response mentioned earlier, that is, "I intend <to take you away> very soon" and so on,[5] one can speculate that the Lord did not want her to pass from this life without the reward for that desire and for that preparation to which he had urged her through those words. For since, as it is written, desires that are deferred increase,[6] in the same way the more they increase, the greater and more worthy the rewards that they deserve to achieve.

---

[2] See Ps 41:2-3.

[3] *plenam confessionem* L.

[4] It is not clear whether her confessor or confessors were incapable of hearing her general confession, or simply not authorized to do so.

[5] See L 42 and 44 above.

[6] Gregory the Great, Hom in Ev 25.2 (PL 76:1190A, C), or Hom in Ev 25.2.58–60 (CCSL 141:207). See above, *Ducam eam*, 6: "Gregory says, 'Holy desires increase through delay, but if they diminish through delay, they are not desires!'"

1. One Sunday, when she was present at Mass and about to communicate, she suddenly experienced such an abundance of divine grace and flood of words that it seemed to her that all that she owed in praise, thanksgiving, lamentation, and prayer,[1] **both for herself and for all those entrusted to her, had been completely fulfilled, so much so that, in marveling at such an overflowing abundance of grace in herself, she wondered if perhaps the time of her release had now arrived. So she said to the Lord, "O my Lord, if I shed my body at this time, everyone will be astonished at my release by such a sudden death." To this** the Lord **replied,** "If I carried out in your passing all that you could <attempt> **out of your nakedness**[2] from your earliest years until now, it would be very little in comparison to that grace that I have conferred on you by my generous loving-kindness alone without your desiring it." And the Lord added, **"Make a quick decision:** either to leave the body now, or to be made beautiful by somewhat longer **chastisings,** even though I know that you abhor the taint of the negligences <committed> in prolonged sickness." Then, submitting to God's great courtesy, she said, "*Your will be done,*[3] my Lord." And the Lord said, "It is right

---

[1] Cf. LDP IV.3.

[2] *pre nuditate poteras* L, *praemeditari potuisti* LDP, a significant discrepancy. For L's reading, cf. *Prae cruore occisorum, prae captivitate, prae nuditate inimicorum capitis*, a variant of Deut 32:42, *De cruore occisorum, de captivitate, nudati inimicorum capitis*, "of the blood of the slain and of the captivity, of the bare head of the enemies." Forms of *nudus*, adj., "naked," are fairly common in LDP: see especially V.8.3 where the word is used metaphorically to express Gertrud's lack of merit.

[3] Matt 26:42.

that the choice should be mine, **so that wherever I choose my dwelling-place to be, in that place no one would resist my eternal preordination, to prevent me from lingering there as long as I liked.** Therefore, if you agree **concerning your life,** to journey onwards in this **pilgrim** body for my love, I shall remain in you like a dove in its nest, and I shall comfort you in my bosom until finally **at the end of your life** I shall conduct you to the delights of eternal spring." And **from then onwards** her desire was moderated, **as she entrusted herself completely to the foresight of the divine will,** and whenever she retreated into herself after this, she heard this verse <sounding> **sweetly in her heart:** *My dove in the clefts of the rock,*[4] **until the negligence of human weakness lost it.**

[4] Song 2:14.

<CHAPTER FORTY-SEVEN = LDP III.65.3–4[1]>

1. Once when she had been bled before Lent these words often came to her: "O most excellent King of kings, most illustrious prince," and others of the same sort. When she had recollected herself early one morning in a place of prayer, she said to the Lord, "Most loving Lord, what do you wish to become of those words that so often come into my mind and spring to my lips?" Holding in his hand a golden necklace composed of four parts, he showed it to her. While she was wondering what the four parts **signified**, she was taught by divine inspiration that Christ's divinity was symbolized by the first part, Christ's soul by the second part, the faithful soul whom he has betrothed with his own blood by the third part, and Christ's spotless body by the fourth part. Also the fact that she saw in this necklace the faithful soul set between Christ's soul and his body gave her to understand the indissoluble cement of love with which the Lord fixes the faithful soul to his own body and soul. Well! suddenly, **with regard to** this necklace, she was inspired with these words by powerful energy:

> You, my soul's life, may the love of my heart be made one with you, fused with strength of loving heat. In all to which it turns without you, let it be left lifeless. For you are the charm of every color, sweetness of every savor, fragrance of every scent, delight of every sound, delicious **tenderness** of close embraces. In you delicious pleasure, from you **copious overflow**, to you charming allure, through you loving influence. You are the overflow of the

---

[1] The final chapter of the first part of LDP III.

Godhead's abyss, O King of kings most worthy, emperor most excelling, prince most illustrious, ruler most mild, defender most strong. You are the life-giving jewel of human nobility, craftsman most skillful, teacher most gentle, counselor most wise, friend most faithful. You: the savory union of intimate delight, O caresser most delicate, paramour most mild, lover most ardent, spouse most sweet, zealot most chaste. You: flowering blossom of prime beauty, O brother most lovable, youth most gorgeous, comrade most joyous, host most generous, servant most courtly. I set you above all creatures; for you I renounce every pleasure, **through** you I meet every hardship, in all these I seek your praise alone. You the quickener of these **and** every good I declare with heart and mouth. In the strength of your fervor I unite my **intent** devotion's intention to the power of your prayer that through the integrity of divine union I may be led to the summit of perfection, every rebel impulse consumed.

2. Each phrase gleamed like brilliant jewels worked into the golden necklace. The next Sunday following, while she was at Mass, about to communicate, and was reciting these words most devoutly, she saw the Lord taking delight in them. She said to him, "Most loving God, since I feel how much you delight in these words, I wish to counsel as many other people as I can to offer you the same song, in their prayers, like a necklace." The Lord replied, "No one gives me what belongs to me! But if anyone recites these words devoutly, **may I** increase in them the grace of my knowledge, and they will receive in themselves the splendor of my Godhead, **which it directs at itself** through the potency of those words, just as someone who holds pure gold up to the radiant sun sees the light reflected in it because it is gold." She soon felt the effect of these words, and when she had finished that prayer, the face of her soul appeared lit up more brightly by the radiance of the divine light, and, so it seemed to her, she received with greater relish the taste of divine thought.

1. While she was intent on celebrating *Esto michi* Sunday with a zeal more devout because of the special grace she had received in the past on the same day,[1] **just as the Lord is accustomed to vary his gifts, so he nonetheless condescended to increase her grace. For during Matins, from the first response until after the eighth, understanding each phrase in its symbolic sense, she took pleasure in the converse of the young man who was miraculously with her.**[2] **When they began the introit of the Mass, that is, *Be thou to me*, and she was striving to offer the Lord her intention through the same words, according to the insight that she had received from him before,** the Lord laid claim to those words for himself, on the grounds that they seemed particularly appropriate because of the provocations of that present time. He said to her, "*Be my protector,*[3] beloved, by resolving that if you had the strength you would willingly defend me from the **reproaches and** injuries with which I am particularly vexed at this time **by the worldly. And if you could strive to do so, concentrate on my not being harmed by such great insults, for you are she with whom,** repulsed by others and longing to rest, **I have decided to recline. And since you are called 'Christian' from my name, that is, Christ, and 'spiritual'**

---

[1] For accounts of earlier graces received on this pre-Lenten Sunday, see LDP II.14.1/L 11 and LDP II.8.1/L 27 above. See also L 51 below (not in LDP) and LDP II.23.13 (not in L).

[2] See L 40 and note.

[3] Ps 30:1.

from my Spirit, you will also conduct me into the innermost places of your heart through devotion and comfort me by making amends with the church for sinners." Then she embraced **the Lord and, embraced in return by his right hand, it seemed to her as if she were stealing into a mountain, and in this way during the whole of Lent until the Easter Vigil, while they were reading the lesson *In the beginning God created heaven and earth*,[4] as often as she returned to her heart, she seemed to be toiling in the mountain with the Lord, out of reverence for the Lord's having toiled in spirit for forty days in the wilderness.**

2. **When the introit of the Mass was repeated, that is, *Be thou to me*, once more she besought divine assistance to supplement her devotion through the same words.** And suddenly she was so ravished from her bodily senses and inwardly united to God that she failed to sit down and stand up with the community. Told by someone **to sit down, and realizing from this** that **her actions were different** from the others', she begged the Lord that she might control her body with his help, lest she should be seen **by others** to stand out through any eccentricity. The Lord replied to her, "Send that emotion of yours that is called love to me, that it may take your place in my presence, and you can concentrate on controlling your body!" She replied, "O most loving God, if one of my emotions can take my place, I certainly hope that the control of my body may be entrusted to my reason, so that I may be the more completely at your disposal!"

3. **And when they were reading in the gospel *Son of David, have mercy on me*,[5] the Lord gently intimated, "Whose words are these?" She replied, "Lord, <they are> Reason's, for she seeks to be enlightened by you in order to carry out what has been imposed on her." Having said this, she was immediately united to the Lord, without any hindrance. Then in the third week of the same Lent, while receiving the holy Body and Blood of the Lord, she was so completely absorbed into God that not only did she perform all her duties with the Lord, but, what is astonishing**

---

[4] Gen 1:1.
[5] Luke 18:38.

and worthy of all reverence, the Lord seemed kindly to extend himself towards everything that was expedient for her. For the longer she was occupied in exterior works because of the function imposed on her, the more gladly she ascribed it to the divine condescension.

<CHAPTER FORTY-NINE **Not in LDP**>

1. Since she had tropologically[1]expounded part of the readings from the book of Esther[2] and had finally added an exhortation concerning daily spiritual communion,[3] one day when she had participated in the solemnities of the Mass the Lord gently greeted her, saying, "Hail, my faithful follower: you give birth to me in the hearts of all those in whom your words are about to be fulfilled by making them fruitful." Then when in the sequence of the same Mass, which at that time was *Verbum bonum*, that verse was chanted, "We beseech you to correct us,"[4] "the Lord of majesty, upon whom rests the governing of the universe"[5]—I mean he whom angels praise, dominions adore, powers fear, *who does not need* our *good things*[6] (as if all one's salvation depended on trust in oneself!)—seemed to be imploring her to expound the generous overflow of the divine loving-kindness to those men who too often stretch the harshness of justice over the sweetness of the divine mercy. Among these things she particularly understood one person, whose unwise timidity the Lord wanted stimulated by her admonitions. But as she had neglected the community

---

[1] That is, figuratively, or more specifically in a way that relates events and personages in the Hebrew Scriptures to those in the New Testament. This technical term does not appear anywhere in LDP.

[2] In LDP Gertrud quotes from the book of Esther on several occasions: see also L 85 below. The book was sometimes read in September at the Night Office (see above, Intro. p. xxxii, n. 26).

[3] There are several references to spiritual communion in L, and none at all in LDP.

[4] From verse 3 of *Verbum bonum et suave*, sequence for feasts of the Virgin.

[5] Bernard SC 68.2 (SBOp 2:197).

[6] See Ps 15:2.

rather often during that week for many reasons, she considered it a weighty trouble, because of the scandal to others, if once again she were to neglect her decision to hold a conversation during that day with the person mentioned, to exhort her. The Lord, kindly sympathizing with her trouble, greeted her gently during the offertory of the Mass,[7] saying, *"Hail, Mary*, that is, bitterness conceived because of me; *full of* my *grace*, for I *the Lord will be with you*, helping you in all things; *you are blessed among women*,[8] that is, among those who, living only to themselves, seem to show no concern for the salvation of others, *and blessed is the fruit of your womb*,[9] that is, of your mouth."

3. After this, mindful and respectful of what has been described, she was quite often eager to take part in the solemnities of the Mass with greater devotion and yearned more frequently for spiritual communion. In a short time, that is, in that very winter, she received such consolation as was truly worthy of all respect: on two occasions she was offered the sacred Hosts of the Lord's Body in the form as taken from the altar, that is, first on the Saturday after *Populus Syon* Sunday,[10] from the royal hand of the Lord. The other time, on the Saturday before the feast of the Purification of the immaculate Virgin, he brought out <the Host>, as it were, from his sweetly flowing breast in which *are hidden all the treasures*[11] of sweetness and loving-kindness. And on each occasion she received in place of the chalice a delightful draught from the loving wound[12] in his side, pierced by the power of charity.

---

[7] This verse is the offertory for several feasts: Wednesday in Rogationtide in Advent, the Annunciation, commemorations of the Virgin in Advent.

[8] Luke 1:28.

[9] Luke 1:42.

[10] Second Sunday in Advent.

[11] Col 2:3. See "the Lord's breast, flowing with sweetness, in which lie hidden treasuries of perfect blessedness," LDP IV.4.3, and "that breast, in which are hid all the treasures of blessedness," LDP V.6.3.

[12] A favorite phrase: see also LDP I.16.1, LDP III.18.27, LDP IV.2.4, LDP IV.13.4, and LDP IV.16.2.

<CHAPTER FIFTY = LDP III.30.39; V.23.3>

1. On one occasion, when the memory of past sins had so cast her down that, **blushing red with shame[1] in the valley of humility,[2]** she was doing all that she could to be inconspicuous, the Lord bent down to her with such courtesy that all the court of heaven, as if astonished, was striving to call him back. To this the Lord replied, "I cannot possibly restrain myself from pursuing her, for she attracts my divine heart to her with such powerful cords of humility."

2. Another day, when **with impatient** desire **she was awaiting the time of her** release, the Lord **added,** "What bride ever hastened with great desire to that place where she knew her bridegroom must cease from adding to her adornment, and in addition where she would not be allowed to prepare any further gifts for her bridegroom?" For after death neither does the soul's reward increase, nor **can** it **offer** anything **further in praise to the Lord.**

---

[1] Cf. LDP IV.17.2.
[2] Cf. LDP II.16.6, LDP III.6.1, and LDP III.26.2.

<CHAPTER FIFTY-ONE **Not in LDP**; LDP IV.16.6>

1. A year having passed, on the Saturday before *Esto mihi* **Sunday**[1] **during Vespers, inspired by divine grace, she was turning over in her mind in thanksgiving God's blessings, one by one, with which she had been surrounded so repeatedly on that very day. At the least she was longing for some opportunity to repay God's great courtesy towards her through more circumspect custody of her senses and affections. Stretching out his arms above her, the Lord made her rest at the loving wound**[2] **of his most holy side, like someone who is hiding something in his bosom to protect it, and said, "I shall** *hide you in the secret of* my *face.*"[3] **The next day she was lamenting during Mass and said, "Lord, you have said that you would hide me** *in the secret of your face,* **and yet I take no joy in so desirable a gift!" In reply the Lord said, "What can you possibly lack? You possess that heavenly treasure chest**[4] **in which lie hidden all the treasures of my divine nature."**[5]

2. Notwithstanding, *the desire of her lips was by no means withheld from*[6] **her for long, but** on the Wednesday **of the same week,** in the name of the church, **she was offering the Lord a prayer for which she had a special devotion, as if** offering herself with <the

---

[1] See L 48.

[2] See L 49, n. 4.

[3] Ps 30:21.

[4] See LDP II.8.4, LDP III.25.2, LDP IV.58.3, and LDP V.10.4.

[5] See L 49, n. 3.

[6] See Ps 20:3.

church> and through it for Lenten amendment. He caught her up amid joyful embraces, in the tenderness of such great serenity that she **was able to bear witness** through her own experience beyond any doubt that Christ the bridegroom was indeed espoused out of great love to his bride, the church, in whose name she was herself striving to approach him at that time. **In addition she saw the Lord offer his deified heart in a form from which she could extract whatever was appropriate through her sighs and desires. And in this way she composed the hours of love and another useful exhortation.**

1. That Lent many people had devoutly entrusted themselves to her prayers before the feast of the glorious Resurrection, and she, weakened by physical illness, knew that she lacked the strength properly to satisfy the requests of each one of them. During the Mass *In nomine Domini*,[1] with what affection she could muster she devoutly besought the Lord that what she could not do in body, his all-powerful mercy would condescend to supply, according to the needs of each of those entrusted to her. Then she saw the Lord pouring out of the treasury of his sweet-flowing breast purest streams, as if ready to impart his blessings to each and every one entrusted to her, according to the capacity of each.

[1] Introit for Wednesday in Holy Week.

<CHAPTER FIFTY-THREE **Not in LDP**>

1. After this, during Mass on the feast of Saint Gothard,[1] she was suddenly aware of a wonderful abundance of divine sweetness, and astonished at the overflow of such great impetuosity, she said to the Lord, "O Father of mercy, unwearying and abundant fount of all grace, tell my soul through well-seasoned knowledge what drives your fatherly love with such bubbling force that its torrent, tasting of honey, penetrates the innermost recesses of my most unworthy heart with such joyful delight." With serene countenance the Lord kindly replied, "Because today is the anniversary of the day that I began to dwell in your heart,[2] which I chose in my flourishing eternity to be surpassingly joyful for me with all delights, the royal generosity of my divine heart is sweetly inclined towards you with a tenderness of such great serenity that I cannot restrain my princely largesse from making you devoutly remember that day by a special prerogative of grace, so that by this I may have a pathway to your heart, by which I may for ever pour into you the gifts of my graces."

[1] 4 May.

[2] This must be the "certain day between the Resurrection and the Ascension," referred to in LDP II.3.1/L 3.1.

<CHAPTER FIFTY-FOUR Not in LDP>

1. On the feast of the Dedication,[1] **during Matins she was concentrating on the seventh response, that is,** *Every precious stone [was your covering: the sardius, the topaz, and the jasper, the chrysolite, and the onyx, and the beryl, the sapphire, and the carbuncle, and the emerald],*[2] **with this prayer, that she might strive to win from the Lord the gift of the nine virtues symbolized by the nine jewels about to be named there, virtues with which the house of her heart would be prepared to be a worthy dwelling-place for the divine presence. Once the response was finished, the Lord added,** *"Upon your walls, O Jerusalem, I have appointed watchmen; all the day and all the night they shall never hold their peace*[3] **from praising the Lord's name." She understood these words as follows:** *"Upon your walls,* **that is, to fulfill your desire;** *Jerusalem,* **that is, vision of peace, or, containing true peace in yourself;** *I have appointed watchmen,* **that is, I have granted <them> from all the glorious choirs of angels;** *all the day and all the night they shall never hold their peace* **from praising the Lord's name, that is, however much you fall short in my praise from human weakness, they shall make up for it, with you and for you." Challenged by these words, she concentrated on what followed with more fervent devotion.**

[1] If this refers to the dedication of the monastic church, the date is unknown; it might also refer to the feast of the Dedication of the Lateran basilica, which fell on November 9. The chapel at Helfta was dedicated on August 10, year unknown.

[2] Ezek 28:13.

[3] Isa 62:6.

2. And while she was persisting in that devotion, when <the sisters'> Matins had finished, a cleric began Matins,[4] on which she took care to concentrate with the greatest diligence. And when they intoned the psalm *Come, <let us praise the Lord>*[5] with a descant, the Lord forewarned her with these words, saying, "Now give me your consent, for I shall begin the game of my divine delight with you." Then she understood from the various voices of the descant singers,[6] that is, through the low and the high, a meeting and parting between God and the soul that was most delectable, but also wonderful and ineffable; that is, how eternal divinity sings on high that unending praise that is incomprehensible to all created beings, and the soul sings in the lower register of its various miseries, and how the Lord, coming down to the soul through love, shows himself to be such that the soul is able to grasp him in accordance with its lowliness. She drank in such great devotion from this that she asserted that she did not remember having ever remained for a longer time in any prayer through knowledge and enjoyment. For she knew, too, that the prayers of the blessed spirits mentioned earlier were clearly present with their own desires.

3. Then after this she inserted these words into her prayer: "I praise you, my sweetest God, for you are unquenchable fire in the seraphim, inescapable knowledge in the cherubim, serene tranquility in the thrones, unconquerable strength in the powers, unmatched nobility in the principalities, limitless honor in the dominions, tireless strength in the virtues, friendly counsel in the archangels, wondrous protection in the angels. Angels, archangels, thrones and dominions, principalities and powers, heavenly virtues, cherubim and seraphim, praise the Lord, saying, 'To you be praise and honor, Lord, for every grace that ever you granted any creature, and specially the person whom you have advanced above all others with glory and honor.'"

---

[4] Clearly the clerics (possibly canons) based in Helfta said the offices at a separate time from the nuns.

[5] Ps 94:1.

[6] Cf. LDP IV.58.7.

<CHAPTER FIFTY-FIVE = LDP V.6.1, lines 1–25>

1. One day, when Dame S<ophie> the elder[1] had received the sacrament of anointing, **for the relief of her soul** <Gertrud> was reciting five *Our Fathers* **in honor of Christ's five wounds during the celebration of Mass** and last of all was praying to the wound in the side, that **with the saving water from his pierced side, which washes away the sins of the whole world, the Lord would purify her from every stain and, with the purple blood of the same loving wound, would mark her out with rewards for virtues.** The woman **for whom she was praying** appeared[2] in the form of a tender young girl, adorned with a halo; embracing her with his left arm, the Lord kindly **inclined his head towards her and, sprinkling her with the purest streams of his heart, pierced through and through, made her *whiter than snow*.**[3] **(But nonetheless <Gertrud> perceived that she had still to wash away one stain while in the flesh.) In addition, the Lord made her wondrously beautiful with the precious blood that redeemed humanity.**

2. And when, during this, the bell was rung at the elevation of the Host,[4] **and she was offering that same Host for the sick woman already mentioned, the sacred Host, touching the sick woman's breast, seemed to adorn her on every side with a kind of golden hue. Indeed, while the bell was being rung at the elevation of the chalice, and she was offering it for her in the same way, the Lord**

[1] Aunt of Sophie of Mansfeld, who succeeded Gertrud of Hackeborn as abbess in 1291.

[2] A rare example of a vision of someone who was still alive.

[3] See Lam 4:7.

[4] *hodie* L.

replied, "I shall also give her to drink inwardly, just as I have made her beautiful outwardly." Meanwhile the clapper[5] was struck, and that vision vanished.

3. Indeed, the sick woman, although very obviously dying, nonetheless survived for a while and finally lived for nearly five months, suffering from time to time from such sickness that it was obvious that she was expiating a fault. So, on that very day on which this sick woman began to feel better, she manifested such heavenly joy that it was possible to surmise, if not in her words, nonetheless in her actions, that the Lord had indeed visited her with his divine consolation. But she strove again and again to explain the gift of God to her, although as her strength was failing she could not utter it completely in words. The next day, when that person who perceived all that has been described was present with three others, and the sick woman was being questioned about the manner of the Lord's visitation, she called that person already mentioned by name and said, "Speak for me, for you know!" When the others said, "We don't know, do we?" the sick woman, pointing at the person we have mentioned with her finger, said her name again and again. When she had begun to explain, as if not entirely seriously, the sick woman picked up the story and completed it. And when the others who were present added some details as if in ignorance, she most steadfastly rejected that. For instance, when she who had known all this in spirit was saying that the sick woman was embraced by the Lord's left arm, the sick woman, smiling with humble kindliness, confirmed that this was so. But when the others added this verse, *His left hand is under my head, and his right hand shall embrace me*,[6] she contradicted them repeatedly, but added of her own accord that the Lord had kindly bent down his blessed head to her. Then when those present added that she had also received a kiss from the divine mouth, she steadfastly denied it. And after this the sick woman explained in detail how the Lord had forgiven her sins and adorned her with virtues.

---

[5] *tabula* L, "monastic clapper," cf. LDP IV.26.1.
[6] Song 2:6; 8:3.

<CHAPTER FIFTY-SIX = LDP V.6.2–3>

1. Then after **a certain amount of time,** on the day before this **same** sick woman's death, **in the morning at sunrise** the Lord appeared seated, preparing a restful place in his bosom, in which he paid particular attention to cleanliness and comfort, and that sick woman appeared at the Lord's left, as if lying on a bed, enveloped in a small cloud, **not bright but not very dark**. Then she who saw this said to the Lord, "She is far from fit for such a glorious place as she is still enveloped in this little cloud." The Lord replied, "I am leaving her here for a while until she is completely purified and fit for my company." And thus the sick woman remained in her death agony throughout that day and night. But the next day **at the hour of her passing,** <Gertrud> saw the Lord bending kindly towards the sick woman with a calm expression and raising her up as if to meet **the Lord.** Then she said, "My Lord, can it be that you are now coming to the desolate soul as merciful father?" He answered her question with a gentle nod of his head.

2. And after a little while, when she had died, <Gertrud> saw her soul in the **same** form of a girl as she had seen her before, beautifully dressed in snow-white and rosy pink garments, joyfully flying up to the place prepared for her. When the **most kindly Father** stretched out his left arm to welcome her, she leaned her head on it with tender delicacy, as if to take her rest. And suddenly, as if **she disliked that rest**, she leaned on the other side **below** his right arm, and immediately raised herself up from there to press a kiss on the **beatific** mouth, **by whose word the heavens were established.**[1] As if unable to reach

---

[1] Ps 32:6.

it, she flung herself on his neck and placed a sweet kiss on the Lord, between his breast and his neck. And thus, having slipped back, weary and panting, onto the Lord's breast, she rested for as long as this verse was being recited in the Commendation: *The prayer of the church commends <her> to you.* At these words she seemed to draw delightful refreshment abundantly from that breast, in which *are hid all the treasures*[2] of **divine consolation and sweetness**. Sweetly revived by this, she drew herself up and breathed freely.

[2] See Col 2:3.

<CHAPTER FIFTY-SEVEN **Not in LDP**>

1. On Saint Stephen's day,[1] when she had composed herself in her place of prayer after Matins, she saw the King of Glory, *beautiful above the son of men*,[2] resplendent with unimaginable adornments, raised up on an imperial throne, gently enticing her, by a *going up of purple*, to the *seat of gold*[3] of his sweetly-flowing breast. This "going up" [i.e., staircase] was marked out by such great glory that it seemed that every bodily pain, however serious, could easily be alleviated in gazing on its delightfulness. And since she suffered from a frequent and uncontrollable pain in her side, she strove to win from the Lord, by her heartfelt prayers, that that continual pain would persist, because it assured her that she would continue to stand in the glory of that staircase. She made one condition, however: that she should not be so heavily burdened as to be hindered from the strict observance of the Order, and particularly from attendance at choir, which she always judged a most joyful thing.

2. From this she perceived that pain that does not include the denial of pleasure[4] bestows much less glory than when a person is burdened with physical pain in body but is also mentally tortured because of deprivation of things in which she takes pleasure, such as fasting, prayer, and the like. For this humbles the soul, and such humility shines before God with wonderful brightness.

[1] December 26.

[2] Ps 43:3.

[3] See Song 3:10.

[4] For this chapter, compare LDP III.3/L 59 below.

Similarly, someone who sweats and toils for love of the Lord, if also tormented mentally because the tranquility of contemplation is hindered, acquires wonderful dignity. But since she was taking very great delight in the pleasing nature of that staircase, fired with compelling desire she said to the Lord, "O strongest God, *draw me*[5] with whatever tight chain you wish, lest, left to my own will, I might be slow to come to you." He replied, "Do not ask for this, for it does not further your interests to be drawn."

[5] Song 1:3.

<CHAPTER FIFTY-EIGHT Not in LDP>

**1. While on that and the following day her mind was preoc-
cupied with these things, on the night of the Holy Innocents, when
she had spent a long time sleepless before Matins, the Lord added
this insight to the vision just described: All those who strive to
climb that staircase spoken about reach it in three ways. The first
are drawn. The second are carried. The third are led. Just as one
who is drawn is not reliant on his own will but is completely in
the power of the person who is drawing, so also is he who is carried, although he is pleasantly relieved from the toil of the journey. But he who is led, if he wishes, can sometimes go on ahead
as if to gather flowers, or can sometimes stand still *in the midst,
covered with charity for the daughters of Jerusalem.*[1]**

**2. For the first, who are drawn, seem to symbolize those who
are tormented by many temptations and tribulations, through
which they are forced to go to God, as Saint Gregory says: "The
evils that oppress us here force us to go to God."[2] The second,
who are carried, seem to denote those who frequently acquire
such great abundance of inner sweetness that however much
tribulation or physical adversity rages at them, they never think
themselves abandoned, knowing that it is written, *I am with him
in tribulation.*[3] Mindful that the Lord's *yoke*, as he himself said,
is sweet and his *burden light*,[4] they say with the apostle, *I can do***

---

[1] See Song 3:10.

[2] Gregory the Great, Mor 5.XXVI.13.

[3] Ps 90:15.

[4] Matt 11:30.

all things in him who strengthens me,[5] for in their love of the beloved they consider any labor or sorrow to be light, or rather exceedingly sweet.

3. The third, who are led, seem to signify those who, in all that is set before them, voluntarily choose what is more burdensome, in some way supporting *the hand* of the Lord *heavy upon*[6] them and considering this to be their consolation, that by afflicting them[7] with pain he is not sparing <them>, for they know that the *present* is a time not of *joy but sorrow,*[8] and that this is the safest path to follow the Son of God, who passed through doing good, *not having,* as he himself said, *where to lay his head,*[9] that is, to lighten his physical burdens. In all tribulation they pay attention only to this: that as much as anyone will have shared in Christ's sufferings in this world, so much the more like him will she be established in glory. Truly, they are gathering flowers that bloom eternally, for their hearts rejoice in the Lord's justice rightly, not falsely. May praise of justice bring such great enlightenment to the soul, when God is praised and loved in his justice: this knowledge is given to none who has not experienced it.

4. These are the true daughters of Jerusalem who, however much the storms of temptations may assail them, nonetheless always delight in calm of mind and stand firm *in the midst, covered with charity for the daughters of Jerusalem:*[10] that is, contemplative souls. They are said to be *in the midst, covered with charity,* because human understanding cannot comprehend how the chastisement of human beings springs from the justice of majesty, the wisdom of divinity, and the overflow of goodness. The bitter taste of that inflowing has no appeal for human affection, but when the mind in ecstasy moves towards God, in that intervening space in the midst it finds that truly all things spring from divine love.

---

[5] Phil 4:13.

[6] Ps 31:4.

[7] *eas* L, i.e., feminine gender.

[8] Heb 12:11.

[9] Matt 8:20; Luke 9:58.

[10] Song 3:10.

5. Also by the staircase's circular shape three grades of those climbing it were symbolized. The first, who go directly to the golden couch mentioned earlier in the center, where the pathway is shortest,[11] **are those the pain of whose tribulations is nothing but the irksomeness of impatient desire that affects the minds of lovers. Because of this** *their tears have been their bread day and night*[12] **and they always** *desire to be dissolved,*[13] **not so much from the body as from all worldly preoccupation, and** *to be with Christ*[14] **in continual devotion and sedulous meditation, and, as much as is possible in this life, to cling to him in the love of indissoluble union. With the prophet they say,** *As the hart pants after the fountains of water,*[15] **and with the bride in the Song of Songs,** *I am wounded with love,*[16] **and again,** *Tell* **my beloved** *that I languish with love.*[17] **And these are such that most easily run headlong "to kisses and embraces that surpass drinks of honey."**[18]

6. The second, who go up on the right, are those who, though sometimes burdened by human tribulations, consider the greatest tribulation to be their human shortcomings, for which they fear to be separated from God. They pay no attention to human opinion, but they fear offending the King of angels, saying with the apostle, *to me it is a very small thing to be judged by you, or by man's day,*[19] **since** *he who judges me is the Lord.*[20] **Or again,** *It is better for me to fall into the hands* **of men,** *<than to sin in the sight of the Lord>.*[21]

---

[11] *in medio* L: if we assume a circular or spiral staircase turning clockwise from the bottom, as most medieval staircases seem to have done, the fastest route would be to climb in the center, closest to the central post.

[12] Ps 41:4.

[13] Phil 1:23.

[14] Phil 1:23.

[15] Ps 41:2.

[16] See Song 4:9.

[17] See Song 5:8.

[18] From the sequence *Dulcis Jesu memoria*, lines 97–98.

[19] 1 Cor 4:3.

[20] 1 Cor 4:4.

[21] Dan 13:23.

7. The third, who come on the left, are those whose trouble is completely from without, such as loss of family, vexation by others, separation from friends, loss of honors and goods, and similar things that they do not suffer at all for love of God but do so completely against their will. The unconquerable goodness of God, however, mercifully condescends to save them through those same tribulations, for he *desires not the death of the wicked, but that he turn from his way and live.*[22]

[22] Ezek 33:11.

<CHAPTER FIFTY-NINE = LDP III.3>

1. She received indisputable evidence that the denial of pleasure in hardship is increase of glory,[1] which she had not understood until then. One day around the feast of Pentecost she was so unbearably tormented by a pain in her side that those near her would have reckoned it more easy for her to die on that day rather than survive, if they had not known that she had quite often recovered from similar pain. Her kindly lover and her soul's true comforter gave her this recompense: that whenever she lay there, suffering want from the negligence of those serving her, the kind and loving Lord himself appeared, whose soothing presence mitigated her pain. But when care from her helpers was more attentive, the Lord stole away and the pain grew more oppressive. By this she was clearly given to understand that the more one is abandoned by human beings, the more one is regarded by the divine mercy. And when the day was drawing near evening and she suffered an excruciating attack, she tried to persuade the Lord that her pain should be relieved. The Lord raised his **delicate** arms and showed her that he wore on his breast, like a jewel, the pain she had endured during the day. Now when she saw that jewel, which seemed perfect and completely flawless, she rejoiced and hoped that from then on her pain would cease. To this the Lord answered, "Whatever you suffer from now onwards will add glory to this jewel." For although it was studded with gems, still it seemed less radiant, like *gold become dim.*[2] Her next source of suffering was the plague, which she now contracted. She was not seriously ill but was wearied more by denial of pleasure[3] than sharpness of pain.

---

[1] See above, L 57.2.

[2] Lam 4:1.

[3] That is, presumably, the inability to perform her favorite spiritual exercises.

1. Since she took very great delight in admiring the purple staircase mentioned earlier[1] **that led to the golden couch of the Lord's sweetly flowing breast, she said to the Lord, "Can it be, my Lord, that your chosen one, the sick Sister Mechtild,**[2] **is also striving to climb this staircase?" He replied, "No: she has made her way there and stands ready for a single great momentary rapture." Then she saw the Lord preparing, as if in his bosom, a most lovely place of repose for that sick woman and gently cherishing her as she leaned on his left side. Then she who saw these things** said to the Lord, "Why, most loving God, do you not hear us **more obviously** when we pray for her?" **The Lord replied,** "Her spirit is so detached from human concerns that **just as you could not be comforted by her, so she** could not be comforted in any human fashion by you." **To this she replied, "And** by what decision, **most merciful Father?"** The Lord replied, "I now possess my secret in her, just as I once possessed it with her." **Another time, when she was awaiting the moment of the same woman's release,** the Lord said, "My innermost majesty **has entered** her." She said, "What death will she die?" **He** replied, "I shall absorb her with my divine power, just as the burning sun dries up a drop of dew." **Then** she asked **the Lord** why he allowed her to wander in her **anterior**[3] senses. The Lord replied, "So that I may be known to work more in

---

[1] See L 57 and 58.

[2] Mechtild of Magdebourg.

[3] A technical medieval medical and scientific term: the anterior (i.e., front) part of the brain received impressions from the senses.

the inmost being than on the outside." She said, "Your grace would quite easily persuade **their** hearts of this." **Then** the Lord responded, "And how will they receive my grace when they rarely or never resort to their inmost being, where grace is usually infused?"

2. After this she prayed that after <Mechtild's> death he would at least exalt her with **miraculous prodigies,** to his own glory, as proof of the divine revelations **that she had composed,** and as an appropriate **refutation of the wicked.** Then, holding the book between two fingers **of his right hand,** the Lord said, "Surely I will not protect my victory without weapons!" And he added, "When it was necessary, I **subdued** peoples and kingdoms by **miracles,** signs, and prodigies. But in the present case **I am not considering such things, because if anyone has acquired knowledge of something similar** through his own experience, **that is, a** similar inflowing **of whatever kind of divine sweetness,** it is easy to confirm in him a carefully considered belief, **because he is glad to have proof that agrees with his own experience. But I** certainly do not tolerate **the perverters of good things** who attack **this book;** I shall prevail against them **when and where I wish."** In this she sensed a wonderful sweetness of the **kindly** favor, with which the Lord welcomes the belief of the faithful, **by which they readily trust** that the generous overflow of divine grace is imparted to the chosen not according to human merits but according to the **boundless** unrestraint of the divine heart.

<CHAPTER SIXTY-ONE **Not in SC**>

1. One day after this, when the community was praying for the sick woman mentioned before, she too was praying the Lord that, for love of his chosen Mechtild, he would at least condescend to exalt her death with signs and prodigies. The Lord answered her, "She herself will not want this." She replied, "Well, we want it!" The Lord said, "Since you are all still living in the body, you could not have everything that you want." However, she saw the Lord assert this with such great gentleness that from then onwards she used to wonder whether the Lord would agree to the wish of the community in this.

1. And when the same sister **Mechtild** of blessed memory was being anointed, <Gertrud>, led by desire, saw the Lord Jesus touching her heart with his **own** hand and saying, "Since that blessed soul, released from the flesh, is plunged into its source of origin, I shall pour out abundantly on all those who are here out of love the swelling waves of my honey-sweet **blessing." And when she was praying with the words, "Fortify her, most loving God, with the sacrament of your sweetest Body and Blood," the Lord replied, "She is mingled with my divinity to such an extent that there is no need for her to receive the sacraments, but my unfathomable judgments do not so command."**

2. Then, when **that sick woman** was dying, and <Gertrud> was concentrating on prayer with the others for a long time, **desiring to know by the gift of God what was then happening to God's chosen one,** eventually she understood that the Lord was **rewarding with** a threefold blessing all those standing around. The first of these was that he would fulfill the righteous desires of them all towards him; the second, that he would tirelessly assist anyone working on the correction of their failings. **In addition** she perceived that by the merits of M<echtild> these two were quite easily bestowed, one after the other, in that place. The third blessing was that **with serene countenance** he **kindly extended over all those present his** generous benediction with **his blessed** outstretched hand.

3. Having seen this, with great devotion she exerted herself in giving thanks that although divine justice, as she feared, had driven her away from the knowledge of those things that the Lord was working in his chosen one because of her unworthiness,

nonetheless his kindly mercy had granted her the perception of what has just been described. And when she thus praised both the justice and the mercy of God with devout love, saying, "I praise you, rock of justice; I praise you, jewel of mercy; I praise you, sun of justice; I praise you, flower of mercy; I praise you, beauty of justice; I praise you, sweetness of mercy; I praise you, loveliness of justice; I praise you, amiability of mercy, for all the justice and mercy that you have ever exercised in any created being, and especially in me, *the offscouring of all*[1] **created beings."**

4. *The Lord of hosts, the King of Glory,*[2] appeared, in form *beautiful above the sons of men,*[3] or rather, above the countenance of angels. He was sitting at the head of the sick woman and [was receiving][4] her breath, which, like a rainbow of golden splendor, stretched from the sick woman's mouth to the divine heart on his left-hand side. And when <Gertrud> had lingered some time in delight at this **lovely** vision, and in the meantime they were reciting the psalm, *O God my God, look <upon me>,*[5] to the end of that psalm, *To thee, O Lord,* **will** *I cry,*[6] the Lord leaned over the sick woman with wonderful gentleness as if about to bestow a kiss on his spouse, and after a little while, raising himself, he repeated this a second time.

5. After this, while they were reading the suffrages **of Our Lady, and among other things this** antiphon *That we may look upon you,*[7] the Virgin Mother appeared, illustrious offspring of a royal house, suitably arrayed in purple garments. Gently leaning over her son's spouse and holding the sick woman's head with her delicate hands, she enabled the trajectory of her breath to travel more directly towards the divine heart. And while they were reciting that short prayer, "Hail Christ Jesu, Word of the Father" **and so on,** the Lord **was** transfigured

---

[1] 1 Cor 4:13.

[2] Ps 23:10.

[3] Ps 44:3.

[4] LDP; *om.* L.

[5] Ps 21:2.

[6] Ps 27:1.

[7] Sixth antiphon for Matins of the blessed Virgin Mary.

by wonderful brightness, and **all** the divine countenance glowed fiery red like the sun shining in its splendor. Astonished at this and ravished from herself, when she came to herself after a little while she saw the shining rose of **heavenly loveliness**,[8] I mean the virginal Mother, press most delightful kisses on her son the bridegroom with sweetest embraces, as if in the wild cry of congratulation on such a joyful union with his new bride. From this she perceived that during this time that happy union had been consummated, which had *brought* that thirsty soul *into the* ample *storerooms*,[9] or rather, **it had been completely intermingled with** the abyss of true beatitude, never to emerge **thenceforward. Nor did she consider it inappropriate that she was hindered by outer things at that moment, for she thought herself by her own estimation completely unworthy to participate in spirit in such joyful and secret delights.**

[8] Cf. LDP III.19.3, 13, and 23.
[9] See Song 1:3.

<CHAPTER SIXTY-THREE Not in LDP>

1. On the day of the holy Epiphany,[1] **becoming somewhat aware of the severity of the divine justice, which demands some fruit from a person for grace bestowed on them, her mind was dismayed by those words that were being sung,** *Where is he that is born <king of the Jews>?*[2] **In soothing her, her kindly lover took care to calm her by the words sung next,** *We have seen his star,*[3] **saying, "You are the star of my splendor, receiving light from me, the true sun, to make up for all your shortcomings."**

[1] January 6, also Gertrud's own birthday.

[2] Matt 2:2. *Magi veniunt ab oriente Jerusalem quaerentes et dicentes, ubi est qui natus est, cuius stellam vidimus et venimus adorare dominum,* "There came wise men from the east to Jerusalem, saying, 'Where is he that is born king of the Jews? For we have seen his star in the east and are come to adore him' "; verse and response for the feast of the Epiphany.

[3] Matt 2:2.

<CHAPTER SIXTY-FOUR = LDP IV.8.1 >

1. On the holy night of the **noble** virgin Agnes,[1] <Gertrud> was greatly pleased to see the Lord glorying with great love and sweetness in that praise with which the whole court of heaven was extolling the words of that virgin, which the church was repeating at that moment. **Mindful of the feast of Saint Katherine, particularly beloved to her since childhood, which had passed,**[2] she said to the Lord, "**Ah, Lord God,** what delightful sweetness could have flowed into my soul on the occasion of **that antiphon, *Wise and watchful virgin*, and of the other** sweet words **sung that night,** if only my weakness had not hindered it!" The Lord replied, "I am keeping it safe for you in myself, and from there you shall draw it now or in the future, all the more sweetly because it will be the less mingled with the foolishness of your own will." From this she understood that no one's salvation is lessened by an obstacle incurred through no **negligence** of one's own. And when in the sixth lection **at the clerks' Matins**[3] the words "A certain person said that Agnes, a Christian from childhood, was so skilled in magic arts that she called Christ her spouse"[4] were being read, she sorrowfully added, "Alas! Lord God, **that** your supreme majesty **endures such indignities** from the human race!" To this the Lord replied, "I am amply recompensed from the voluptuous **love** that united **her** with me." Grant **therefore, bestower of gifts,** to all chosen **for special grace**, to cleave to you by the charm of such great

---

[1] Vigil of the feast of Saint Agnes, January 20.

[2] November 25.

[3] See above, L 54.

[4] Saint Ambrose, Ep 1 (PL 17:737A).

trustworthiness, **delight in** which leads you to consider of little weight all the injuries that those who speak against you inflict on you. **Amen.**[5]

[5] In LDP this closing prayer is Gertrud's response to the Lord.

<CHAPTER SIXTY-FIVE = LDP V.8.1–3>

1. When M.[1] of blessed memory was in her death agony, <Gertrud>, summoning all her **emotions within her,** was trying to discover through God's grace what was happening with respect to the dying woman. **And although she labored** for a long time, she could not **obtain** anything except that **the sick woman seemed to have** a minor problem **because** she had sometimes taken pleasure in outward things, such as that her bed was draped with embroidered fabric with designs in gold. **For even if there were more faults, because she acknowledged them she was not held accountable for them, for according to Augustine, when people acknowledge their faults, God forgives them.**[2] **Hence it could be that she did not recognize that particular fault and so was held accountable. After this, since <Gertrud> persisted for some time, she received this answer from the Lord, "Remember the words of that sick woman and reckon according to faith how mercifully I am treating her."**

When on that very day Mass was being celebrated for **the dead woman after the Commendation**, and at the elevation of the Host <Gertrud> was offering **the sacrifice** for **the dead woman with all the devotion that she could**, although she did not see the dead woman's soul, she nonetheless perceived that it was **nearby from the eager attractive force that she sensed being drawn out from the divine heart.** So she asked the Lord: "O Lord, where is she?" He replied, "She is coming to me, dazzlingly white." She realized

---

[1] "M. B." in LDP. The absence of any title such as *domna* or *soror* suggests that this woman was not a nun.

[2] Augustine, Enarr in Ps 44:18; see also LDP V.22.1.

from this that **that assistance** that had been **given** her in the love of God, before her death **and at the hour of her death,** had helped her so much that, **radiant and purified from every stain,** she had flown up.

2. The next day, on which she was about to be buried, <Gertrud> was praying for her **in the same way** during Mass, and she saw her on the Lord's left, as if sitting at table for a banquet, and everything that was being offered on her behalf in prayer, devotion, and the like was being placed before her **on the table** in the likeness of various dishes. **And** when**,** at the elevation of the Host, **she was making an offering for the dead woman in the same way as on the day before, and the Lord was setting before <the dead woman>,** in the likeness of a drinking vessel, **what was being offered for her,** she had scarcely tasted it when she was immediately pierced to the marrow by the innate sweetness of the divine. She **herself** was **completely** transformed into such a state of **sweetness** that, raising her clasped hands, she prayed **with devout love** for all those who had **resisted** her in this life in thought, **words, or deeds**, for she rejoiced that **from such things her reward had increased the more abundantly**. And when **the one who saw these things asked,** in astonishment, why she did not pray for her friends **as well as for her enemies, she understood that the more powerfully she prayed, the more sweetly and intimately she prayed for her friends** from her heart to the heart [of her beloved].[3]

3. Another **time,** when she was reflecting that she had **voluntarily** renounced all the reward **with which she could be enriched** through God's mercy in the practice of good works **so as to give it up for the increase of** the reward of dead woman, she said sorrowfully to the Lord, "I hope, **my** Lord, that your loving mercy **may** often **turn its fatherly glance on** me, naked and poor as I am." To this the Lord replied, "What can I do for one who is naked out of love, except cover him with my own fleece and work with him more urgently, so that he may recover the more quickly **whatever he has laid aside** through love?" Then she said, "However much you work with me, I must still

---

[3] LDP; *om.* L.

come to you naked, for, **overcome by charity and trusting in the unbounded[4] overflow of your generosity,** I have renounced **not only the past, but also all the future rewards of your gifts.**" The Lord replied, "Although a mother allows her fully clothed daughters to sit at her feet, she puts her arms around the naked little boy on her lap, wrapping it in her own clothes." He added, "And what then do you have, sitting beside the depths of the ocean, that is any the less than others who are sitting by the sources of brooks?" That is, those who to a certain extent **are reliant on** their own deeds sit by the sources of brooks, but those who, **overcome by love and humility,** have completely emptied themselves possess God, the depths of complete blessedness.

[4] *continentissima* L, emended to *incontinentissima*; compare LDP V.29.4.

<CHAPTER SIXTY-SIX **Not in LDP**>

1. One day while she was watching some people[1] receiving communion who[2] were approaching not of their own accord but compelled by her, wondering whether this pleased or displeased the Lord, she diligently asked the Lord in prayer. She received this answer, "Being closer to me, you offered them at that time the gift that I gave."

2. At Quinquagesima,[3] she was intent on taking part in the Mass, in which she had often received divine blessings, and they had arrived at the place where they sing in the introit of the Mass, *For <you are> my firmament*.[4] The Lord added, "*You are my firmament* because I shall work more urgently in you, through you, and with you, just as a hand, covered by a glove, is unseen when it is stretched out to work." <Gertrud> did not understand at all what was being conveyed by these words, until on the Wednesday of the same week a task was imposed on her to which she thought herself encouraged, not in vain, by those words.

3. Then one day in the presence of the Lady Abbess and some of the senior nuns she had spoken firmly about the task imposed on her, and having left she had attended Mass. She remembered that she had spoken before her seniors less respectfully, even boldly, she feared, and these thoughts hindered her. Then she perceived the Lord saying to her in spirit, "Don't be afraid. It is I who prompted you to speak those words." Comforted by this, she was no longer distressed.

[1] *aliquas* L, i.e., feminine gender.

[2] *qui* L, i.e., masculine or common gender.

[3] *Esto mihi* Sunday.

[4] Ps 70:3.

<CHAPTER SIXTY-SEVEN **Not in LDP**>

**1. When they were reading this sentence in the passion accord-
ing to Luke,**[1] *With desire I have desired,*[2] **the Lord seemed to offer
her his sweet-flowing breast, saying, "Drink! This is yours, for I
put it aside for you at that time, and I am keeping it for you still."
Leaning on the Lord's breast, she drank so copiously from the
nectar-sweet torrent of his divine heart that she seemed strengthened not only in spirit but also in body. Mindful of a particular
person, she said to the Lord, "Offer her, too, most merciful God,
a pleasing taste of such saving sweetness." The Lord replied, "I
shall pour it out for her, from which she will profit." When in the
same place was read,** *Father, forgive them,*[3] **the Lord, embracing
her with his right hand, said, "If I did this for my enemies, amidst
sorrows, what do you think I shall do for you, my bride, amidst
delights?"**

[1] Read on the Wednesday in Holy Week.
[2] Luke 22:15.
[3] See Luke 23:34.

<CHAPTER SIXTY-EIGHT = LDP IV.26.4; **not in LDP**>

1. On Good Friday, when around Prime she was rendering devout thanks to **Christ, who for our sins** was willing to be judged by **an earthly judge**, she saw the **Only-begotten** of God himself, serene in perfect joy, sitting on the imperial throne with the **heavenly** Father, who with wonderful sweetness was soothing him for all the insults and blasphemies suffered for the **salvation and** redemption **of the human race**. She saw each one of the saints pay homage to the Son of God himself, kneeling with the greatest gratitude **for his trial, because** they had been freed from eternal damnation.

2. **Then, while they were reciting the verse** *Arise, Lord,*[1] **immediately the King of Glory himself, arising from his imperial throne, kindly offered with his almighty hand a generous blessing by making the sign of the Holy Cross over the whole choir, beginning from the acolytes who were serving at the altar and moving on to those who were singing, and finally ending with those praying in the tower.**[2]

---

[1] Sung at Prime: see below, L 86.

[2] The sole reference in any of the Gertrudian texts to a tower at Helfta.

<CHAPTER SIXTY-NINE = LDP IV.26.5>

1. **The same day**, when they were reading **those words** *I thirst*[1] in the passion **according to John, she perceived** the Lord holding out a chalice **with his delicate hands** as if to catch tears of devotion for himself in a cup **from the eyes of the reader. And the more the attention of the one who was weeping turned towards greater mysteries, the greater the care with which they seemed to be collected. Feeling** her heart **swelling with sweetness of such great devotion that she found it not only easy but, rather, extremely delightful to shed fervent tears copiously,** she **said to** the Lord, **"O, sweetest Lord,** how **do you** receive it **from me that right now I am holding back tears that I would find it most sweet to shed? But I wish the gift of your grace to remain a secret between you and me, lest if it were made known to others through my tears, it would be mingled with some impurity. And although it would be nothing to me, even if I had a thousand lives, that they should be consumed for your sake in an instant, nonetheless I hold back these tears to spare my head,**[2] **lest I should be hindered from your service for too long."** Then she saw a most pure little stream, **as if of ethereal splendor**, flow into the Lord's mouth from the heart of her soul, and meanwhile she **understood** the Lord's reply **in this manner**: "This is how I **shall drink in** the tears of devotion that are held back with such purity for my sake."

[1] John 19:28.

[2] That is, to prevent a headache: see LDP V.1.28.

2. When fifteen[3] *Our Father*s were being recited in honor of the Lord's five most holy wounds, the Lord appeared, offering her the noble jewels of his sweetly flowing wounds, blossoming in rosy splendor, to kiss. They were as blood-red and as fresh as if they had been inflicted on the Lord's body on that very day.

---

[3] Gertrud's devotions to the wounds more usually involve five recitations of the *Our Father*: see, e.g., LDP IV.21.5 and V.4.23.

<CHAPTER SEVENTY Not in LDP>

1. Before Matins on the night of the most glorious Resurrection, the King of Glory, king of famous victory, appeared, offering her once again his wounds, flowing with honey, to be kissed. While she was kissing them with great devotion and thanksgiving, there came into her mind a desire to compound, to the best of her ability, an excellent ointment with which she could anoint[1] those sacred wounds. To carry this out she decided to renounce of her own free will all sensual pleasure to compound that ointment for soothing the Savior's flowering wounds already mentioned. That is, if she could possess or desire to possess in abundance all delight of the eyes in the loveliness of all colors and in the flower of all the world's springtime growth, and all pleasure in songs accompanied by organs, sweetly sounding melodies, and the melodiousness of everything the universe contains that soothes human hearing, and the pleasures of the other senses, she would most willingly renounce them that she might proffer more sweetly, from such delight of her five senses, an ointment for the Lord's five wounds.

2. While she was intent on these things, the Lord added, "Never could you provide me with a sweeter ointment than to cherish my wounds within you." Although she did not yet understand this in a spiritual sense and was preparing to carry it out, she received this insight, that she should concentrate on following her Lord's example more especially in the five senses, in reverence for his

---

[1] Cf. LDP II.5.3/L 6.3 above.

five wounds: that is, in resisting all the temptations of the enemy she should work valiantly at completely overcoming them in herself. Next, that she should be zealously on her guard, with holy and perfected affections, to admit no evil deed after that. Then she should enhance her way of life with honorable virtues through God's grace. Finally, just as the Son of God desired unceasingly the praise of God the Father with fervent love at every moment, so too she should fervently desire the divine praise without pause, with the loving gratitude of her inmost heart.

<CHAPTER SEVENTY-ONE **Not in LDP**>

1. As she was sick on the feast of the apostles Peter and Paul,[1] having been hindered by other occupations, she was wondering whether it would be better for her to receive the divine sacraments or to abstain from them, and meanwhile she was brought some food.[2] Turning to the Lord she said from the depths of her heart, "O Jesu, my most kindly Lord, with your blessed mouth you declared yourself to be *the living bread*,[3] and also you give all food its efficacy. Look! I am duly taking this food to restore my strength to your eternal praise, in the fervor of that love with which you offered me your life-giving Body and Blood." Then taking what was put before her, she began to eat and immediately felt the Lord's most delightful embrace and sweet kiss gently bestowed on her as he said, "Who can drag me away, united to you like this?" Thence strengthened in both body and spirit, she was delivered from that physical weakness under which she was laboring at that time.

[1] June 29.

[2] Accepting food would of course preclude her receiving communion.

[3] John 6:41.

<CHAPTER SEVENTY-TWO = LDP III.31.1>

1. A procession that had been decreed because of the exigency of the weather had taken place, and as the convent was returning to choir the cross was carried before them. She understood that the Son of God was speaking from the cross and saying **these words**: "Here am I with my army, come to beseech you, God the Father, in the form in which I reconciled all human **wrongdoing**." With these words she was aware of the heavenly Father, calm with such a kindly readiness to be pleased, as if every human fault had been very worthily expunged one hundred times over. Then God the Father was also seen to raise the cross into the clouds with these words, "This shall be *the sign of the covenant between me and between the earth*."[1]

[1] Gen 9:12.

1. When **after this** they were singing the sequence, *Hail, bright <star of the sea>*,[1] **for the same dire need**[2] **at the Mass,** *Drop down, you heavens, from on high*,[3] **and the convent was kneeling at that verse,** *Hear us and save us*,[4] **the tender and delicate** Virgin appeared, **supremely glorious, and together with the community knelt before her son** with clasped hands **and bowed her head. Raising her head with his worshipful hands, the King of Glory showed that he received her supplication most graciously.**

2. Also, another time when the same sequence was being similarly chanted, she saw the Mother of the Lord sitting beside the King of Glory on the imperial throne. In prayer she said, "O Lady **and Mother of Mercy,** why are you not praying **with** us?" The blessed Virgin replied **kindly with serene countenance, "Why is it necessary to plead, since I can most excellently command my Son?" And thus** the royal Virgin stretched out her hand **and, holding her son's chin,**[5] **she made him bend towards her and delighted him with sweet words and gestures.**

---

[1] *Ave, praeclara maris stella*, composed by Hermannus of Reichenau, ca.1050.

[2] See L 72.

[3] Votive Mass of the Virgin.

[4] *Audi nos . . ., Salva nos*, stanzas 12 and 13 of the sequence *Ave, praeclara maris stella*.

[5] A conventional gesture of affection: see below, L 75, 95, and 195.

<CHAPTER SEVENTY-FOUR **Not in LDP**>

1. During the first Mass on the feast of Saint Laurence,[1] while the Host of the most sacred Body of Christ was being consecrated according to the canon, turning over in her mind the superlative excellence of that most worthy work, she said to the Lord, "This work, my sweetest Lord Jesu, by which you sacrificed yourself to God the Father for our salvation, so far exceeds my littleness that I cannot approach it with understanding, not even in the least! Look, meanwhile as best I can I am sinking down into the deepest valley of humility[2] that is my desert." And since she had thus plunged herself into the abyss of humility,[3] because she deprived herself of all the gifts, both spiritual and physical, conferred on her by the divine generosity for God's praise, and was almost annihilated, after a little while the Lord, in the ardor of his loving spirit, drew her to his deified breast as if on a spice-laden breath of air. And when she had remained in that vital state granted her by divine grace for a while, she beheld the deified heart of Jesu, the Son of God, in the presence of divinity in the likeness of lamps,[4] bubbling furiously like cooking oil:[5] the delicious smell of its steam was offering the divinity an inestimably sweet aroma. But the droplets that seemed to leap out of that furious boiling were conferring on the heavenly court wonderful

---

[1] August 10.

[2] A phrase used five times in LDP and even more frequently in L: see L 50, n. 1.

[3] See LDP II.22.5.

[4] See LDP III.25.1, III.26.1, and III.26.2 (not in L).

[5] See LDP IV.4.4 (not in L).

refreshment and the dignity of inestimable glory. In that bubbling she perceived boiling together the devotion of all those who from loving affection were completing to the Lord's praise the procession decreed because of the exigency of all on that day.[6] Indeed, she understood that in its very center, which seemed to burn like a rush in a lamp,[7] was accepted only their devotion that, withdrawn from all outer sensory pleasures, was not mingled with any human delight, such as pleasure in harmonious sound, sweet melody, and the like.

[6] Probably the same procession mentioned in L 72 above.
[7] See LDP IV.54.1/L 80 below.

1. During the first Mass on the vigil of the Assumption of the most glorious Mother of God,[1] at the collect, "God who <chose> the virgin womb,"[2] with heartfelt love at the words "May he make us rejoice to take part in her feast," she was praying that through the intervention of the Virgin Mother she might deserve to celebrate that feast in a way praiseworthy to God. The Lord, welcoming her desire, informed her that she would celebrate the impending feast according to his most praiseworthy good pleasure, and indicated to his mother that she too should provide her with assistance. Then she was swept, as it were, beneath the undefiled Virgin Mother's red cloak. And while she was turning over in her mind how best she could celebrate that feast to God's praise, as she knew that she had not prepared herself at all with special prayers and other virtuous exercises, as very many were accustomed to do, she received this answer from the mediatrix *of God and men*:[3] "I grant you my own preparation, by which I had been perfected before my death, to supplement your merit, for that preparation far excels all human efforts." After a little while, while she was remembering that some people symbolize suffering by a red garment, she grew somewhat afraid, thinking that she was once again to labor under some sickness. The Lord, gently consoling her, said, "Do not be afraid of what may happen to you. Be confident that you will celebrate this feast in a way

---

[1] That is, August 14.

[2] Collect for the Vigil of the Assumption.

[3] 1 Tim 2:5; see LDP II.7.1.

most pleasing to me." Then, in accordance with her premonition, an acute pain followed and, following the pain, severe weakness of heart. These sufferings lasted during the vigil and the day of the Assumption, so that afterwards she dared rightly assert that suffering pleases God most excellently.

2. That very day, during Vespers, when the condescension of the divine loving-kindness praised her for the merits of the Mother of God as if they were her own, she marveled at how she could be extolled for these, insofar as, in her opinion, she could not possess anything at all herself, because of her worthless and wretched indigence, other than the assistance provided by the Mother of loving-kindness. To this the Lord added, "Then consider my inestimable goodness, incomprehensible to all human understanding, since I sometimes seek out in so many different ways undeserved opportunities to benefit my chosen." Now while she was experiencing through grace, from the Lord's wonderful gentleness, the effect of those words with which the most kindly Mother of the Lord had shared the superabundance of her merits, she desired to give her devout thanks and was eager to greet her, reverently and properly, with the sweet-flowing words and varied musical notes of the chant. The Lord added, "I shall pour into you every single word and note from my purest and sweetest inmost being, so that you may extol my mother on high more properly, purely, and sweetly according to your desire." From this she later perceived that this is God's good pleasure, when amidst acute suffering someone is intent on the sweetness of the divine in-flowing.

3. On the same day when they were chanting the antiphon "Hail, Queen <of heaven>" after Compline, by means of the phrase, "thy merciful eyes," she was hoping that she might be granted physical health. The Lord, leaning towards her and holding her chin, as if smiling softly to himself, reproved her importunity and said, "Do you not know that I look upon you with my most merciful gaze when you are physically chastized and mentally distressed?"

<CHAPTER SEVENTY-SIX = LDP III.4>

1. Around the feast of Saint Bartholomew[1] she fell into such **inner** darkness, as a result of a certain disordered depression together with impatience, that she had largely lost the delight of the presence of God, until **on the tenth day, that is,** on the Saturday, she rejoiced to see the clouds of darkness moderated by the intervention of the Virgin Mother of God when the antiphon "Mary, star of the sea" was being **chanted** in her honor. On the following Sunday, when she was rejoicing that God in his kindliness was caring so gently for her, and was recalling her past impatience and her other failings, she became extremely annoyed with herself, **rightly so,** and began to implore the Lord, with great dejection of spirit, to correct her. As if because of the great number and extent of the failings that she had **censured** in herself, in desperation she said to the Lord, "Ah, most merciful Lord, put an end to my evil deeds, to which I apply neither limit nor end. *Deliver me and set me beside you, and let anyone's hand fight against me.*"[2]

The kindly Lord took pity on her desolation and showed her a garden, very small and extremely narrow, full of all kinds of flowers in bloom, which was fenced around with thorns and had a tiny stream of honey flowing through it. He said to her, "Would you prefer that pleasure that you could enjoy among those beautiful flowers to me?" She replied, "No indeed, Lord God." Then he showed her a muddy little **place**, but covered with a meager amount of green growth, having here and there a few tiny flowers of no value but a little color. He

[1] August 24.
[2] Job 17:3.

asked her the same question about this and said, "Surely you would not prefer these things to me?" She turned away from it angrily and said, "Far be it from my soul that I should prefer something false and worthless, not good but evil, to you the only Truth, greatest, constant, steadfast, and everlasting Good."

The Lord said, "Why **then** do you doubt whether you are in charity, in which anyone is proved to be who abounds in so many good things and, as Scripture witnesses, *Charity covers a multitude of sins*?[3] This is why you did not prefer to my will your own, by which you could live an easy, honorable life, without any trouble, finding favor in **everyone's** eyes and a reputation for every kind of holiness. For this is what I showed you in the likeness of the **little** flowering garden, and I offered the pleasure of a fleshly life in the green growth of that muddy place." She replied, "How I wish—how many thousand times I wish—that in my contempt for the worthless little flower-garden you showed me I had completely renounced my own will. But I am afraid it was its narrowness that persuaded me to spurn it the more easily."

The Lord replied, "Thus is the abundance of my loving-kindness accustomed to constrict worldly comforts through remorse of conscience for those whom he has chosen, so that they may quite easily hold them cheap." Then she, renouncing all pleasure, both heavenly and earthly, with the utmost constancy, leaned on the bosom of her beloved with such great pressure and constant adherence that it seemed to her that the force of all creation would not be strong enough to **move her away** even a little from that resting-place where she was rejoicing to drink in, from the **flowing liquid** of the Lord's **breast**, life-giving savor, sweetness far surpassing balm.

---

[3] 1 Pet 4:8.

1. A person had been troubling her abbess because she pre-ferred to have a confessor from outside, saying her reason was that there was no way she could possibly make her confession to her own confessor, even if her soul were heading for perdition. When <Gertrud> learned about this, she prayed for her as stren-uously as she could, that if it could be <found> in the divine will, the Lord in his loving-kindness would provide her with such a confessor who could console her, and that he would influence the minds of the superiors to agree to this. Then one day she received this answer from the Lord: "If superiors yield to their subject, they enrich themselves but do their subject little good." That is, when superiors yield to the wishes of their subjects, they enrich themselves with works of charity, by stooping to their neighbors, and with humility, for they become subject to those over whom they are set as of right. But they do their subjects little good, for there is no deed so good that could be healthy for the soul when it happens according to the voluntary choice of one's own opinion, against the voluntary agreement of rational superiors.

2. And since she was concerned to learn more, she said to the Lord, "Then which of those confessors, to whom I believe her choice inclines, would be more healthy for her soul?" The Lord replied, "She cannot confess to anyone against her own[1] confes-sor's wishes, without its being wrong. If however she confesses to the one on whom the superiors quite readily agree, it is more

---

[1] That is, the one currently assigned to her.

conducive to the salvation of that woman's soul, but if she confesses to the one whom she has greatly preferred, greatly will the work of charity and the virtue of humility shine forth—in her superiors!" She said, "O Lord God, since it would have been very easy for you to have taught me this with your closing words, why have you drawn it out with such an intricate discussion?" The Lord replied, "The intelligence that I have created is obliged to serve me." That is, the superiors, whom God has set over his people and to whom he has given the intelligence for that task, are bound to think carefully and search out what is evil and what is good, and also what is better, and their subjects are bound to agree with them simply and humbly. And this is the royal road, the safest road on which one could never go astray.

<CHAPTER SEVENTY-EIGHT Not in LDP>

1. Some time having passed after this, while she was praying for the person mentioned earlier, she received this answer from the Lord: "See how great is the thick mist of the darkness[1] of her own ideas and her own opinions that she is collecting in her bosom by turning away from me!" She said, "O most merciful God, help her, for you alone, to whom nothing is impossible save only to be unable to have mercy on wretches,[2] can help her time of need." Then the kind and gentle Lord, rising up from the royal throne but not stepping forward, said, "If only she would get up, casting aside the darkness that has collected in her bosom, I would be ready to meet her." She replied, "Does not Bernard, who loved you, say of you, 'When we flee, you pursue us; we turn our back and you meet us face to face'?"[3] The Lord answered, "It is not fitting for me, the creator of light, to approach such great darkness." But she, pitying the woman for whom she was praying, said to the Lord, "Most merciful God, will you at least offer her some help?" The Lord replied, "Look, I am sending her my representative, her confessor, with my seal, that is, the power of absolution. If she listens to him, she will certainly gain my favor." Then she said, sorrowing, in the deepest affection of her heart, "Father of mercies, have mercy on her, for her case seems to me more one of suffering than of guilt." The Lord replied, "She

---

[1] See LDP II.1.1.

[2] See LDP III.49.1.

[3] Unidentified, but the same quotation, also attributed to Bernard, appears in LDP II.3.3.

has turned her suffering into guilt through rebellion, for when I offered her my hand through the intimate advice of some of her superiors, she refused to agree. For if she had humbly offered me her hand in agreement at that time, I would most easily have raised her up."

1. On the Sunday on which the souls of relatives of the community were collectively commemorated, after having received holy communion she was offering that Host to the Lord for the relief of the souls just mentioned. Immediately she saw a vast crowd rise up from the lowest depths of darkness, just as sparks are scattered by fire, some like stars, but some like something else. Asking whether that large crowd was made up of our relatives, she received this answer from the Lord: "I am your closest relative—father, brother, and spouse—therefore my special friends are your very close kin, whom I do not wish to be excluded from the collective commemoration of your relatives, and so they are intermingled with them and are freed with them."

2. The next day, while Mass was being celebrated, after the oblation of the Host she perceived that the Lord was saying, "We have shared a banquet with those *who were ready*[1] to come here. But now let us *send portions*[2] to those who could not yet be present." The year before on the same day, when the bell was rung for Vigils, and, as granted her by the Lord, she was taking part with devotion, she saw a snowy-white lamb, as the Paschal Lamb is usually depicted, as if standing; it was pouring rosy streams of blood into a golden chalice from its wounded heart and saying, "I myself am about to offer a drink to all those souls for whom a banquet is prepared in this place today."

[1] Matt 25:10.
[2] Neh 8:10.

3. Again, when a brother from the order of Friars Minor was celebrating Mass for the dead, in reverence for that friar's devotion she was eager to take a more devout part in the Mass and was reciting the concluding collect, "We beseech you, merciful God, that the souls of our community" and so on. At the words "May light perpetual," she saw five souls, gleaming with golden color, fly up to on high from the depths.

4. When working at the composition of a sermon, on one day she was too preoccupied with it and had failed to concentrate on her prayer both after Matins and also during Mass. Repenting of this, at the elevation of the Host she offered God the Father the task mentioned earlier together with that most holy and acceptable Host. Then she saw her kindly Lord himself holding up the offering just mentioned, like a present, and showing it to the whole company of heaven with these words, "Look what I have just been given: my beloved gave it me!"

5. After this when, as a result, so she thought, of the task of dictation already mentioned, she felt faint and was suffering from vertigo,[3] she was chewing cloves for relief and was offering the Lord this, too, for his eternal praise. That same most companionable lover of men and women bent down and, as if refreshed by the spicy scent of those cloves, showed that he took wonderful delight in that pleasure.

6. O most truly benevolent Lord and most faithful friend! He showed openly on both these occasions how eager the devouring flame of his burning heart's divine love made him to receive from us something from which he can enrich the salvation of our souls, when he showed that he welcomed so greatly these small offerings!

---

[3] Glossed in Middle Low German as *swindel* in L.

<CHAPTER EIGHTY = LDP IV.54.1 >

1. On the night of the feast of the Eleven Thousand Virgins,[1] while *Behold, the bridegroom is coming*[2] was being frequently chanted, inspired **to greater devotion by these words** she finally said to the Lord, "O **sweetest and only object of my pilgrim soul's desire,** since **on this night we have chanted** of you **so many times,** *Behold, the bridegroom is coming,* how will you come, **or what will you do with me? Or** what will you bring **me when you have come?"** The Lord answered, "I am already working with you and in you." **And when he raised her up from his feet, before which she seemed to have prostrated herself, he said,** "Where is your lamp?" She replied, "Look, my Lord, I offer you my heart instead of a lamp." And the Lord said, "I shall **assuredly** fill it to overflowing with the oil of my divine heart." To this she said, "Where then shall I find a rush?"[3] The Lord replied, "The rush will be your devout intention, which you must direct towards me in **every** work."

[1] October 20.

[2] Matt 25:6; *Ecce, sponsus venit: exite obviam ei*; verse for Matins of the feast of the 11,000 Virgins.

[3] See L 74 above.

<CHAPTER EIGHTY-ONE **Not in LDP**>

1. On the day before the feast of the Dedication,[1] **when around None she was recalling what could be allegorically**[2] **celebrated on that feast, the Lord kindly bent down and, drawing her soul into his divine heart, stood upright. After a little while he once again leaned down and, replacing <her soul> in her body, rendered it such that, having been greatly refined by various trials, it might shine more splendidly like a sparkling jewel, after the end of this exile, in the heavenly Jerusalem.**

Now on the following day she was experiencing less than her usual sweetness of devotion. Attributing this to her unworthiness and praising the beauty of divine justice, when at length she was going to receive the life-giving sacrament, she said to the Lord, "Look, my Lord! now I am coming to you in union with that purest innocence, most burning love, and deepest humility, which your Only-begotten won for me with his most holy life." Then the Lord gladdened her with this reply: "Say <rather> that you will go forward ennobled by your connection with the royal marriage-chamber, where I united you to me yesterday in my divine heart."

[1] See L 54, n. 1.
[2] *spiritualiter* L.

<CHAPTER EIGHTY-TWO **Not in LDP**>

1. On the feast of All Saints[1] **they were reciting this verse in the seventh lection about Christ's priests: "The good things that they taught were not only for themselves in the future but also, according to the apostle, they strove in** *reproving, entreating, rebuking*[2] **to sow them in the minds of those subject to them." Thinking, rightly so, of our superiors, she said to the Lord, "O Lord God, if the holy confessors about whom these words are recited pleased you in such things, how could our superiors displease you in similar things?" The Lord replied, "The former pleased me, and indeed the latter please me, or rather they please me the more. Just as a light shines more brightly in darkness than in sunshine, so everything that they do appears more welcome to me from the humility with which they darken themselves."**

[1] November 1.
[2] See 2 Tim 4:2.

1. When **the convent was told that** brother S<eguinus> was dying, she had been busy elsewhere and had **failed** to pray for him, **as would have been right,** until his death was announced **after the introit of high Mass.** She was **completely stunned, remembering** that he **greatly** deserved **our** prayers, for more than the other brothers, to the best of his ability he had always shown himself well-disposed and loyal to the community in his work. So she began to pray the Lord the more strenuously **that her neglect should not disadvantage the soul of that brother, but** that for his loving-kindness's sake, *according to the multitude of his mercies,*[1] he would reward that loyalty to the community that <brother Seguinus> had shown so often. **While she was laboring in such <prayers> as far as the preface of the Mass,** she **then finally** received a reply from God's kindliness: "Because of the community's prayers I have already rewarded that loyalty **that you emphasized** in three ways. For it often did his heart good to benefit someone from his natural benevolence, and now all those feelings of pleasure, each and every one of which warmed his heart after a kindness, are **all** gathered together in his soul and make him joyful. In addition, he also possesses the happiness of each of the hearts that he ever made happy with some kindness, such as a penny for a beggar, or a present for a child, or an apple or **something suitable, however small**, for an invalid. In addition I have given him the joy of certainty, **by which** he knows that I welcome these things **mentioned earlier**. Moreover, if there is anything that he needs for his salvation, it will be promptly provided."

[1] Ps 105:45.

<CHAPTER EIGHTY-FOUR = LDP III.14>

1. The Lord is everywhere so eager for the salvation of his chosen ones that it is sometimes his custom to burden them so much with ordinary things that an extraordinary accumulation of merits accrues to them from then on. So on one occasion he made the confession she was about to make so burdensome[1] that it seemed to her that she was quite incapable of carrying it out by her own efforts. So with what devotion she could, she commended **that confession** to the Lord in prayer. And for this she received the following reply from him, "Do you entrust this to me with such complete confidence that you will expend no further effort to carry it out?" She answered, "Yes, I have complete—more than complete—trust in your omnipotence, **wisdom,** and kindliness, my most loving Lord, but I think it wrong to inflict injury with my sins **if, by not** making the effort to ponder them in the bitterness of my soul, I shall have shown you **no <desire of>** emendation." When the Lord gladly accepted these words and she had completely devoted herself to recalling her own sins, she saw herself with her skin somewhat torn **and** as if she had been rolling in thorny stubble. When she was exposing this wretched condition of hers for healing to the Father of mercies, as a most experienced and trustworthy physician, he kindly bent down and said to her, "With my divine breath I shall heat up for you the bath[2] of confession. When you have been washed in it, you will stand before me spotless **as I wish.**" Longing to strip herself for this bath she said to the Lord, "So

---

[1] One wonders if Gertrud's confessor was the same as the one to whom the nun in L 77 and 78 objected so strongly.

[2] See RB 36.8, "The sick may take baths whenever it is advisable, but the healthy, and especially the young, should receive permission less readily."

far, my Lord, do I lay aside all human favor for love of your splendor that you would find me ready even if I had to publish all my wrong-doings to the whole world." Then the Lord covered her with his own garment as if she were naked and, holding her to his bosom, made her wait until the bath was ready.

2. As the time of confession **loomed**, while she was **in great anguish and excessively weighed down because she foresaw that the delay of her own confession would be noticed**, she said to the Lord, "Since the loving heart of your fatherly mercy knows very well how hard it is for me to make this confession, why do you permit me, kindly God, to be weighed down even more by **the attentiveness of those lying in wait**?" The Lord replied, "Girls who are bathing are helped by the hands of those who rub them down; so you are advanced by the annoyance of **those who are watching**."[3] Then, as there was displayed on the Lord's left a bath, as it were, giving off great heat, he also showed her on his right a certain garden with most charming delights, in bloom with all kinds of flowers. But more especially there appeared in this garden the most beautiful roses without thorns, which exuded a life-giving sweetness in the fresh vitality of their vigorous flowering, and by their marvelous attractions they drew those that came near. He indicated that she might enter this charming garden if she preferred it to the bath that she pleaded was too hot for her. To this she replied, "By no means, Lord! I shall unhesitatingly enter the bath that you have heated for me with your divine breath." And the Lord said, "May this be your eternal salvation."

3. She understood therefore that the garden signified the inner sweetness of divine grace that, when the gentle *south wind*[4] of love is sweetly blowing, rains down the nectar-dew of loving tears on the faithful soul and suddenly makes her *whiter than snow*[5] and com-pletely sure not only of forgiveness of her sins but also of the accu-mulation of superabundant merits. From this she knew that it was

---

[3] Making one's confession at Helfta would not, of course, have been particularly private, and presumably there were others waiting their turn.

[4] See Song 4:16.

[5] See Lam 4:7.

most welcome to the Lord that because of his love she should choose the more burdensome task, abandoning the more pleasant. And when, **after this, she had set about her confession**, she was aware that the Lord of his great courtesy was there. Yet **by his decree** that confession became a great burden to her, so much so that she labored with the greatest difficulty in mentioning those things that some people, as if boasting, do not blush to **lay bare before** everyone.

4. **For** it should be known that the soul is purified from all sin in two ways in particular. In the first way through the bitterness of penitence and all that goes with it, denoted by the bath. In the second way, through the delightful conflagration of divine love and all that goes with it, signified by the charming garden. After confession, she was fixed in contemplation of the wound in the Lord's left hand, as if she were resting in exhaustion after a bath, until she had performed the penance laid upon her by the priest. But since this penance was of such a nature that it had to be postponed for a while, she was very concerned whether, before its satisfaction, she might not be granted more intimate and free access to her sweetest and most loving Lord. And so during Mass, when the most sacred Host was being offered by the priest as the surest, most efficacious reconciliation for the faults of all humanity, she offered it to the Lord in thanksgiving for the blessing of the bath and in acceptable reparation for all her faults. When this had been accepted, she too was accepted into the bosom of the most kindly Father, and she there felt that *the orient from on high had truly visited* her *through the bowels of his mercy*[6] and **loving-kindness**.

---

[6] See Luke 1:78.

<CHAPTER EIGHTY-FIVE **Not in LDP**>

1. Then, since she had postponed part of that confession we have mentioned for good reason, the Lord instructed her that by God's loving-kindness the completion of that confession[1] would become, as it were, an unguent to increase beauty, just as we read in the book of Esther that the women chosen by King Assuerus used *oil of myrrh*[2] **and other unguents to increase their beauty. Next, when she had entrusted her concerns to the Lord, at the elevation of the Host during Mass with greatest kindliness the Lord assigned all the angelic spirits to serve her, that by their help she might be borne towards <the completion of the confession>.**

2. But even though that confession was protracted even further, and entrusted to the Lord again and again, he nonetheless added no other consolation to strengthen her further. Rather, he allowed her to be greatly troubled in various ways, and also by other outward trials. Finally, after her confession was completed, at the time and place of prayer, as if exhausted by travails and troubles she ran to the humanity of Jesus Christ, rushing into his embraces, as it were, with these words: "Here I am, coming to you, *whom I love, whom* **alone** *I sought* **through that confession;** *whom I have* **ever** *desired.*[3] **And now, O my only, true and supreme rest, say to my soul,** *Turn into your rest*[4] **by recalling your Lord's**

---

[1] That is, of the sacrament as whole, including the penance.

[2] See Esth 2:12.

[3] Response for the common of Virgins: see LDP IV.54.3.

[4] Ps 114:7.

blessings, for *I am your salvation.*[5] Say this to me, my most loving Lord, that I may hear, and *all my bones shall flourish*[6] with love, and all the inner parts of my marrow, permeated with the sweetness of your consolation, will burst out in praise and say, *There is none among the gods like unto you, O Lord; and there is none according to your works.*"[7]

3. During this she became aware that at her right hand, as if from the Father's omnipotence, there had appeared a support, and that she was encircled on every side. Then from the left, too, as if from the goodness of the Holy Spirit, there blew a gentle breeze that encircled and greatly strengthened that support and, surrounding her with something like a wall, decreed that she should dwell there from thenceforward. Then in the same place she resolved that for some time afterwards it would cause her great pain to accept comfort from anyone by any word or sign, or even speak a word to someone, however necessary. Indeed, during Mass, when she was offering the holy Host for the emendation of her sins, she seemed to be leaning her head against Jesu's breast and from it to be completely covered with the red hue of a rose in bloom.[8] And at once, while praying for someone, she saw her similarly suffused with a rosy hue, but the redness suddenly turned pitch black. Then on that very day something happened that afflicted both women: she was strengthened in patience, but the other collapsed in impatience. By this she was clearly given to understand how much salvation patience bestows and, on the contrary, how much condemnation impatience brings.

---

⁵ See Ps 34:3.
⁶ Isa 66:14.
⁷ Ps 85:8.
⁸ See LDP III.15.1/L 87 below.

<CHAPTER EIGHTY-SIX **Not in LDP**>

1. And so, when this much-discussed confession had been completed, since she thought the penance enjoined on her insufficient, she requested her confessor that when he was first to celebrate Mass, mindful of her in offering the Host he should also offer her for emendation of all her sins and compensation for her negligences. Then she awaited that Mass with great desire. But the next day, around the end of the first Mass, she perceived the Lord saying to her, "Prepare yourself for spiritual communion, for you too are about to receive communion and to make an offering in the way that you desire the priest to offer on your behalf." She rejoiced greatly from these words and was raised up in fervor of spirit. When they were chanting the verse "Arise, Lord," at Prime, she said to the Lord, "Arise, most kindly lover, and prepare me, according to your best pleasure, for yourself so that I may communicate worthily." The Lord replied, "If you entrust yourself completely to my preparation with confidence, you are already prepared, for what I do brooks no delay." And with these words he offered her his Body with his blessed right hand, in the form of bread, just as it is received from the altar, and, in place of receiving the chalice, he pressed her face to his lordly breast. After a while, when she raised her head, she saw her face all ruddy, as if sprinkled with blood. But since she did not understand what that ruddiness symbolized, she was afraid that some trouble was threatening,[1] but she was confident that nothing but good could come to her from the kindliness of God.

---

[1] For the idea that the color presages suffering, see L 75 above.

1. During the **high** Mass **that she had awaited with such great longing,** at the moment of the elevation of the Host, as if half asleep, she was less intent on her devotion. But at the sound of the sanctuary bell, she suddenly as it were woke up and saw the King **of Glory,** the Lord, holding with both his hands a tree that was, as it were, cut off near the ground, laden with the most beautiful fruit and giving out rays like a star of marvelous brightness from every single leaf. And when he shook this tree at the court of heaven, **they** rejoiced marvelously in its fruit. Then after a little while the Lord planted that tree in the midst of the garden of her heart, that she might strive to increase its fruit, and she might rest beneath it and thereby be refreshed. While she had returned to herself and was undertaking this task, she soon began, in increasing the fruit, to pray for a certain person who had annoyed her very recently: she suggested that she should choose to undergo yet again the bitter sorrow that she had just experienced[1] so that the grace of God should be given more generously to the one who was troubling her.

Meanwhile she suddenly saw on the top of the tree a flower of the most lovely color, which was about to bear fruit if she carried through her good intention. For by that tree was symbolized charity, which abounds not only in fruit of good works but also in the flowers of good will, and even in the shining leaves of sweet **affection**. From this the citizens of heaven take extraordinary delight, when one human being condescends to another and strives to alleviate the needs

---

[1] Possibly as recounted at the end of L 85.

of neighbors, as far as possible, to God's praise. Also at the very moment of the elevation of the Host, she received wonderful adornment of gilded clothing over that rosy color she had received the day before, when she leaned on the Lord's breast.[2]

[2] See L 86 (which, it should be noted, is not in LDP, unlike L 87).

<CHAPTER EIGHTY-EIGHT = LDP III.15.2>

1. The same day, **while they were singing** None, the Lord appeared in the guise of a vigorous, delightful young man, asking her to offer him nuts, gathering them from that tree. To do this he lifted her up and placed her on a branch of the tree. At this she said, "Sweetest youth, why do you ask this of me, who am as weak in strength **and in virtues** as in gender, when it would be more suitable for you to offer them to me?" "Not so," he said. "The bride who is, as it were, at home in her own house with her parents can act with greater confidence than the bashful bridegroom, who for the sake of visiting only sometimes turns aside to her. But if the bride is at all considerate towards the groom's bashfulness, when he takes her into his own house he will promptly pay her welcome recompense for everything."

By this means he led her to understand how unreasonable is that excuse by which some people say, "If God wanted me to do that, he would certainly give me the grace to do it," since it is quite right that in this life a person should, as it were, crush her own opinion for God's sake and not consent to her own will in anything that concerns her own convenience. And in the future this will be most graciously rewarded.

Since she wanted to offer him the nuts, the young man climbed up to her. He sat down, told her to crack the nuts, extract the kernel, and prepare them for him to eat. He let her understand by this means that it is not enough for a person to crush their own opinion so as to benefit an enemy, unless they themselves also search out an opportunity to put it into effect. For the purpose of all this was to indicate by these nuts that, namely, one should do good to **one's persecutor**. And so the Lord showed her nuts, which **are** bitter **and have a** hard

shell, growing on the same tree as apples! For the love of one's enemies ought to be mingled with the sweetness of God's savor, by which
anyone would be ready to suffer death for Christ's sake.

<CHAPTER EIGHTY-NINE **Not in LDP**>

1. On one occasion[1] **she was so weighed down for certain reasons that, strenuously restraining the tears that kept breaking out during the day, she turned to the Lord when it was late and said, "I shall offer you those tears that I held back so much beyond my strength for your sake, my Lord, as the sweetest wine to drink since first you allowed me to take part in the joyful banquets of your consolations. Or at least, drink them in, as you showed you were drinking in the tears held back for your sake on Good Friday."**[2] **Then, relying on this, when she was rendering thanks to God on the next day during Terce for the crown of thorns on his most sacred head, the Lord intimated, "Anoint the wounds of my head with that pleasing ointment that you put to one side for me yesterday."**[3] **And immediately she welcomed love, in the guise of an instrument: each time she pierced her own breast** [4] **and each time she dipped her finger in the profoundest depths of her heart,**[5] **she soothed the punctures in the Lord's most sacred head that was kindly leaning towards her. She saw the Lord accept this as a most sweet and welcome ointment.**

[1] The Easter Monday following the Good Friday referred to below.
[2] See L 69.
[3] See L 70.
[4] Possibly a reference to the pelican: see LDP III.18.12/L 130.
[5] *intimis cordis medullis* L: see LDP IV.14.6.

<CHAPTER NINETY = LDP IV.59.1–2>

1. After the chapel had been consecrated,[1] while the response *I saw the holy city*[2] was being chanted at Matins, the Lord appeared in the form of a bishop, **sitting** on his throne against the wall facing the altar,[3] gathering his **clothing** about him, as if he had chosen that place for himself to dwell **frequently**. While she was looking at this, she considered how far away **he appeared** from that place that she had herself chosen **in which to be free for such special devotion, and to taste how sweet the Lord is**.[4] She seemed to be drawn closer to him with great desire, **surmising that he would much more properly single out the altar, dedicated to creating his most holy Body and Blood, by his presence and indwelling, and also that place**

[1] There are several references to a chapel in LDP, but there must have been more than one at Helfta: this chapter and the corresponding LDP IV.59.1 implicitly refer to the chapel's dedication as having just taken place, whereas LDP III.17.1/L 100 refers to the anniversary of its dedication on the feast of Saint Laurence (August 10). The latter could well be the chapel that Burchard of Querfort, son-in-law of Helfta's founder, Burchard of Mansfeld, built in honor of Saint John the Baptist and Saint John the Evangelist, as a burial place for members of his family in 1265 (see Paquelin II, 726).

[2] See Rev 21:2-3: *Vidi civitatem sanctam Jerusalem novam descendentem de caelo a deo paratam et audivi vocem de throno dicentem: ecce, tabernaculam dei cum hominibus et habitabit cum eis*, "I saw the holy city, the new Jerusalem, coming down out of heaven prepared, and I heard a voice from the throne saying, Behold the tabernacle of God with men, and he will dwell with them"; response for Matins of the feast of the Dedication.

[3] The traditional position of the episcopal throne was in the apse, behind the high altar.

[4] See Ps 33:9.

near the altar that was more suitable not only for her own prayer but also for all those intent on devotion, especially since he himself was the one who *leads his spouse into the wilderness, that he may there speak to her heart*[5] and, like someone bashful fleeing human company, would entrust all that he had to his more intimate friends.

She received this answer in response: "Since *I am he who fills heaven and earth*,[6] how much more **do you think** I fill this building? Do you not know that the place that the arrow pierces is watched more attentively than the place where the bow is drawn? Thus you should know that I act with more powerful love not in that place where I appear physically,[7] but rather in that place where my treasure, **my panting heart in its entirety, and also my love and** the pure and pleasing eye of my divinity, are present." And miraculously he touched the holy altar, as if it were beside him, with his outstretched hand, saying, "And this place is here." And he added, "Anyone who seeks my grace in hope of salvation will find me the more manifestly in my blessings, and anyone who seeks my love in faith will experience me the more sweetly in their inmost being." Through these words, **and through the fact that he appeared near the entrance to the sanctuary, and nonetheless asserted that his love was strongest in a place of greater intimacy, it was shown** that there is a great distance between those who seek salvation not only of their body but also of their soul according to the inclination of their own will, and those who entrust themselves completely in quiet confidence to the providence of divine love.

2. Again, while **the communion verse** "*My house <shall be called the house of prayer>*"[8] was being chanted in the Mass, the Lord seemed to touch her breast with his right hand and to burst out in these words, as if from **excess of love**: "With pure **heart** I say to you: *Everyone that asks, receives, **and he that seeks, finds, and to him***

---

[5] Hos 2:14; see Prologue: also quoted in LDP V.1.4.

[6] Jer 23:24.

[7] That is, the episcopal throne in the apse.

[8] Matt 21:13; communion verse for the feast of the anniversary of the Dedication.

that knocks it shall be opened."[9] And stretching out his arm **as if from above**, he extended his hand in the midst of the sanctuary, as if continuously **about to hold blessings to distribute**. Again, while **in the same chapel** the antiphon, *The foundations of this temple*, was chanted at the *Benedictus*, there appeared on top of the walls angelic spirits, beautiful, elegantly dressed, **and lovely in form**, who had been assigned to guard the church, to repel the attacks of their enemies. Touching each other with their golden wings, they repeated a sweet song in praise of divinity. One by one they seemed to come down from on high to the depths, to show that they were assiduously visiting their fellow citizens in that place with kindly love.

[9] Luke 11:10.

<CHAPTER NINETY-ONE **Not in LDP**>

1. One day when going to holy communion she was repeating these words on the way: "Now I await you, most kindly king, now I worship you, now I am standing before the sight of your divine majesty,"[1] and so on, and through these was acknowledging her great worthlessness and unworthiness. It seemed to her that God the Father was looking upon her in that same worthlessness and insignificance and saying with astonishment, "Are you the one who is asking for this magnificent gift?" She pretended she was not and, longing to hide her face for shame, replied, "No, no, Lord, holy Father, I would never have presumed to do this, but the Lord of glory himself, your Only-begotten, prompted me." God the Father kindly answered with a serene countenance, "Do not be afraid, but approach in confidence, for the will of my Only-begotten alone is wholly sufficient for your every reward, and it alone in its perfection makes worthy everyone whose approach it has preordained."

2. Again, another time when about to communicate, she was concentrating on these words, "Hail, food for my pilgrimage,"[2] and perceived three ways in which this sacrament of the Lord works especially as food for the journey in someone receiving it worthily. First, that just as a traveler is sustained and strengthened by food to complete the journey, so one who worthily communicates is fortified in all good. Second, because from that

---

[1] Cf. LDP IV.38.3.

[2] Part of the elevation prayer *Ave, principium nostrae creationis* (H. A. Daniel, *Thesaurus Hymnologicus*, 2 vols [Leipzig, 1844], II.329).

strengthening he becomes so terrible to his enemies that, as if completely terrified, they become impotent to attack the soul. Third, that the soul becomes beautiful with such great purity and special claim to rewards that all the court of heaven awaits its arrival with a joyful dance of wonderful exultation.[3]

[3] See LDP I.11.2.

<CHAPTER NINETY-TWO **Not in LDP**; LDP IV.9.8>

1. Lying in bed on the holy day of the unspotted Virgin's purification,[1] **while she heard the community as it processed, she addressed this complaint to the Mother of Mercy: "Ah, queen of mercy and glory, look! Right now the entire community is honorably and devoutly following you with hymns and praises as you carry so noble a burden.**[2] **And I alone, held back by ill-health, am forbidden to follow you." The gracious Virgin kindly replied, "All these are following me with corporeal footsteps; you alone are processing with me in spirit."** And when the verse "Pray for us, **mediatrix**" and so on[3] was being chanted in the chapel **before the altar**, the glorious mother, **placing** her tender son on the altar, **prostrated** herself devoutly before him as if about to pray for the community. **Her** royal child in his turn prostrated himself as a sign that not only did he welcome her prayers but also he willingly consented to every wish of so dear a mother.

---

[1] February 2.

[2] That is, the Infant Jesus.

[3] *Ora pro populo, dei genetrix*, "Pray for the people, Mother of God"; verse for the feast of the Purification.

<CHAPTER NINETY-THREE Not in LDP>

1. On the Sunday on which the Lord's passion is read during the Mass "Judge,"[1] **the Lord, provided with white priestly robes and a red chasuble, appeared on the altar as if standing opposite the priest who was celebrating Mass. Intent on the Host that seemed to link him and the priest, he said, "That priest is acting visibly in the person of my human nature, and I am working with him invisibly through the power of my divine nature." For the Lord seemed as it were to hold up <the Host> so that after its consecration was completed he showed God the Father all his chosen at once as a pleasing reconciliation and acceptable offering. Also, she understood through the sign of the cross that its four parts [drew]**[2] **four kinds of the chosen to union with the sacred Host, that they might be offered all at once to God the Father with it and through it. The first part symbolizes the chosen already triumphant in heaven. The second part, those suffering in purgatory. The third and fourth parts symbolize those still militant on earth: the perfect and the imperfect.**

2. Astonished at God's great courtesy, by which he so kindly joined his chosen to himself, she said to the Lord, "How could consecration by gestures and those words join your chosen to you in such great purity, dignity, and holiness that you offer them in union with yourself to God the Father?" The Lord answered, "You should honor and admire that power that transforms that tiny substance into me, creator of heaven and earth, much more

[1] Palm Sunday.

[2] *attrahi* L.

than that power that is able to draw the chosen to me." Then after the consecration was finished, stretching out his finger over the Host the Lord added, "Anyone who has now received this possesses with truth and certainty every good thing that my divine nature could find in all the chosen, both in heaven and on earth." In these words she perceived that although the whole body of the church is given life by this sacrament through communion, nonetheless the distance between those who receive [communion] and those who abstain is infinite.

<CHAPTER NINETY-FOUR **Not in LDP**>

1. While because of the lack of the money that they needed the community was fleeing to the aid of the Virgin Mother by praying together, she saw that noble empress standing in the beauty of her virginal modesty before her Son, raised up on his throne, and praying for the community's poverty by the implication of these words, *They have no wine*.[1] The Son replied, "This time I do not say to you, My mother, *what is that to you and to me, woman?*[2] but I say to you that mine is the power and the kingdom, over which you will rule with me as you wish, sitting beside me." And when she who saw these things said to the Lord, "Once again, my Lord, you are allowing our administrators to experience anxious sorrows," the Lord replied, "Once again I am causing the love of my divine heart for them to grow!" She said, "If you intend to assist our poverty eventually, merciful Lord, at the intervention of your most loving Mother, at least do so more quickly, so that our administrators may be less burdened." The Lord said, "If I lessen the difficulty of their task, I must also lessen their compensatory reward."

[1] John 2:3.
[2] John 2:4.

1. On one occasion when praying for someone who was troubled, she saw the Lord gently holding the chin of the person for whom she was praying, and saying, "I shall bless him." Drawing confidence from that gentleness, she was also intent on praying for another person entrusted to her. But the Lord, soon changing his gentleness to severity, swiftly deprived her of all the grace that she had in praying.

<CHAPTER NINETY-SIX = LDP III.16.1–2>

1. While the community was chanting the Mass "Hail, holy Mother"[1] in honor of the Mother of God on the last day before the divine rites were to be suspended, amid the words of prayer she spoke to the Lord, "How will you console us, most kindly God, for our present trouble?" The Lord answered, "I shall increase my delights among you. Just as a husband enjoys his wife more freely in private than in public, so your sighs and desolations shall be my delights. Indeed, progress in my love shall increase among you, just as hidden fire **disperses** more widely. Moreover, just as rising water suddenly overflows with a rush, so shall my delights in you and your love in me overflow, to the increase of both."

Then she asked, "And how long will this interdict last?" The Lord replied, "As long as it lasts, **the profit** too will last." She rejoined, "It would seem shameful to great princes if one of the lowest of the low, of utter worthlessness, were admitted to their confidences. In the same way it could seem unfitting for you, the King of kings, if the secrets of your divine providence were revealed to me, *the offscouring of all*.[2] I believe that is why I have not been given an assurance, even though the end of all things is known to you before their beginning." The Lord replied, "Not at all, but it is out of the grand design for your salvation; for although I raise you up through contemplation, sometimes admitting you to my confidence, I also sometimes shut you out to safeguard your humility, so that when you do receive it

---

[1] *Salve sancta parens*; introit for Masses of the Virgin outside Eastertide and Advent.

[2] 1 Cor 4:13.

you may discover what you are thanks to me, and when you are again deprived you may realize what you are in yourself."

2. During the offertory, that is, "Remember, Virgin Mother," at these words, "that you may ask good things for us," while she was concentrating on the Mother of every grace, the Lord intervened, saying, "It is not necessary for anyone to ask on behalf of you all, as for my own part I am entirely pleased with you." But she, remembering numerous failings, both her own and those of certain others, and being unsure **in what way** the Lord could assert that he was **very** pleased **with her in all things**, understood how the Lord was gently saying, "My natural goodness influences me so that I see the better side, and I embrace with my entire divine nature, raising up the less perfect to the more perfect." Then she said, "Generous **God**, how can you impart to me, so unworthy and unprepared, **the mighty workings** of your grace that are now so great and so full of consolation?" The Lord replied, "Love compelled me." She said, "Where now are those stains that I contracted as a result of my heart's impatience, into which I fell a little earlier and made rather obvious in my words?" To this the Lord said, "The fire of my divine nature has completely consumed them, for in any soul on which I rest in my grace and favor I consume every stain." Then she said, "Most merciful God, as long as your grace so often forestalls my unworthiness, I would like to know if such faults as the impatience I mentioned and others like it will have to be purified in my soul after my death." When the Lord kindly failed to answer, she added, "Truly, Lord, if *the beauty of your justice*[3] demands it, I would freely and willingly go down even into hell that I might by this means more worthily make reparation to you. But if it greatly exalts your natural goodness and mercy that all things should be consumed by your love, I shall demand with complete frankness that your love should purify every stain in my soul, far beyond what is deserved!" The Lord kindly granted this in accordance with the fullness of his loving-kindness.

---

[3] Jer 50:7.

1. On the next **Sunday, the divine rites having been suspended**, while Mass was being celebrated for the local people, **and the time for communion had come,** she said to the Lord, "Do you not pity us, most merciful Father, in that now, because of those material goods by which we ought to be sustained in your service, we are deprived of the precious good of your Body and Blood?" The Lord replied, "And how could I feel great pity if, when I am leading my bride towards flowery and charming places of refreshment, turning aside **momentarily** to some more barren place before we arrive, I would with my own hand straighten out some disorder in her clothes or finery, so that I might lead her in the more fitly?" Then she said, "My Lord, how can those people who have imposed this burden on us possess your grace?" The Lord said, "Let it be. I shall deal with them on this."

2. Then, about the time of the offering of the Host, **the living and spotless Body of the Lord**, when she was offering that same **sacred** Host to the Lord for his eternal praise and for the salvation of the whole convent, the Lord, taking that Host into himself and breathing forth life-giving delight from his inmost being, said, "From this breath I shall feed them with divine nourishment."

3. And although she had taken great delight in these words, shortly afterwards she lost [it] to a certain extent. Leaning on her Lord's breast she said, "Although our situation does not seem wretched to you, my Lord, remembering my wretchedness, however, I completely renounce all outer consolation, and totally immerse myself in you, the abyss of divine consolation." Receiving

her with wonderfully gentle love, as if from the inmost depths of his heart, the Lord showed himself wounded by compassion. Moved by this compassion and as if completely melted, she desired totally to devote herself so that she could at least in some way soothe the Lord lest, following the greatness of the compassion that he was displaying, he would also exercise forceful vengeance against those who had oppressed the community.[1]

---

[1] This expands the Lord's somewhat enigmatic remark at the end of the first paragraph, but the role it gives Gertrud in assuaging the Lord's anger is perhaps too close to that of the Virgin Mary to survive Sister N's revision process.

1. On the third Sunday of this interdict, when she once again longed to receive the Lord's Body with a great desire, around the time of communion, sorrowing, she said to the Lord, "Remember, most loving Father, that very rarely, or rather most unwillingly, would I fail to receive that sacred salvation to suit my own convenience, if not prevented by force. And now, my Lord, with all the strength of my inmost being I beg you not to frustrate my desire. But as no force can resist you, out of the most generous overflow of your loving-kindness, offer me the life-giving food of your most holy Body and Blood." The Lord replied, "Draw it out from my inmost being through desire." Throwing herself impetuously on the Lord's breast, she drew [it out] so strongly that she felt as if she had indeed received the Lord's Body, just as it is received from the altar. By its power she sensed all her inner being so changed that throughout the day it seemed to her quite unbearable to turn aside to other, extraneous, things.

2. Then she said to the Lord, "O Lord God, since you who are infallible truth had made known to me, even though most unworthy, that you planned to increase your delights in us,[1] and enlarge our love for you, how is it that some women are complaining that they are growing very cold in their love for you?" The Lord replied, "I contain in myself all good, and to each one I shall grant the appropriate portion at the appointed time."

---

[1] See L 96.1.

<CHAPTER NINETY-NINE **Not in LDP**>

1. During this time on another day when, once again, the convent was accustomed to receive communion, while she was offering the Lord her desire and that of the whole community, the Lord appeared seated, and around him a great number of angels. The Lord seemed to extend to each one of them the form of the Host, just as it is consecrated on the altar, entrusting it to each of the angels to provide from their share for the members of the community committed to them.

2. And when they were reading in the gospel, *I have compassion on the multitude*,[1] she pointed out to the Lord that he had inclined to mercy when the crowds had endured a three-day fast, and she asked him why the community's having been deprived for many weeks now of the comfort of his most holy Body and Blood did not incline him to greater mercy and loving-kindness. The Lord replied, "I fed that crowd at that time, for it was not appropriate to send them away to their own homes while starving.[2] But as for you, I shall allow you all to leave me for a short while."[3]

3. Then while she yearned in the same way for communion of the Body of the Lord with a heart full of desire, there appeared, as it were, a bird flying in the air above her head that seemed to

[1] Mark 8:2: in the Middle Ages, from the gospel for the seventh Sunday after Trinity. As Trinity Sunday can fall on any date between May 17 and June 20, we can date this vision roughly as June or July.

[2] *famelicam* L, added in the margin by a correcting hand.

[3] That is, without being fed, unlike the crowd in the gospel reading.

carry the sacred Host in its mouth. Seeing it and quite unable to follow it, she burned with greater desire and, coming to herself, was afraid lest she had deserved this inability to follow the Host because she had been working very hard externally the week before and had recollected herself internally too infrequently. Then, with the help of God's grace, she raised herself up to the wound in the side of Jesus Christ, considering that there is a source continually flowing to wash away all filth, even though up till then she had imagined that the force of God's grace violently removed every kind of filth from the soul. From this she sensed inwardly that the divine mercy, gently flowing from the Lord's breast into her soul, was sweetly cleansing her efforts from every stain. Cleansed in this way and *made whiter than snow*,[4] she saw the Lord leaning towards her with wonderful gentleness and offering a kiss from his mouth that flowed with honey, and during this kiss she received as it were half the sacred Host, while the Lord kept back the other part, absorbing it as if consuming it. Much astonished at this, and eager to find out the reason, she received this answer: "You will know later."

[4] Ps 50:9.

1. On one Sunday that coincided with the feast of Saint Laurence,[1] and also with the commemoration of the dedication of the chapel, during the first Mass she was praying for certain **people** who had devoutly entrusted themselves to her prayers. She saw come forth from the throne of heaven to earth a branch of a green vine; by the shoots of its leaves an ascent was provided from the bottom to the top. She understood that this ascent was faith, by which the chosen rise up to heavenly things. And then she recognized that in its heights, as if at the left hand of the throne, very many members of the community were there, and the Son of God, as if in the presence of the heavenly Father, was standing with proper reverence at the time that the community would have been about to receive communion, if the interdict had not prevented it.[2] She greatly desired that the life-giving sacrament should be offered spiritually both to herself and to the others present, out of the divine mercy that no human power can withstand. Then she saw the Lord Jesus **dipping** the Host that he held in his hand in the heart of God the Father[3] and bringing it out tinted a rosy red, as if reddened by blood. In great doubt because of this, she pondered in her heart what this meant, since red denotes suffering,[4] and God the Father could never be reddened by any mark

---

[1] The feast of Saint Laurence (August 10) fell on a Sunday in the years 1281, 1287, 1292, and 1298, but the text here apparently refers to the interdict (1295 or 1296). Was Helfta perhaps interdicted on another occasion?

[2] See previous note.

[3] The only reference in either L or LDP to "the heart of God the Father," as opposed to the heart of Jesus.

[4] Cf. L 75 and 86.

of suffering. While she was brooding on this, she failed to notice that she was experiencing the effect of her aforementioned desire, except that after a while she understood that the Lord had accomplished a respite of repose for himself in the hearts and souls of every one of those women whom earlier she had recognized raised on high. How this had happened, however, she could not know.

2. Meanwhile, mindful of someone who had entrusted herself humbly and devoutly to her prayers just before Mass, she prayed for her, that the Lord might make her partaker in this honor just described. To this she received the following reply: "No one can come so far along the ascent of faith shown you unless raised up through trust, which that woman for whom you are now praying does not have." She replied, "Lord, it seems to me that humility, to which you customarily infuse more abundant grace, lessens her trust." The Lord replied, "I shall come down and impart my gifts both to her and to others settled in the valley <of humility>."

Next the Lord of hosts was seen to come down as if by a red ladder and after a while appeared in the middle of the chapel altar robed in pontifical vestments,[5] holding in his hands a pyx like those in which the consecrated Host is usually kept. And throughout the whole Mass he remained seated, facing the priest, until the preface. So great a crowd of angels were in his service that all the chapel on the Lord's right (that is, the north end) seemed full. They were displaying a particular joy because they were encompassing **as if** with affection those places where devout prayers had frequently been offered by their fellow citizens, that is, the community. On the Lord's left (that is, towards the south) stood just one choir of angels; a choir of apostles and separate choirs of martyrs, confessors, and virgins joined them. When she perceived this and recollected that *incorruption brings near to God*,[6] she understood that between the Lord and the blessed virgins was shining a special splendor of snowy whiteness, which united the virgins to the Lord more than the other saints, with a **sweet** caress and intimacy of astonishing joy. She also understood

---

[5] Cf. L 90.1.
[6] Wis 6:20.

that some rays of **similar** brightness were stretched out to members of the community as if there were no barrier between them and the Lord, although many solid walls separated them from the chapel in which he was seen.

3. And while she was taking extraordinary pleasure in this, concerned for other members too of the community she said to the Lord, "Since your generous loving-kindness, Lord, has now given me the graces of such incredible sweetness, what do you give to those who, perhaps at this very moment sweating at external activities, do not enjoy similar graces?" The Lord replied, "I anoint them with balsam, even though they are, as it were, drowsy." When she weighed up **the** force **of these words,** she was greatly astonished at how those who made an effort in **such things** and those who did not could possess so equal a reward: for balsam renders incorruptible those bodies anointed with it, and it makes very little difference whether those anointed are awake or asleep! She also received this more comprehensible analogy as an example: that is, that when a person eats, by which the whole body is strengthened in every individual member, nevertheless only the mouth delights in the taste of the food. In the same way, when a special grace is granted to those who have been chosen, out of God's unrestrained loving-kindness, **virtue and** merit also are increased for all members <of the church> and especially for those belonging to the same community, with the exception of those who deprive themselves of it through envy and ill-will.

4. **Praise and unbounded thanksgiving be to God, giver of every grace, for these and other things that were bestowed on his servant** through both words and deeds and also through chants **during the time of this Mass, to be understood with wonderful delight! For** while *Glory to God in the highest* was being intoned, the Lord Jesus, our great **high priest and true** pontiff, sent a divine breath like a burning flame towards heaven, to the glory of the Father. And at the words *and on earth peace to men of goodwill*, he sent forth the same breath, in the guise of snowy splendor, towards those present, **or rather to all the faithful. While before the preface they were chanting,** *Lift up your hearts*, the Son of God **seemed to rise up on the altar** and, as if through his powerful magnetism, **to attract**

the desires of all those present. Then turning towards the east, pavilioned about on every side with a phalanx of countless angels, he stood with raised hands and offered up the prayers of the faithful to God the Father in the words of the preface. After this, while they began the **first** "Lamb of God," the Lord raised himself on the altar with all his power, and at the second "Lamb of God" flowed with his unsearchable wisdom into the inmost depths of every single person there. And at the third "Lamb of God," collecting himself on high **with his inestimable sweetness**, he presented the prayers and desires of all in his self-offering to God the Father. Thus, out of the abundance of sweetness he granted with his own blessed mouth the kiss of peace to all the saints present, offering this privilege before others to the company of virgins, so that after the kiss of the mouth **they** also **might plant** an intensely sweet kiss on **his** breast. And after this the Lord, **gathering himself together on the altar,** offered himself, as if completely overflowing with the honey-sweet love of divinity, to the community, saying, "I am wholly yours. Then enjoy me, all of you according to your desire." After this she **who saw these things** said to the Lord, "Lord, though **in this Mass** I am replete with inconceivable sweetness, nevertheless when you sit on the altar you seem further away from me. Thence through the benediction **that will conclude** this Mass bring it about in me that my soul may feel united **and firmly joined** to you." This the Lord carried out in such a way that through the Lord's embraces she felt **herself held tight in the Lord's arms and** pressed to his breast, both sweetly and vigorously.

1. On the vigil of the most joyful Assumption, when she was greatly burdened by the interdict that has now been mentioned so often, and during Vespers was setting out before God, the Father of mercies, the community's trouble over this and other tribulations that were weighing upon them, she received this consoling reply: "Truly, as you are not destined to remain in this life for long, my loving-kindness urges me to help you all so that you can deserve that incomprehensible glory that is prepared for you in heaven, and so you must be burdened by such varied troubles."

2. **The following day**[1] **during Mass,** when at the elevation of the Host she understood that the Lord was saying, "I come that I may sacrifice myself to God the Father on behalf of my members," she replied, "My most loving Lord, surely you are not allowing us, your members, to be **torn away** from you by this curse of excommunication with which those who are trying to take away **what is ours** are threatening us?" The Lord replied, "If someone is capable of understanding the quintessence of my inmost being, by which you cleave to me, let him cut you off from me!" And the Lord added, "The curse of excommunication imposed on you for that reason will do you no more harm than an attempt to cut something with a little **pine** knife, which is quite unable to penetrate but just leaves a slight knife-mark."

---

[1] That is, the feast of the Assumption (August 15). In LDP this paragraph is out of temporal sequence as it precedes the previous chapter, datable to August 10.

3. After this she saw the Lord, *father of orphans,*[2] **calling all the community to him by giving a sign with his most blessed hand and placing before them, in the form of a golden disk, his most blessed heart filled with those wafers under whose form the Body of Christ is consecrated on the altar: all those sitting around were each to take as much as they wished. By this he indicated that the desires experienced that day with groaning, compared to the reception of the sacrament, weighed as strongly with the Lord as the difference between taking enough and being offered an individual share.**

4. Then after Compline when the convent was reciting the antiphon *Hail, queen,* **the Mother of Mercy appeared, who is the consolation of the desolate, drawing her desolate daughters to her, as if about to supply whatever they sorrowed that they had lost, in that they were forbidden to celebrate that feast with the usual joy of communion and song. She was like mothers in this world who tenderly love their daughters, and when they see them distressed because they have stopped them from attending banquets elsewhere, those mothers provide a banquet for their daughters at home, from their own resources!**

---

[2] Ps 67:6: see LDP IV.48.9.

1. On the eighth Sunday of the much-mentioned interdict, she was preparing herself for spiritual communion during Mass as best she could and was often repeating these words with desire, "Ah, Lord, when will we come to you, our troubles gone?" The Lord appeared as if sitting behind a wall, in the midst of which she saw a narrow door, set quite high up, but the further down it reached, the wider it became. He said, "Whichever of you humbly attributes her guilt and affliction not to others' impiety but to their own deserts comes to me through this door, not on rare occasions but very often." Within the wall on each side of that door stood two vigorous young men: if they saw someone in the door lying at their Lord's feet, it was their duty to raise them up immediately and take them to be embraced by the Lord's joyful embraces. She understood that the young men were Desire and Love.

2. Shortly afterwards, while she was praying for those entrusted to her, she saw very many go inside that wall, and then she asked the Lord as great High Priest to give spiritual communion both to her and her other spiritual dependents from the power of his Body and Blood, as from the violence of a hostile power they were forbidden to receive it sacramentally from the priest. Then the Lord seemed to send forth something from his blessed mouth, just as an oven spits out sparks, from which all those present might draw into themselves the food of the saving Host. Then she said to the Lord, "Surely, Lord, you are not giving communion to all our community?" He replied, "No, but only those who desire it, and those who would like to desire it. The others who[1] belong to the community will gain great profit from this: for the first time they will be granted a strong desire, like that of someone who has little interest in food, but when enticed for some time by a delicious odor begins to take pleasure in eating."

3. And when she also saw within that wall that person who was about to receive communion because of her sickness,[2] she said to the Lord, "Lord, what will you do for that person?" The Lord replied, "I shall bend over her, as a mother is accustomed to bend over her little child above the cradle, and from that she will drink in my likeness, just as they say a baby drinks in the likeness of its mother's character and morals through the nourishment of milk." She responded, "O Lord, if that woman earned this benefit of your grace because in the evening she so carefully instructed messengers to forewarn the community to pray for her, how greatly do I neglect my salvation, wretch that I am, for however much I desired it, I would be ashamed to take up the attention of so many people!" The Lord replied, "From that very fact, too, my loving-kindness perfects my glory and your beauty. For although gold shines splendidly, when set with jewels it displays more gracious loveliness; thus out of shamefastness and humility combined, which sometimes make you fear afterwards that you have neglected something, I perfect your beauty, changing all things to good for you."

4. Now when the sick woman mentioned had communicated and the priest had left, shedding tears both from sorrow and from desire, <Gertrud> returned to her place of prayer. The Lord intimated, "Why are you weeping, beloved?" She said, "Because I saw you and walked after you, the Lord and love of my soul, and did not deserve to receive you." The Lord replied, "And do you not think that you possessed me sufficiently, when during the earlier Mass and again till now you enjoyed my presence when I came down to you for your heart's delight?" She said, "But that

---

[1] *Ceteri . . . qui* L, i.e., masculine gender.

[2] The interdict exempted the seriously ill.

I do not have, because I cannot say, 'Now the body of my beloved has been united with my body.'" When the Lord ignored this, she broke out in burning tears from the depths of her burning heart and said to the Lord, "Why, my beloved, do you allow me to be so tormented?" And the Lord answered, "Because the joy of the hoped-for consolation is closer, a greater abundance of pain must issue forth."[3]

[3] *Quia proprius est sperate consolacionis gaudium, ideo necesse est ut maior uis doloris excurrat* L, clearly alluding to Ps-Bernard, *Meditatio in Passionem et Resurrectionem Domini*, 15.38, *sed prope erat insperatae consolationis gaudium, ideo tota vis doloris et plorationis excurrat* (PL 184:766).

<CHAPTER ONE HUNDRED AND THREE **Not in LDP**>

1. Around the end of this much-mentioned interdict on the feast of the Nativity of the blessed Virgin, the Lord seemed to look upon the community with such unspeakably loving kindliness, companionable friendliness, and delightful tenderness, to hear their prayers and share his own good things with them, that it surpasses all human understanding how the Lord could ever share himself with those now reigning with him in eternal life with even sweeter love. It should be explained through a simile; however, no suitable words could be found for the praise and thanksgiving owed the Trinity, ever to be worshiped. May we trust the glorious Trinity itself to respond in a way that befits its own most courteous loving-kindness!

<CHAPTER ONE HUNDRED AND FOUR = **Not in LDP**;
LDP IV.51.5, lines 10–20; **not in LDP**>

1. On the day of the glorious Virgin's Nativity,[1] **while they were chanting the verse** *Hear us* **in the sequence,** *Hail, bright <star of the sea>*,[2] **<Gertrud> saw the gracious Virgin herself sitting beside her royal son on the regal throne.** She said to her, "Mother of Mercy, why **do you not rise up so that in your accustomed way you might** pray for us?" The blessed Virgin replied, "In my heart I am speaking to the heart of my beloved on behalf of you all." Then when the same verse was repeated, the royal Virgin stretched out her slender hand toward the convent and arose, as if drawn by their **prayers and** desires; together with the community she stood before the Son to implore him. The imperial Son, kindly rising up in his turn, first bent his knee at the following verse, that is, "Save us, <for whom your Virgin Mother prays,>"[3] saying: "**You need not ask for anything, for all that you desire, O my dearest children, you can command, for I am so overcome by your love that** I am ready to grant all your desires."

2. And when after the gospel, a bell was struck during the creed at the exposition of the Host,[4] **the Lord said, "I now expose to my dear children that blessing [i.e., the Host] that, the sweeter it becomes in the sweetness of my divine heart, so much the more**

---

[1] September 8.

[2] See L 73.1, n. 1.

[3] *Salva nos, Jesu, pro quibus Virgo Mater te orat*, stanza 13 of the sequence "Hail bright star."

[4] Unexplained. A liturgical practice unique to Helfta?

often it is moved by their groans and desires." Next, when they were chanting *The sun of righteousness* after the offertory, she begged the Queen of Heaven to give her something that she could worthily offer in praise of her blessed son; the glorious Mother took the necklace on her own breast, shaped like a tree, made of golden pearls and having a single jewel of ethereal hue below. When <Gertrud> wanted to offer this to the Lord, she realized that it was his best pleasure that she should wear it on her breast as an adornment, not for her own but for God's glory. The golden pearls of this necklace were the most loving intentions that the blessed Virgin had in all her actions for the love of God, for whose praise she did all things. The gem set below was humility, which governed all the intentions of the same blessed Virgin, just as branches get their fruit from the root. But since she saw no other jewel in that necklace, she was striving to obtain both from the Lord himself and also from his mother more gems that would separate the golden pearls, to increase its beauty. Finally while they were reciting *The peace of the Lord be always with you*, the Lord, bending towards her in gentle sweetness, offered her a kiss with these words: "My mother had jewels of varied virtues because her soul was sweetly greeted by my divine nature, and for this reason I make this promise to you too." Then she saw the necklace that has been described, adorned with a variety of multifarious jewels. This necklace is worn by all who direct their intention towards divine love.

<CHAPTER ONE HUNDRED AND FIVE = LDP IV.52.5–6>

1. On the day of the Exaltation of the Holy Cross,[1] when during Mass she was again offering the Lord at the elevation of the cup the past trouble of the community,[2] she received this reply: "I shall drink—indeed I shall most certainly drink—this cup that the fervor of devotion and your desires have sweetened so much for me that as often as you offer it to me, I shall never cease drinking until you have me completely drunk, ready to hear all your prayers." And when she said, "Lord, how could we proffer this to you?" she was taught that any who, meditating on their wretchedness, offer it to the Lord to his eternal praise, and regret that they have not longed fervently as is fitting, and decide that, if it were possible, they would willingly bear in their heart every torment that ever the human heart can have in desiring the Lord, then they offer the Lord their God the cup of a drink more welcome to him than sweetness of nectar and balm.

2. Anyone can do the same when held back from communion or some other service of God, by saying, "O torrent from the living source! O aromatic savor of divine sweetness! O most delicious drunkenness of all blessedness! Look! I drink to you in the fullness of your being a droplet of my wretched poverty. Because of it I sorrow so long (but less than is right), and have ever sorrowed, that I am restraining my starving soul from your sumptuous feasts since of my own free will, alas, I block the path of your grace by my own vice! And now, creator and re-creator[3] of my substance, you who

<hr>

[1] September 14.

[2] That is, the interdict.

[3] See Anselm of Canterbury, *Proslogion* 14, and *Meditationes* 7 and 11 (*S. Anselmi Cantuariensis Archiepiscopi Opera Omnia*, ed. Franz Schmitt [Stuttgart: Friedrich Fromann Verlag, 1968]).

alone have the power to do all that is impossible to your highest praise, grant that my heart may be in perfect harmony with what I say. For I would willingly contain up to the day of my death every anguish of the desires that the human heart has ever suffered for your love in following you, from the beginning of the world until its end, so that I might provide you with my soul as a more worthy shelter, and in addition might make reparation to you that the unattainable worth of your grace **was** manifested again and again so incalculably to those who are so ungrateful and unworthy."

<CHAPTER ONE HUNDRED AND SIX = LDP III.5 >

1. On the feast of Saint Matthew the apostle,[1] since the Lord *had prevented her with a generous blessing of sweetness*[2] at the elevation of the chalice, she was offering that same chalice to the Lord in thanksgiving. She began to **turn over** in her heart that she had done very little in offering that chalice, if she did not expose herself to endure sufferings for Christ's sake. Thus in an impulse of strength she raised herself from the Lord's bosom, where she seemed to be taking great delight, and flung herself on the ground like a worthless corpse with these words: "Lord, I **wholly** expose myself to suffer all things that could be a source of praise for you." At this the Lord immediately rose up in haste and lay down beside her on the ground. As if drawing her to him, he said, "This is mine!" By virtue of his presence, reviving, she raised herself to the Lord and said, "Yes, my Lord, I am *the work of your hands*."[3] The Lord said, "A new gift is yours: that my love for you is so tightly bound up with you that without you I cannot happily live." In her astonishment at the great condescension of his words she said, "Why do you say that, my Lord, when having deigned to take pleasure in your own creation you would have an unlimited number, both on earth and in heaven, with whom you could happily live, even if I had never been created?" The Lord replied, "He who has always lacked a limb is not tormented by the pain of one who had it cut off in adulthood; so I shall never, from the moment that I set my love upon you, suffer us to be separated from each other."

[1] September 21.
[2] See Ps 20:4.
[3] Job 10:3.

<CHAPTER ONE HUNDRED AND SEVEN = LDP III.6>

1. On Saint Maurice's day, when Mass had been celebrated as far as the secret, when the Host is **accustomed to be** consecrated, she said to the Lord, "That work that you are now about to do, Lord, must be worthy of such priceless and surpassing honor that my wretched self dare not even look upon it. So, sinking out of sight, I shall **hide** myself in the deepest vale of humility that I can search out, awaiting my portion **in that same place**, for thence shall come forth salvation to all the chosen."

The Lord replied, "When a mother wants something embroidered to be worked in silk or pearls, sometimes she sets her little child in a higher place to hold her thread or her pearls for her, or to give her some sort of help. In the same way I have set you in a higher place to make you take part in this Mass. If you gladly applied your will to this, however difficult the labor, you were willing to serve so that this offering may share its full effect in all Christians, living and dead, according to its dignity; then in your way you have helped me best in my work."

<CHAPTER ONE HUNDRED AND EIGHT = LDP IV.58.1–3>

1. When, on the feast of the Dedication, *The queen of Sheba came to King Solomon* was being read **in the eighth lesson** at Matins and, further on, *with precious stones of virtue*,[1] pierced to the heart she said to the Lord, "Woe is me, most kindly God; how may I, such a little thing, come to you, when I do not see in myself the trace of any virtue whatsoever?" The Lord replied to this, "**Even if you do not ascribe to yourself the merit of any virtue, you are surely aware** that you are **very often** distressed by the opposition of your detractors?" She said, "I do know, Lord, that—alas—as my faults demand I am often a source of scandal to my neighbors." The Lord said to her, "Then take each and every word of your detractors in the place of virtues, and, adorned with them, you shall come to me and I shall kindly welcome you, compelled by my compassionate loving-kindness. The more your way of life is unjustly criticized **and disparaged by people**, the more fully my heart **will come** down to you with loving caresses, for through this you become most like me, for I always had opponents **and critics** in what I did **and said**."

2. Then, **while they were chanting** the response *Bless, <O Lord,>*[2] the Lord led her to **the** place **of the tabernacle**, astonishing beyond description, that is, the heart of Jesus Christ,[3] which was disposed like the building in which the feast of the Dedication was **to be cele-**

[1] See 1 Kgs 10:1-2.

[2] *Benedic, domine, domum istam quam aedificavi nomini tuo, alleluia*, "Bless, Lord, that house that I have built to your name, alleluia": antiphon for Matins of the feast of the Dedication of the Church. See 1 Kgs 8:44.

[3] See LDP V.1.23.

brated. When it seemed to her that she had entered it, **because of an** inconceivable overflow of delights **that immediately on her entrance was smiling at her from that place of divine pleasure,** she **turned and** said to the Lord **in astonishment**, "My Lord, if you had led **my spirit** *in the place* **of which it could be said that once** *your feet* had *stood*,[4] **my strength would fail in thanksgiving because of my unworthiness. Therefore how may I now grow strong so that I might attempt** to respond to you for that amazing condescension **in bringing down to my littleness that supercelestial tabernacle in which dwells all the fullness of divinity in physical form**?" To this the Lord replied, "Because you **have not refused** me the more worthy part of your being—your heart—**but rather showed it to me, according to my delight**, I **have deemed** it appropriate that I too should show you my heart to complete your delight. For I am *God, all in all*,[5] life, strength, knowledge, food, clothing, habitation, and the other things that a loving soul can desire." Then she said, "It was a gift from you, my Lord, whenever my heart could consent to you in **any good** thing, **so what could it then deserve, worthy of such a reward**?" And the Lord said, "It is natural for me that anyone whom *I go before in blessings of sweetness*[6] I shall also come after in blessings of rewards; and if anyone coöperates with me, so that as a result I may make him fit according to the good pleasure of my heart, consequently I shall also conform myself to him according to every good pleasure of his heart."

3. While she was mentally strolling among these delights, **that heavenly, or rather** divine, treasure house around her appeared constructed **with four walls** from squared gems of varied color; **all were** bonded together with gold in place of cement. And while she was inspecting them more carefully, **as if** *through a glass in a dark manner*,[7] she saw a wonderful **sparkling** play **of light** in each and every one. Through this she understood how in the life to come

---

[4] See Ps 131:7.
[5] 1 Cor 15:28.
[6] See Ps 20:4.
[7] 1 Cor 13:12.

dignity of spiritual grace in any of the chosen will provide delightful pleasure to all the blessed. For through the deployment of the gems already mentioned she understood the predestination of all the chosen in the divine heart, **but especially of our community**, and that the chosen are bound to support each other reciprocally, just as in a wall one stone supports another. But through the fact that the bonding of the gems was of gold, she understood that that support of the faithful for each other ought to be provided from charity and purely for God's sake.

1. On Saint Stephen's day during the response *De torrente* *<passionis>*[1] **she was thanking God for the blessings that had been bestowed some years before on the same day,**[2] **in the vision of the purple stairs and the golden couch.**[3] **On that occasion the Lord also added the insight that three groups of people are allowed to rest on that most excellent couch. For the first are those whom God finds delighting in God's grace because they feel that in nothing can they take greater pleasure than** *to be still and see*[4] *that the Lord is sweet.*[5] **As if drinking sweet milk from** *the breasts of* **the Lord's** *consolation,*[6] **they cry out with the prophet,** *But it is good for me to adhere to my God, to put my hope in the Lord God.*[7] **But the second, having advanced further towards perfection, devote themselves to the Lord's praise with complete concentration, for love of him whom they cherish. They burn so greatly with zeal for souls that they think it little or nothing to interrupt periods of quiet contemplation from time to time, that they may gain divine praise and profit of souls more fruitfully. Repaying them with his customary loving-kindness, the Lord interrupts their anxious cares with swift showers of sweetness, and thus their whole life happily alternates between praise of**

---

[1] Response for the feast of Saint Stephen.

[2] See L 57 (about four years previously).

[3] See L 57, 58, and 60; datable as possibly 1292.

[4] Ps 45:11.

[5] 1 Pet 2:3.

[6] See Isa 66:11; see also the introit for the fourth Sunday in Lent.

[7] Ps 72:28.

God and their own spiritual progress. The third are those who, although lacking inner consolations, are nonetheless faithful and constant in God's service; because they, too, are able to excel in such things they are supported by the gold couch.

2. Then during Mass, when as best she could she was preparing to receive communion, she saw herself on the purple stair mentioned above, climbing rather slowly, and after a little while she came across a young man, very lovely, dressed in a golden tunic that seemed overlaid with a reddish color. When she asked the significance of that garment, she received this reply: "That gold color signifies my immortality, because of which I am completely incapable of suffering. But the reddish color with which it is overlaid shows my compassion, with which in all your sufferings both of body and spirit, compelled by love I have compassion on you with most loving affection." And the young man added, "Lean on me to climb these stairs more easily with my support." When she moved on, leaning on him, that most joyful companion,[8] relieving her of all the journey's toil, added in friendly conversation, "Do you not notice how slowly I go forward in condescending to you? Therefore it is right that if I sometimes take longer strides in accordance with my nature, of which it is written, *he has rejoiced as a giant to run the way,*[9] so you should not refuse to keep up with me, for my longing to lead you to the beautiful repose to which we are hastening drives me on." That is, the young man's assertion that he was moving forward rather slowly with her indicates that the Lord sometimes condescends to human weakness and purifies with more gentle chastisements, as she showed quite clearly on that occasion. In that he predicted longer strides, he forewarned her of more serious trials to be endured. Then the youth added, "Remember how during the whole time of that sickness I gave you relief by visiting you with my grace: on every single feast day, I met you as if in the middle of that stair with springtime growth of all kinds of flowers and made you sit down

---

[8] See also L 40 above, and the quotation there from Bernard, SC 31.3.

[9] Ps 18:6.

with me as it were for a game,[10] so that after a while you could move on more quickly?" That is, although she was barred from the service of God for a whole week by sickness, when on feast days she was continually yearning to receive the sacrament of the Lord she seemed to be so greatly strengthened that, however hard she toiled, she never felt any weakness or infirmity until after the completion of the Divine Office.[11]

[10] See L 54 for a reference to a "game," but that chapter says nothing about the purple stairs.

[11] See L 148.

<CHAPTER ONE HUNDRED AND TEN = LDP III.7;
not in LDP>

1. On Holy Innocents' day,[1] while she was hampered by the turmoil of her thoughts in her preparation for communion, she was asking divine help on this. This was the answer she received from God's most courteous mercy: "If anyone, attacked by human temptation, takes refuge with confident hope under my protection, he is one of those of whom I can say, *One is my dove*,[2] as if *chosen out of thousands*,[3] who *in one of her eyes has wounded my divine heart*,[4] so much so that if I knew I could not help her, this would be such a source of sorrow to my heart that all the delights of heaven could not assuage it. For in my body, which is united to my divinity, my chosen have always an advocate, who compels me to have compassion on their various needs."

She replied, "My Lord, how could your immaculate body, which contains no internal contradiction, compel you to have compassion on us in our anxieties that are so varied?" The Lord replied, "It is easy to persuade someone who is understanding. For the apostle said of me, *it was necessary for him in all things to be made like unto his brethren, that he might become merciful*."[5] And the Lord added, "*One of* the *eyes* of my beloved with which she had *wounded my heart*[6] is

---

[1] December 28.
[2] Song 6:8.
[3] Song 5:10.
[4] See Song 4:9.
[5] Heb 2:17.
[6] See Song 4:9.

the sure trust that one ought to have in me, that truly I have the power, the knowledge, and the will to be faithfully at her side in all things; this trust acts with such force on my loving-kindness that it is quite impossible for me to leave **them.**"

She said, "My Lord, since trust is such an unfailing good, which no one can possess unless you have given it, how can someone who lacks it be at fault?" The Lord replied, "Anyone at all can overcome his faintheartedness to a certain extent, at least on the evidence of Scripture. For he can say, if not with his whole heart at least with his mouth, that prayer of Job's: 'Even if I have been plunged into the depths of hell, you shall free me from there,'[7] and that other prayer, *Although you should kill me, I should trust in you.*"[8]

2. Again, she was praying for someone else who was so heavily oppressed that from that oppression he feared an opportunity for evil. She was reassured on this count by God's generous loving-kindness, that it would be much more an opportunity for eternal salvation than for anyone's damnation. Guided by feelings of compassion, she desired the Lord, imploring him with prayers, that that same person who was oppressed, having been attacked by temptation, should have his burden lightened in this through God's mercy, so that she might also understand how that oppression would result in his salvation. The Lord replied, "If I relieved him from his burden in any respect I would also diminish his reward from the same source, for his prize increases in proportion to all that brings him low; either he is afraid of displeasing me or he is diligent in pleasing <me>."

---

[7] Response, Summer Histories, from Job. *Historiae* (histories) were passages from the historical part of the Hebrew Scriptures read in summer during the night office (see Introduction, p. 32, n. 22).

[8] See Job 13:15.

1. One day when she was in bed and, unable to be present at Mass, was about to receive communion, she said to the Lord with troubled heart, "Look, most loving **God**, I can attribute the fact that I am prevented from being present at Mass today to your divine providence. How can I now prepare myself for receiving your most holy Body and Blood since, as it seems to me, the supreme preparation for me is always attention to the Mass?"

The Lord replied, "Since you impute this motivation to me, pay attention to me and I shall sing you sweet and loving nuptial songs. Hear me say, then, that you are redeemed by my blood and consider that the entire period of thirty-three years in which I toiled for you in this exile had no other reason for its existence than as a preparatory mission for your betrothal. Let this serve for the first part of the Mass."

"Hear me say that you are endowed with my spirit and **know** that, just as for all those thirty-three years, as **was said earlier**, I toiled for you on that mission in body, so in spirit I celebrated our most delightful and longed-for nuptials that united me to you. Let this serve for the second part of the Mass."

"Hear me also say that you are filled with my divinity and know that my **Godhead** has the power, amid the outward troubles of the body, to provide inward spiritual delights that are most welcome. Let this serve as the third part of the Mass."

"Hear me say further that you are made holy by my love, and **know** that your ability to please me comes entirely from me, not at all from yourself. Let this serve as the fourth part of the Mass."

"Hear me say last of all that by my bonding you are exalted and know that since *all power is given to me in heaven and in earth,*[1] nothing can prevent me, if it so pleases me, from raising you up with me for my good pleasure, just as it is appropriate for the woman who shares the king's bed to be called queen and to be honored. Delight in meditating on this, and from now on do not claim that you had to go without Mass!"

[1] Matt 28:18.

<CHAPTER ONE HUNDRED AND TWELVE **Not in LDP**>

1. When she was very distressed one day for some reason and around Terce on the following day was concentrating on prayer, she perceived that the Lord was gently saying to her, "That hour is now at hand when I carried my cross with great shame for your salvation; in recompense for this I now wish to take my pleasure with you. So you must lay aside the cross of the trouble that threatens you and rest within me." Then she said, "Why, sweetest God, have you allowed me to be so unbearably oppressed?" The Lord replied, "Because it was not good for you to possess without a burden that consolation that you had recently received from someone for such a reason, lest perhaps, having been raised up, you might fall. Thence from now onwards you will carry your burden quietly, patiently, and humbly, and you will not put it down except at that hour when you enter into your inmost being, to live with me in spiritual joy."

1. On the first Sunday after **the feast of the shining and ever-tranquil** Trinity, the Lord appeared to her sweetly **sleeping** in a garden, charming with flowery greenness, as if *lying in the midday*,[1] *surfeited from wine*[2] of charity, so to speak. Flinging herself at his feet, she kissed them affectionately again and again as was her custom. She caressed her beloved in various ways but for three days could win none of her customary enjoyment of him. And so on the fourth day during Mass she was unable any longer to bear her beloved's sleeping. She rose from his feet and in a paroxysm of ardor rushed at his breast, for which she burned with desire. By the power of her love she strove to break in on her beloved's sleep. Aroused by this, the Lord gently embraced her with both arms and, drawing her strongly to himself, said, "Look! now I am holding what I desired. For just as the fox wanting to catch birds flattens itself on the ground as if dead, and the little birds fly more freely above her, so I too, burning with love for you, followed this example, by which I gain total possession of you when you launch yourself at me."

[1] Song 1:6.
[2] Ps 77:65.

<CHAPTER ONE HUNDRED AND FOURTEEN = LDP III.9>

1. It had been divinely revealed to someone[1] that the Lord would deign to release a great company of souls from the pains of purgatory through the community's prayers. To gain this end, a special prayer had been enjoined upon the whole community. Just like the others, the woman who is the subject of this book was completing the prayer enjoined upon her on the Sunday on which the company of souls already mentioned were to be released from their pains, and was offering herself to the Lord as devoutly as she could for the salvation of souls. Since she had drawn nearer the Lord and beheld him in his glory like a king bestowing rewards but could not clearly make out what the Lord seemed to be so busy about, she said to him, "Most kindly Lord, on the feast of Saint Mary Magdalene[2] **that has passed** you made known to me, unworthy as I am, that you were constrained by your own loving-kindness to lay all your kindliness at your feet so that very many, by the example of that blessed sinner, but your lover, would fling themselves in humility at your feet on that very day. Deign, too, in your mercy to make plain what you are doing now, for it is hidden from the eyes of my understanding."

The Lord replied, "I am distributing gifts." By this she understood that the Lord was distributing the community's prayers for the relief of souls. However, she could hardly see the souls themselves, even though they were there. Then the Lord added, "Don't you too want to offer me the riches of your reward to add to what I have to give?" She melted with pleasure at these words, not knowing that the entire

---

[1] Possibly this refers to Mechtild of Hackeborn, who is never identified by name in L.

[2] July 22. This vision is not in L, but see LDP IV.46.2.

community was doing this very thing at the suggestion of the person already mentioned, to whom the promise had been made concerning setting free of souls. She gratefully accepted what the Lord had requested, as if it were something he particularly wanted from her, and replied with cheerful heart, "I offer you, Lord, not only my own spiritual possessions, which are worth next to nothing, but also those of the whole community from the common life that I share with them, claiming them as my own in their entirety through your grace. This I do of my own free will, with great joy, in union with the perfection **of your most holy life**." This the Lord accepted with great kindness.

2. Then the Lord, as if at leisure, stretched a cloud over her alone and himself; **bending** down to her, he said tenderly to her, "Concentrate on me alone and enjoy the sweetness of my grace." Then she said, "Why, my sweetness, my God, do you deprive me so completely of that gift that you have so obviously bestowed on that person previously named—the gift of revelation of souls—although you kindly condescend to make plain to me so many of your secrets?" The Lord replied, "Remember that you quite often vilify yourself because you think yourself so unworthy of the gift of my grace, **in that** you reckon that it is bestowed on you as if on a hired laborer, who is induced to serve by money, and as if, without that gift, you would render me no fealty. For this reason you place others before yourself—others who, induced by no such gift, nonetheless seem completely loyal to me. I have made you like them in this respect so that, while you have no privileged knowledge concerning souls but still labor faithfully for them, you too may not be without that worth that you extol in others."

3. While he was speaking she realized, as if in a state of ecstasy, with what wonderful and inexpressible condescension the divine loving-kindness sometimes comes down to the human level **in** copiously **expending** its grace, and sometimes refuses lesser things to protect humility, which is the foundation and defense of graces. She also realized how the Lord causes both of these to *work together unto good to them that love*.[3] And because of her great thankfulness and

---

[3] Rom 8:28.

wonder at God's infinite goodness towards her, as if out of her mind and reduced to a state of collapse, she flung herself on the Lord's breast and said, "My Lord, my insignificance cannot **bear** that weight!" Then the Lord diminished the magnitude of that knowledge, and when she regained her strength she said to the Lord, "Because, most kindly Lord, the incomprehensible, unsearchable wisdom of your providence demands that I do without this gift, from now on I shall never desire it further."

4. She added, "But surely, Lord, you don't hear me when I pray for certain of my friends?" As if confirming with an oath the Lord said, "By my divine power, I do indeed." She said, "Therefore I now pray for that person who has been entrusted to me again and again." At once she saw something like a little stream of crystalline purity come forth from the Lord's breast and flow into the innermost being of the person for whom she was praying. Then she asked the Lord, "Lord, what use is this to that person, since she herself is not aware of this inflowing?" The Lord replied, "When a doctor administers a medicinal potion to someone who is sick, it is not at the time that he drinks the potion that **all** the bystanders see the invalid restored to health. Nor does the invalid himself feel immediately that he is cured. Nonetheless the doctor who understands the power of the potion knows very well how it should benefit the sick man." She said, "Why, Lord, do you not take from **him his** unruly temperament and other failings, for which I have so often entreated you?" The Lord replied, "It was said of me as the child Jesus, *He advanced in wisdom, and age, and grace with God and men.*[4] So may **he**, who is advancing from one hour to the next, create virtue from vice; I shall take from **him** all that is human so that after this life **he** may behold all that I have prepared for the **man** whom I have arranged to raise above the angels."

5. As the time drew near at which she was to receive communion, she besought the Lord that he would deign to advance the time of his grace for as many sinners (who were nonetheless destined to be saved **at some time**, for she did not presume to pray for those destined to

---

[4] Luke 2:52.

be damned) as there were souls released from the pains of purgatory through the prayers of that person who has been mentioned repeatedly, and who had on that very day joined the choirs of heaven. The Lord corrected her faintheartedness and said, "Does not the high worth of the presence of my immaculate Body and precious Blood deserve that even those who are in a state of damnation should be called back to a state of better living?" Pondering his generous liberality in these words she said, "Since your inestimable loving-kindness deigns to descend to my unworthy prayers, I pray your majesty, in union with the love and longing of all your creation, to grant me as many souls of living sinners, who are currently in a state of damnation, as the number of souls **mentioned earlier** that you have already granted me, so that they for whom you particularly deigned to be prayed may **be converted** to your grace, at whatever time and in whatever place it may be. Nor do I choose any of my friends, relations, or kinsfolk." The Lord kindly accepted this suggestion and assured her this would be so.

6. Then she said, "I would like to know, Lord, what you wish me to add **to this prayer for them**." Receiving no reply she said, "Lord, I suppose that my faithlessness does not deserve to receive an answer to these questions, for you, who *know the hearts of all*,[5] realize that I am so negligent that I would quite likely not carry out anything you enjoined on me." Then the Lord with a serene countenance replied lovingly, "Trust alone can most easily obtain all things, but if your devotion does not shrink from something extra, recite three hundred and **fifty** times *Praise the Lord, all ye peoples*,[6] to make up the measure of my divine praise, which has been slighted by those very souls."

---

[5] Acts 1:24.
[6] Ps 116:1.

<CHAPTER ONE HUNDRED AND FIFTEEN = LDP III.10>

1. On the feast of Saint Mathias,[1] since she had made up her mind not to receive communion because she was **greatly exhausted** for many reasons, during the first Mass she was concentrating on God and herself. The Lord showed himself to her with as strong an emotion of friendship as ever friend could render friend with tender emotion. She however was not at all satisfied by this, for she was accustomed to more potent favors bestowed in more potent fashion. She longed to be completely ravished from her own being and to be given over to her beloved, who is called *a consuming fire*,[2] and, melted by the fire of that very charity, to become one with that love in an intimate bonding.

And since she could not work for this at that time, turning away to the praise **of the Lord her lover,** she returned to another form of devotion to which she was accustomed, rendering high praise: that is, she extolled the vast bounty of the Trinity, **ever to be worshiped**. First, for every grace that has ever flowed from its profound **overflow** to the benefit of the saints. Second, for every grace granted to the most worthy Mother. Third, for every grace poured into the most holy humanity of Jesus Christ. She prayed to all <the saints>, as a group, and to each individually, that each one of them, **approaching the tabernacle of** the radiant and ever-peaceful Trinity, might offer in recompense for her own sins of omission all that devotion and preparedness with which **they had ever been prepared in this life to receive any divine grace as individuals, and specially that with which,** on the day of their own assumption, they stood before the

[1] Celebrated on February 24 in the Middle Ages.
[2] Heb 12:29.

sight of the Lord's glory in a state of perfection to receive their eternal reward. This she did by reciting three times *Praise the Lord, all ye peoples*[3] and so on—first for All Saints, second for the blessed Virgin, third for the Son of God. At this the Lord said, "How are my saints who make such an offering on your behalf **to make recompense**, since you intend to omit that offering that you are accustomed to make in thanksgiving for them?" At this she became silent.

2. Then at the offering of the **sacred** Host with a great *desire she desired*[4] to find an offering that she could worthily offer God the Father to his eternal praise. This was the reply she received from the Lord to this request: "If you were to fit yourself today to receive the sacrament of my life-giving Body and Blood, you could most certainly obtain that threefold blessing for which you prayed at this Mass: that is, to enjoy my most loving sweetness and, melted by the fire of my Godhead, to flow into me just as gold is fused with silver. From this you would have a most precious alloy that you could most worthily offer God the Father to his eternal praise, and **from that** all the saints would have most fully their complete reward."

Overcome by these words, she was inflamed by so great a desire that it would not have seemed hard to her to fly to the most saving sacrament even through the midst of swords.[5] When she was thanking God after she had received the Lord's Body, the lover of men and women himself, **touched inwardly from his own kindliness by the sweetness of charity**, spoke to her as follows: "Today by your own will you decided to serve me with the others with straw, *clay and brick*;[6] **thus** I chose you to be among those who would most sweetly take their fill of the delicacies of my royal table."

---

[3] Ps 116: compare L 114.

[4] Luke 22:15.

[5] Possibly a reference to Statius, *Thebaid* VII, lines 280–81: *macte animo iuvenis! medios parat ire per enses / nudaque pro caris opponere pectora* (*Thebaid, Volume I: Thebaid: Books 1–7*, ed. and trans. D. R. Shackleton Bailey, Loeb Classical Library 207 [Cambridge, MA: Harvard University Press, 2004], 418–19). This first-century Latin epic poem was very popular in the Middle Ages and a standard part of the educational curriculum.

[6] Exod 1:14.

And when on the same day another person had refrained from holy communion for no good reason, she said to the Lord, "Why, most merciful Lord, did you allow her to be tempted in this way?" The Lord replied, "Is it my fault that she has **drawn** the veil of her unworthiness over her eyes for so long that she **could not** discern the **kindliness** of my fatherly affection?"

1. Hearing one day the announcement of an indulgence of very many years that could be gained for almsgiving, she said to the Lord with devout heart, "Lord, if I were at this moment endowed with great riches, I would most willingly offer many pounds of gold and silver so that I might be absolved from my sins through that indulgence, to the honor and glory of your name."

The Lord kindly replied, "Then by the authority of my divine nature, accept full remission for all your sins and omissions." Immediately she saw her soul shining in snowy brightness, free from every spot. Then, after some days, when she examined herself and found her soul still shining with the same brightness that she had known before, **struck dumb, she feared** that she was deceived in such a display of her soul's innocence. For she **certainly** thought that the purity that had earlier been revealed, even if it had been genuine, nonetheless seemed somewhat clouded as a result of her continual lapses into omissions and frivolity, which she had quite often committed from human weakness. The **loving** Lord **kindly** comforted her sense of desolation with these words: "Do I not keep for myself a greater power than I have conferred on my creatures? For I have endowed the sun with such power that, if a white cloth has acquired a stain, it suddenly vanishes as a result of the power of the sun's heat and intensity, and the cloth is restored to an even brighter whiteness than before. How much more will I be able to preserve a soul at which I, the sun's creator, have directed the glance of my mercy, undefiled from every speck of sin or omission? For I purify every stain in it by the force of my white-hot love."

<CHAPTER ONE HUNDRED AND SEVENTEEN =
LDP III.22; **not in LDP**>

1. Another time, prevented because of sickness from keeping the full rigor of her Order, she had sat down to hear Vespers. From simultaneous longing and sorrow of heart she said to the Lord, "Would it not be more praiseworthy for you, Lord, if right now I were **present** among the **community** in choir, with time for prayers and toiling at the other regular exercises, than as I am now, held back by this weakness and negligently wasting so much time?" **She received this answer**, "The bridegroom surely does not seem to you to take less pleasure in his bride when he enjoys her in privacy and delightful quiet and often drinks of her desired embraces than when he takes pride in her going forth in all her finery for public display?" From this she understood that when the soul is engaged in eagerness of good works to the glory of God, at that time it goes out in public in all her finery, as it were. But at another time it rests as in private with its spouse when it is prevented by physical troubles from such pursuits. For then, **drawn away from** the delights of its own senses, it is abandoned to the divine will alone. And thence the Lord takes so much the greater pleasure in a person the less that person finds anything in himself in which he can vainly take pleasure or **even** pride.

2. Again, another time when she asked the Lord why he allowed her to be prevented so often from holy communion, prayer, and other good works, he replied, "When the bridegroom has said to his bride, 'Go into *the greater privacy of the bedchamber*[1]

---

[1] See Bernard, SC 31.7. *Ducam eam* contains twelve quotations from this sermon.

and wait for me until I come to you there in accordance with my promise,' if she has dutifully obeyed the bridegroom, how could she deserve blame for neglect?" Inwardly instructed by these words through the Spirit, she began to fear that she offended more through indiscreet rigor than through some degree of relaxation, when she felt that it was not imaginary but a genuine necessity. In particular, she considered that vainglory and one's own pleasure are subtly and intimately associated with indiscreet rigor, but the dejection and humility that so often attend discreet relaxation that happens painfully, against one's own will and purely to God's praise, are the most reliable way to preserve God's grace. From then onwards she used to assert that by divine declaration bodily weaknesses are rightly called "the greater privacy of the bedchamber," for they completely put to flight human pleasure, because only with difficulty are the dearest friends of Christ Jesus allowed to feast on such delightful gifts. They are sure that they will more gladly accept from the Lord both physical and mental sufferings in preference to all strenuous spiritual exercises.

<CHAPTER ONE HUNDRED AND EIGHTEEN =
LDP III.32.1 >

1. When in the Mass for the Dead they were chanting the words *My soul has thirsted*[1] and so on in the tract "As the hart," she was meditating **with dejected heart** on her lukewarmness **and negligence.** She said to the Lord, "Alas, Lord, that my desires for you, my true **and only** good, are so lukewarm that it is so rarely appropriate for me to say to you, *My soul has thirsted for you.*"[2] **She received this response**: "Not rarely but quite often you may say to me that your soul thirsts for me, for the loving-kindness of love, by which I love human salvation, drives me always to count my chosen as having desired me, whatever good things they desire, since every good lies hidden in me and flows out from me. For instance, if a person[3] desires health, security, ease, wisdom, and so on, I often count him[4] as having desired me so that I may greatly pile up the merit of his reward. I make an exception if he has deliberately turned away, **as if** he desired wisdom so that he could take pride in it, or health **by which** he could carry out evil." And the Lord added, "Therefore it is very often my custom to weigh down my closest friends with weakness of body and desolation of mind **or some other tribulation,** so that when they desire to gain the contrary good things, the burning love of my heart is able to reward **these women**[5] more generously according to the good pleasure of my open-handedness."

[1] Ps 41:3.
[2] Ps 41:3.
[3] *homo* L.
[4] *eum* L.
[5] *eas* L, i.e., feminine gender.

<CHAPTER ONE HUNDRED AND NINETEEN =
LDP III.32.2>

1. Similarly, another time she was divinely inspired and understood that sometimes the Lord, whose *delights are to be with the children of men,*[1] finds nothing **of worth** in a person in which he can take pleasure and appropriately deign to be present with him. Then he sends troubles or trials, both physical and spiritual, so that as a result he may have the opportunity of staying with him. For the Scripture of truth[2] says, *The Lord is near those that are of a troubled heart.*[3] In consideration of this and many similar things, **without a doubt** loving gratitude of human littleness is forced to cry out with all the affections of the heart those words of the apostle: *O the depths of the riches of the wisdom and of the knowledge of God! How incomprehensible are his judgments, and how unsearchable his ways*[4] that he has devised for the salvation of the human race!

[1] Prov 8:31.
[2] See William of Saint-Thierry, *Meditationes* 2.12 (PL 180:209A, 242C).
[3] Ps 33:19.
[4] Rom 11:33.

<CHAPTER ONE HUNDRED AND TWENTY = LDP V.24>

1. **Suffering from extreme weakness, on a day when she was present at Mass, intending to communicate**, she asked the Lord if she was about to pay the debt of the flesh as a result of the infirmity that was weighing her down. She then received this answer: "When a young girl has seen the bridegroom's messengers coming more often, and **most of all if she perceives them** negotiating about what pertains to the completion of the marriage, it is right that she too should prepare herself in those things that fit her for the nuptials. In the same way it is appropriate that when you experience sickness you should not **put off** any of those preparations that you would want to make before death." Then she said, "And how could I know in advance that desirable hour of your coming, when you will lead me out of the prison of this **death**?" The Lord replied, "I shall have two from among the princes of the heavenly court cause to resound in both your ears **with sweet-sounding voice** through golden trumpets, *Behold the bridegroom comes; go forth to meet*[1] **Christ the Lord**."

2. She said, "What then will be my steed when I am conducted along that royal road to be presented to you, my one and only sweetest **and best beloved spouse, with such joy?**" The Lord replied, "The powerful attraction of divine desire, aimed at you from the depths of my love, will lead you to my realm." Then she added, "What saddle shall I then have, my Lord?" And the Lord said, "The complete **confidence** with which you await every good thing from my most generous loving-kindness will provide you with a saddle in this journey." She said, "What bridle will direct me?" The Lord replied, "The

---

[1] Matt 25:6.

most fervent love that leads you to long with all your heart for my embraces will act as your bridle." Then she said, "Since I do not know anything else about riding, **I am unable to ask any** further questions concerning the means by which I am to travel on that desirable road." The Lord replied, "However much you seek to discover now, in eternity you will rejoice to have found far more, and this is the source of my delight, that human intelligence could never search out anything as great as what I regularly prepare for my chosen."

1. While a certain friar was preaching in the chapel, among other things he had said, "Love is a golden arrow: if a person has shot something with it, in some way he claims it as his own. Therefore, anyone who neglects heavenly things and lavishes his love on earthly things is **shown to be very foolish." And when the preacher was saying this and similar things, from the depths of her heart** she said to the Lord, "Would that I possessed that **golden** arrow **of love as a gift from you**, for then without delay I would pierce you, my soul's only love, **so that I would the more easily** keep you, **as if rendered powerless by the wound, with me** for ever!" While she was saying this, she saw the Lord holding a golden arrow aimed at her and answering **what she had just said** as follows: "You **plan** to wound me, if you had a golden arrow; therefore, since I do have one, I intend to **transfix** you so much so that you will never return to your former state of good health!" The arrow just mentioned seemed bent three times: in the upper part, in the middle, and towards the end. By this she was taught the threefold power that Love produces in the soul by wounding it.

2. For when the first section has pierced the soul, it wounds it in such a way that it renders almost all **earthly and** transitory things tasteless to that person, as happens with the sick, so much so that from then onwards that person can **never** take pleasure or find comfort in any such thing. The second, in piercing it, **wounds** the soul **in the manner of someone suffering from fever,** who from the intensity of the pain seeks medicine with the greatest impatience;

thus <**the soul**>[1] burns with excessively impatient desire to cleave to God, since it seems completely impossible to live and breathe at all apart from **God. Finally** the third, piercing the soul **in this way, also** leads to such inconceivable things that no description can be given, **nor can anything further be said,** other than that the soul, separating from the body, is joyfully plunged into the torrents of the Godhead, delicious as nectar.

---

[1] *ista* L, i.e., feminine gender, presumably to agree with *anima*, "soul."

<CHAPTER ONE HUNDRED AND TWENTY-TWO =
LDP V.25.3>

1. After the **vision**[1] just described, influenced by human emotions, she importunately desired to pay the debt of the flesh in the place just mentioned, that is, in the chapel, as if the physical place would facilitate spiritual things. And since she sometimes included this in her prayers, one day she received this answer from the Lord: "On the passing of your soul I shall cherish you under the protection of my fatherly nature, just as a mother makes her dear child rest in her bosom, covered by her garment, while she sails across raging seas. And after you have paid the debt of death, I shall make you delight in lovely fields of heavenly verdure, just as a mother does not want her **daughter**, whom she wishes to be safe from danger, to be without hope of safety in a port." Then she, giving thanks to God and refraining from that childish wish, entrusted herself completely to Divine Providence.

---

[1] *exhibicionem* L; cf. LDP II.12.3.

1. Then another time she grew so weak from meditating on her unworthiness that she was quite incapable of exerting herself in God's praise or for the enjoyment **of God in any way.** At last, by the Lord's freely given mercy, through communion with the most holy life of Jesus Christ, she was so moved that, it seemed to her, she went forward in accordance with her desire and stood before the Lord, the King of kings, in that beauty in which Esther, it is thought, stood before King Ahasuerus. The kindly condescension of the Savior spoke to her with these words: "What is your command, lady queen?" She replied, "I beseech you, Lord, and desire with all my heart that your most praiseworthy will may be accomplished in me *according to your best pleasure.*"[1] Then the Lord, enumerating one by one all those people who had entrusted themselves to her prayers, said, "What then do you ask for her, for her, and for her, who **on this occasion** have specially entrusted themselves to your prayers?" She replied, "All I wish to ask on their behalf, Lord, is that your most **acceptable** will may be accomplished in all those people." After this the Lord spoke again, "And what do you want me to do for you?" She replied, "This is my **most** earnest wish, taking precedence over every delight: that your most gentle, most praiseworthy will may be accomplished in me as in all creation. And to accomplish this may I be found most ready to expose any part of my body to any suffering whatsoever." To these words the most benign loving-kindness of God,

---

[1] See Eph 1:9.

which had gone before her in longing and rewarded her in following after, replied, "Because you have been so zealous in furthering my will with such loving devotion, according to my customary benevolence I reward your effort with this gift: that you may appear as pleasing in my eyes as if you had never in the least disregarded my will."

1. Another time while they were chanting these words at Matins, Behold, *the eyes of the Lord are upon the just*,[1] **mindful of a certain person whom she had known to be oppressed by sickness at that time, she saw the gaze of the divine loving-kindness directed at that person with such gentle kindliness that she thought one could not desire to have any greater pleasure than to deserve to give thanks for the bestowal of God's gaze on others in the way in which she had seen it just then. Thence through this she perceived how great is the blessedness of heavenly spirits, who are invigorated by such inestimable delight through thanksgiving for the rewards of others.**

2. Again, on another occasion while they were chanting the verse in the psalm, *The words of the wicked **have prevailed over us**[2]* and so on, she **was divinely instructed** that when someone guilty from human frailty is **reproved** for her guilt, if too much is said, the words call forth God's mercy and increase the guilty one's reward. **That is, for shamefast minds it should be enough for the ones who reprove simply to say to them, "You have done wrong; do your penance, and be careful in future." If any more is said, it increases their reward from God's most generous loving-kindness. But for the shameless and thick-skinned, who deserve harsher correction according to Gregory, whatever is added over and above their correction does not increase their reward at all.**

---

[1] Ps 33:16; antiphon for the feast of All Saints.
[2] Ps 64:4.

1. When they were beginning the Mass "Come and show <your face>,"[1] the Lord, as if all honeyed with the sweetness of divine grace, exhaling a life-giving **or rather** divine breath, appeared **to come down** from the lofty throne of his imperial glory, **so that through the feast of his sweet-flowing Nativity he could pour the inflowing of his divine grace more directly and copiously into anyone who desired it.** Then she prayed for those entrusted to her, namely that the Lord would vouchsafe each one more powerful grace, and received this reply: "I have given each a golden reed of such power that with it anyone may draw to herself from the depths of my deified heart anything she desires." She understood that this reed was one's own will. Through it a person can claim for herself every spiritual good, both heavenly and earthly. For instance, when aroused by desire a person wishes to be able to render God as much praise, thanksgiving, service, and **felicity** as any of the saints has rendered him, the vast goodness of God accepts this wish as if **already** performed. But the reed, too, is ennobled with a golden color while the person thanks God that he has vouchsafed so noble a will, with which one can be infinitely more enriched than the whole world with all its strength can perform.

From this she understood that all the **members**[2] of the community who were standing around the Lord were drawing in the divine grace,

---

[1] Introit for Ember Saturday in Advent, i.e., the Saturday following the feast of Saint Lucy, December 13.

[2] *singulos* L, i.e., masculine gender: LDP reads *singulas*, feminine gender.

each according to their capacity, as it were through the reeds bestowed in them. Some appeared to draw directly from the depths of the divine heart, others through the hands of the Lord, **and others from the feet, and others from various other limbs. But wherever they were drawing from, nonetheless all that they received came from the heart, flowing with honey.** So the greater the distance at which they drew from the heart, the more difficult it was for them to obtain their desires. And the nearer to the Lord's heart they tried to come, the more easily, sweetly, and abundantly they drank. By those who[3] drank immediately and directly from the Lord's heart are symbolized those who completely conform and subdue themselves to the divine will, desiring above all that the most praiseworthy will of God concerning themselves may be completely performed, in both spiritual and physical things. And these move the divine heart towards themselves with such great efficacy that **when the proper time** foreordained by the Lord **has arrived,** they will receive a flood of divine delight as fully and delightfully as they have unreservedly entrusted themselves to his will. But by those who were trying to draw something through the Lord's other limbs are signified those who according to their own desire attempt to win certain gifts of grace or fruits of virtues **from the Lord**, following the disposition of their own good pleasure. The more they rely on their own will, and the less they entrust themselves to divine Providence, the harder they have to work for what they desire.

---

[3] *Hos qui* L, i.e., masculine gender.

1. Before the feast of the Lord's Nativity, she offered the Lord her own heart in these terms: "Here is my heart, Lord, withdrawn from every created thing; I **present** it to you with my whole will, praying you to wash it in the virtuous water of your most sacred side, and to array it most fittingly in the precious blood of your sweetest heart, and to make it most becomingly fit for you in the warm spicy breath of your divine love." The Son of God appeared, offering God the Father her heart united with his own divine heart in the likeness of a chalice, its two parts joined together with wax. When she saw this, she said to the Lord with suppliant devotion, "Most loving God, grant that my heart may be always at hand, like the flasks that are brought for lords' refreshment, so that you may always, as you please, have it clean for pouring in and pouring out whenever you wish, for whomever you wish." The Son of God kindly accepted this and said to the Father, "Holy Father, may this heart pour out, to your eternal praise, all that my heart contained for dispensation in my human nature." From then on, when she quite often offered her heart to the Lord through the words written above, it seemed to her that it was replenished sometimes in such a way that its outpouring through praises and thanksgivings was fit for the increase in joy for the dwellers of heaven, sometimes in such a way that it was also suitable for those on earth, for their progress, as was clear from what follows. For she understood from this time on that it was the Lord's pleasure that she should **write down** such things for the profit of many.

<LDP III.30.22> 1. Once, when she was turning over in her mind the trials of her past life, she asked the Lord why he allowed her to be troubled at that time by certain people. She received this reply from him: "When the father's hand wants to correct his son, the rod cannot resist him. So I would like my chosen never to blame the people by whom they are purified, but always regard my fatherly love. For I would not allow **even** the lightest breeze to blow against them if I were not looking to their eternal salvation, which they shall receive in reward. But let them feel compassion for those who for the sake of their own purification are sometimes defiled."

<III.30.3> 2. **Again, through the response** in Advent, "Behold, the Lord our protector will come, the Holy One of Israel, **having the crown on his head,**"[1] she understood that if anyone is disposed with her entire will to desire in her heart that every section of her life, both in prosperity and in adversity, should be ruled according to the most praiseworthy will of God, with such a thought by the mediation of God's grace she confers as great an honor on the Lord as he who places the royal crown on his head confers on the emperor.

<LDP III.30.4> 3. Again, from that verse that is read in Isaiah, *Arise, arise, stand up, O Jerusalem,* **you that have drunk at the hand of the Lord the cup of his wrath; you have drunk even to the bottom of the cup of dead sleep, and you have drunk even to the dregs,**[2]

---

[1] Response for second Sunday in Advent.
[2] Isa 51:17; antiphon for Tuesday, third week in Advent.

and so on, she understood the profit that accrues to the church militant from the devotion of the chosen, specifically when a single loving soul turns with its whole heart to the Lord, with its entire intention that, if it had the power, it would most gladly make reparation to God for every injury that is a detriment to his honor, and thus, burning with **loving** torches in prayer, it clings caressingly to God, it pleases him so much that at length he is conciliated and spares the whole world **for the sake of a single man**. This is what is meant by the words, *You have drunk even to the bottom of the cup.* For by such means the severity of justice is completely transformed into the serenity of mercy. But by the words that follow, *You have drunk even to the dregs*, it is implied that there can be no redemption for the damned, who deserve the dregs of justice.

<LDP III.30.23> 4. **Again,** another time, because of the difficulty of **something**, she was saying to God the Father, "Lord, I offer you this task through your only Son, in the power of the Holy Spirit, to your eternal praise." Through her understanding she sensed the power of these words, specifically that for this intention she was miraculously ennobled above human reckoning, and whatever was offered **through that** became acceptable to God the Father. To provide a comparison, just as anything seen through green glass appears green and anything seen through red glass appears red, and so on, anything offered through the Only-begotten **appears** most pleasing and acceptable to God the Father.

<LDP III.30.24> 5. **Again, while** she was asking the Lord in her prayer what good it did her friends to pray for them so often, when she saw in them no **result** from her prayer, she was instructed by the Lord by this analogy: "When a little child is brought back from the emperor endowed with vast estates, which of the onlookers immediately sees any fruit of that endowment in the boy's appearance? Nonetheless it is no secret to the witnesses what sort of person he will be, and how great, from the riches granted him. Therefore do not be surprised that you cannot physically discern the fruit of your prayers, which I lay out to their greater benefit according to my eternal wisdom. The more often a prayer is made for someone the more greatly he is blessed, for no fruitful prayer will remain fruitless, although its manner of fruition remains hidden from humans."

<LDP III.30.5, lines 1--3> 6. Again, from that verse in Isaiah, [*If
. . .*] *you glorify him, while you do not <go> your own ways, **and
your own will is not found to speak a word, then will you be delighted in the Lord, and I will lift you up above the high places of
the earth, and will feed you with the inheritance of Jacob your
father*,[3] she understood that anyone who orders his words and deeds
by deliberate thought, and nonetheless considers that there is no
utility in them and refrains from what he would perhaps have liked,
obtains from this a threefold blessing. First, that it is given him to
take a more pleasing delight in God, as it says, *You will be delighted
in the Lord.* Second, that harmful thoughts **have** less power against
him, as it says, *I will lift you up above the high places of the earth.*
Third, that in the life eternal the Son of God imparts more fully to
him than to others the fruit of his most holy life, in which he resisted
every temptation with noble victory and conquered gloriously, as it
says, *And I will feed you with the inheritance of Jacob your father.*

<LDP III.72.4> 7. Since it is human to pray more often for the
sick, once when she was about to pray for a particular sick man she
asked the Lord what **prayer would greatly please him to be made**
on behalf of **the sick man**. The Lord replied, "Just say two prayers
for him with devout heart, that is, pray that I may preserve his patience. Second, pray that every moment during which he is to suffer
I may lead him to more welcome praise of me and more useful profit
for the sick man's salvation, according to what from eternity charity
has pre-ordained in my fatherly heart." And the Lord added, "As often
as you repeat these words, you increase both your own merit and that
of the sick man, just as when a painter paints over a picture the
original color is intensified."

<LDP III.30.5, lines 13–20> 8. Again, in the words of Isaiah,
Behold his reward is with him,[4] she understood how the Lord himself
in his love is the reward of the chosen, presenting himself so sweetly
that the mind of the lover can assert with utmost truth that he is rewarded most worthily, far beyond every desert. *And his work is before*

---

[3] Isa 58:13-14.
[4] Isa 40:10.

him,[5] **that is, he who** entrusts himself totally to divine Providence and desires the will of God **in his own heart** already, by the grace of God, appears perfect in the eyes of God.

<LDP III.30.6> 9. Again, from the verse *Be sanctified, sons of Israel, **and be prepared***,[6] she understood that if anyone, in true penitence for all her sins of omission and commission, with her whole heart bows in obedience to the commandments, in the eyes of God she is truly found sanctified and prepared, just as that leper was purified to whom the Lord said, *I will: be made clean.*[7]

<LDP III.30.25> 10. Again, as she wished to know what would be the fruit of directing one's thoughts to God, she was taught as follows: when someone directs his thoughts to God in meditation or reflection, before the throne of glory he presents to **the Lord** a mirror, as it were, of wonderful brightness, in which the Lord gazes most gladly at his own image, for he is the dispatcher and director of all good things. When a person sometimes toils with some difficulty at such tasks because of obstacles, the harder he toils the more delightfully that mirror appears adorned in the sight of the Trinity, ever to be worshiped, and of all the saints. And this shall remain forever to the glory of God and the perpetual exultation of his soul.

<LDP III.30.26> 11. Again, **on the feast of the Lord's Nativity** when she was prevented from chanting by a headache, she asked the Lord why he quite often allowed this to happen to her on feasts. She received this reply: "Lest perhaps raised up by the pleasure of harmony you should be found less fit for my grace." She replied, "Your grace, Lord, could **well** prevent that lapse in me." The Lord said, "It is more profitable for a person that the opportunity for a lapse be removed through the crushing weight of troubles, for from that her reward is doubled, that is, for patience and for humility."

<LDP III.30.7> 12. Again, through the verse *Sing to the Lord a new song*,[8] she understood that everyone who sings with devout con-

---

[5] Isa 40:10.

[6] Response for the vigil of the Nativity.

[7] Matt 8:3.

[8] Isa 42:10; used on numerous occasions, including the Nativity.

centration sings a new song to the Lord. For being already renewed because he receives grace from God by which he is able to concentrate on him, he will be acceptable to God.

<LDP III.30.8> 13. Again, from the verse *The spirit of the Lord is upon me,*[9] and later, *That I may heal the contrite of heart,*[10] she understood that since the Son of God had been sent by the Father to heal the contrite of heart, he was accustomed to make contrite his chosen with some burden, sometimes small, even concerning external matters, so that he might have an opportunity **to heal** them. But when he has turned to the soul for that reason, he does not heal that burden by which the heart is perhaps made contrite, for it is not harmful, but rather he heals whatever he finds in the soul that is damaging.

<LDP III.30.27> 14. Again, drawn one day by excessive love, she was saying to the Lord, "O, would that I had such a fire, Lord, that my soul could be melted like a completely liquefied substance, so that I could pour it all the more precisely into you!" The Lord replied, "Your will is such a fire for you." From these words she understood that a person possesses through her will the full effect of all desires that look towards God.

<LDP III.30.9> 15. Again, from that verse *In the splendors of the saints*[11] she understood that the light of the Godhead is so great and so incomprehensible that if each of the saints, from Adam up to the most recent, singly perceived a single insight so bright, profound, and extensive that no creature could ever possibly grasp it, so that no one could **participate** in their own insight with another, even if the company of saints were a thousand times larger, nonetheless the Godhead would remain unspent forever, beyond all reach of understanding. And this is why it does not say "in the splendor" but *in the splendors of the saints; from the womb before the day star I begot you.*[12]

<LDP III.30.10> 16. Again, while they were chanting of a martyr, *If any man will come after me,* **let him deny himself, take up his**

---

[9] Isa 61:1; used at various times in late Advent.
[10] Isa 61:1.
[11] Ps 109:3; chant used at Christmas.
[12] Ps 109:3.

cross and follow me,[13] she saw the Lord walking along a path charming with green growth and the beauty of flowers, but narrow and harsh with the thickness of thorns. She saw the likeness of the cross go before him, conveniently making the path wider by a separation of the thorns from each other, and she saw **the Lord** turn back with a serene countenance, inviting those behind him and saying, *If any man will come after me*, and so on. In the midst of this she understood that to each one their own trial is their own cross. For instance: for some the cross was that they were compelled by the goads of obedience to something that went against their wishes, but for others, that they were hampered from what they wanted by the burdens of weakness, and thus other people have other trials. Everyone must take up their own cross to show their willingness to suffer gladly what goes against their wishes, and nonetheless as far as possible let them not neglect to fulfill anything they know to be more praiseworthy to God.

<LDP III.30.28> 17. **Again,** since she often strove to obtain from the Lord by her prayers the eradication of vices, both in herself and in others, it often seemed to her that she could not entreat it more completely than to ask that the loving-kindness of God would mitigate that compulsion that results from evil habit—that is, that he would make it as easy for her to resist vice as if no difficulty had accrued from habit, which is called "second nature." For in this too she recognized the admirable plan of the divine loving-kindness concerning the salvation of the human race: for in order that an accumulation of eternal glory may accrue to someone more fully, he allows him to be quite heavily attacked by very many vices so that he may the more happily exult in his triumph.

<LDP III.30.29> 18. **Again,** she had heard this statement enunciated, that **certainly** no human being is saved without the love of God, **which the one to be saved** must at least **have from God, so that** out of love he may repent and refrain from sin. She therefore reflected in her heart that many depart this world who seem to repent more out of fear of hell than love of God. The Lord **slipped into her thoughts**, "When I see on their deathbeds those who have ever been

---

[13] Matt 16:24.

sweetly mindful of me, or have done some good work, in the very throes of death I manifest myself to them as worthy of love with such kindliness that they repent from the depths of their heart ever having offended me, and thence they are saved at that moment through such repentance. Therefore I would wish to be glorified by my elect for that courtesy, specifically that among my generic acts of kindness they should thank me also for that particular one."

<LDP III.72.5> 19. **Again, when from time to time she prayed** for certain office holders, she understood that quite often the Lord took greater pleasure in those office holders who held the status of prelate, in that although they had it, they were *as if they had not,*[14] that is, they exercised the power of prelature as if it had been granted them for a day or an hour, and were always ready to give it up at any moment. However, they were often concerned about the usefulness of their work, how they could to the best of their abilities gain the greatest praise for God, as if always saying in their heart, "Come on, hurry! Do not fail to do this for God's praise, and then gladly lay aside the burden of office when you have performed to the best of your ability everything you know is a source of praise for God and of salvation for your neighbor."

<LDP III.30.30> 20. **Again,** sometimes while meditating she began to recognize her inner ugliness and to **be** so dissatisfied with herself that, anxious and troubled, she carefully considered how she could ever please God,[15] who saw so many stains in her. For where she detected one, the piercing eye of divinity perceived an infinite number. She was divinely consoled on this topic by this reply: "Love makes pleasing." She understood from this that if love has such power among earthly beings that sometimes the ugly, because of love, are pleasing to those by whom they are loved, and are also from time to time so pleasing that lovers, through the force of love, long to be like their beloveds, how then should we despair of him who is the God that is love, that he could not by the force of love render pleasing those whom he loves?

---

[14] See 1 Cor 7:29.
[15] 1 Cor 7:32.

<LDP IV.5.4–5> 21. **On the feast of the Lord's Circumcision,**[16] **while she was praying** for a certain woman who **had entrusted herself, asking** her to beg the Lord that, just as people in the world customarily give each other gifts at New Year, he would grant her fidelity to God with her whole heart, for better and for worse, the Lord kindly replied, "Because she has the will and the desire to ask such things from me, I have accepted this gift from her, which I find wonderfully welcome. But as it is also fitting for me to give her a gift in return, as she asks, let this be between her and me, both for her profit and for my pleasure, so that my share may shine to my glory and she may adorn her own share with my help minute by minute. For just as a mother while teaching her daughter constructs a piece of embroidery with her daughter's hand but with her own skill, so with my eternal wisdom I shall construct this gift by means of that person."

Also she perceived that the pearls and jewels with which a present should be adorned were holy pursuits and desires and various thoughts tending towards God, such as of the fear and love of God, of hope and joy and the like. God did not neglect a single one from which he might work the soul's eternal salvation. Then she prayed for more **of her friends, that the Lord would also give them such a New Year's gift; among these women was** one who **before the feast** had been troubled by a disturbance that <Gertrud> had caused **altogether** unwittingly, **for whom she was specially praying**. The Lord replied, "*I have enlarged*[17] her bosom through the disturbance that happened earlier, and I have made her hand more fit to receive <my gifts> fully and appropriately." Then she said, "Alas, Lord, that I, wretched as I am, was your scourge in the purification of that friend of yours." And the Lord said, "Why say 'alas'? For everyone who purifies my chosen in this way is a gentle scourge in my hand, because she did not mean to bring them trouble but wholeheartedly sympathized with them, and her own merit is increased by the purification of the other."

---

[16] January 1.

[17] Ps 4:2.

<LDP III.30.15> 22. **Again,** from the words that are chanted of John, "He has drunk deadly poison,"[18] and so on, she understood that just as the virtue of faith preserved John unharmed by poison, so the consent of the will keeps the soul unspotted, however poisonous may be what makes its way into the heart against one's will.

<LDP III.30.31> 23. Again, when she greatly desired, in accordance with the words of the apostle, *to be dissolved and to be with Christ*,[19] and on this was uttering many groans to God from the depths of her heart, on one occasion she was comforted by this reply: as often as she conveyed **as if** with her whole heart her desire *to be delivered from the prison of this death*,[20] and in addition kept steadfast her will *to abide in the flesh*[21] **as long as it pleased the Lord**, the Son of God would add all his own most holy way of life to her own way of life, and thence she would miraculously appear perfect in the eyes of God the Father.

<III.31.2> 24. Again, **one** time while wild winds were greatly afflicting the people and with the others she was invoking God's mercy again and again for this, but was aware of no result, **finally** she said to the Lord, "How can you, most kindly **and compassionate**, put off for so long the desires of many when I, although unworthy, have such confidence in your loving-kindness that <I believe> I alone could sway your mercy to greater things?" The Lord replied, "It would not be astonishing that a father allowed his son to ask him for a penny, if each time he had a hundred marks set aside for his son. Thus do not be astonished that I put off hearing you all in this matter, for each time you pray **to me** for it, even with the least word or thought, I put aside for you far more than a hundred marks from the treasures of heaven!"

---

[18] From the sequence for the octave of Saint John the Evangelist, "Verbum dei, deo natum," *Analecta Hymnica Medii Aevi*, vol. 55, ed. Clemens Blume (Leipzig: O. R. Reisland, 1922), Nr. 188.

[19] Phil 1:23.

[20] See Rom 7:24.

[21] Phil 1:24.

<III.30.32> 25. **Again,** one day, when she was reflecting on the many varied graces infused in her from God's generous loving-kindness, she **considered** that she was wretched and unworthy of every good thing. For she had received so many countless gifts from God but had **lost** them so carelessly that it seemed she had harvested *no fruit*[22] whatsoever from them, neither in herself through fruitfulness or through thanksgiving, nor in others among whom, if they had known of it, there would have been a reason for edification **or thanksgiving,** or improvement of divine knowledge. She was **divinely** comforted on this point by this insight: sometimes the Lord does not pour forth the gifts of his graces on his chosen in such a way that he demands that they harvest worthy fruit from every single one, since human frailty often prevents this. But since the overflowing generosity of God cannot contain itself, even though he knows that a person is unable to make use of every single one, nonetheless he assiduously heaps up the accumulation of graces, that in this way he may grant to that person accumulation of blessedness in the future. Similarly as often happens with earthly **gifts**—which are sometimes granted to a little child who does not know how to expect any use from them, so that later on as an adult he may have an abundance of goods—so the Lord, when he bestows a grace on his chosen in this life, is preparing for and granting them some of that eternal fruition with which they will be blessed in heaven.

[22] Luke 8:14.

1. Another day when about to communicate, she drew back from it even more than usual because of her unworthiness. She implored the Lord to receive the holy Host on her behalf in his own person and incorporate it with himself and **from there** breathe into her out of the noble respiration of his most delightful breath, minute by minute, as much as he knew was appropriate to her littleness. Thence when she had rested for a while in the bosom of the Lord, as it were beneath the shadow of his arms, in such a way that her left side seemed to lean against the blessed right side of the Lord, a little later she raised herself up and perceived that from the loving wound in the Lord's most holy side she had contracted a pink scar on her left side.

2. After this when she was approaching to **take the life-giving nourishment**, the Lord himself seemed to receive that sacred Host with his divine mouth. Passing through his inmost being it emerged from the wound in **his** most holy side and, like a dressing, fitted itself over that same life-giving wound. Then the Lord said to her, "See how this Host unites you to me in such a way that it covers up your scar from one side and my wound from the other, and becomes a dressing for both of us. You should change this dressing every day, as if cleaning it, by reciting devoutly the hymn 'Jesu, our <redemption>.' "[1] After this it was his pleasure that, in proportion, as it were, with the growth of her desire, she should increase her devotion day by day, so that on the first day she read the hymn once, on the second she read it twice, and on the third day thrice, until the day when she again received communion.

---

[1] Ancient hymn for the feast of the Ascension.

1. Another day, when she was about to receive communion the desire came upon her to plunge herself into the deepest valley of humility and lie there hidden, out of reverence for that astonishing courtesy by which the Lord shares his precious Body and Blood with his chosen. Then that deepest humiliation by which the Son of God descended into the limbo **of hell**[1] to lay it waste became clear to her. Then **resting on** the union of that descent, it seemed to her that she had descended to **its** depths. And there, sinking down as much as she could, she understood that the Lord was saying to her, "In the reception of the sacrament I shall **attract** you to me in such a way that you will draw with you all to whomsoever extends the fragrance of your desires, inconceivable **beyond measure** in your garments."

2. After this promise, when at the reception of the sacrament she longed that the Lord would grant her as many souls from **the place already mentioned** as the number of parts into which the Host was broken in her mouth, and **thence** tried to break it up into very many parts, the Lord said to her, "That you may understand that *my mercies are over all my works*[2] and that there is no one who can exhaust the abyss of my loving-kindness, look, I grant that by the ransom of this life-giving sacrament **as many armies of souls may follow you as the numbers of parts into which you would ever wish to break it."**

[1] Cf. LDP III.46.7.
[2] See Ps 144:9.

1. **One day**, after she had received communion, while she was withdrawn into the inmost depths of her being, the Lord appeared to her in the guise of a pelican, just as it is usually painted, piercing its heart with its beak. When she said in astonishment, "My Lord, of what are you trying to convince me through this analogy?" the Lord replied, "To consider by what incalculable goads of love am I compelled when I offer you such an outstandingly noble gift: for if it were not improper to say so, I would rather remain dead after giving this gift than withhold this gift from a loving soul. Also, consider in what an excellent way your soul, having received this gift, is restored to life that lasts eternally, just as the little pelican chick is restored to life from the blood of its father's heart."

2. Again, one day when a sermon on divine justice was being preached at great length, she took it so seriously that she trembled and greatly feared to approach the divine sacraments. By the goodness of God these words put heart into her: "If you fail to look upon my goodness that has been shown you in innumerable ways with your inner eyes, at least see with your physical eyes that, **although enclosed in a small pyx,** I am coming to meet you. Know for certain that the rigor of my justice is thus completely enclosed in the gentleness of my mercy, which I worthily extend to the human race in the sustenance of this sacrament."

1. Again, another time but at a similar moment and on a not dissimilar occasion, his divine loving-kindness enticed her to taste the sweetness of his delight with these words: "Note the tiny form of this substance in which I manifest to you all my divine and human natures, and compare its size with the size of the human body, and from that gauge the courtesy of my goodness. For just as the human body surpasses my body in size—that is, **the form of the substance** in which I communicate myself—so my mercy and love **cause me to contract** in this sacrament that I may allow the loving soul to have the advantage over me **as much** as the human body has the advantage over my body in size."

2. **Again**, while the saving victim was being offered, the Lord again further intervened to commend his great courtesy, saying, "Do you not observe that the priest who is offering the Host has pushed up his arm band out of reverence for the sacrament, and is handling my Body with his bare hands? Understand from this that although, as is right, I look with kindly regard on those efforts that are made to my glory, such as prayers, fasts, vigils, and the like, nonetheless (even if it does not seem so to the less perceptive) I present myself to my chosen with a stronger emotion of compassion when, driven by the stings of human weakness, they flee to my mercy, just as there you see the priest's hand of flesh as more intimate **with the Host** than his arm band."

3. **Again,** another time when the bell was ringing at the reception **of the sacrament** and the chant was being intoned, feeling herself less prepared than was right, she said to the Lord, "Here you are,

Lord, coming to me already, and why have you not sent me the jewels of devotion, as you **well** could have, so that I might come to meet you more fitly prepared for you?" The Lord replied, "The bridegroom sometimes takes greater pleasure in seeing the white neck of his bride than when it is hidden with a necklace, and he takes even more pleasure in touching her well-***turned hands***[1] than in seeing them adorned with gloves. So I sometimes take more pleasure in **progress in** humility than in the grace of devotion."

4. Again, when **one day** many of the community, being prevented,[2] refrained from communion, after she had received the mysteries she was for that reason rendering the Lord more devout thanks, saying, "Invited to your banquet, I have come giving thanks **that you condescended to invite me, rather than many much more worthy, to your sacred feast."** The Lord spoke with most ravishing words, *sweeter than honey and the honeycomb,*[3] saying, "Know that I longed for you with my whole heart." Then she said, "Lord, what glory does your divinity delight to gain from my chewing your spotless sacraments with my unworthy teeth?" The Lord replied, "The love of one's own heart makes a friend's words delightful; thus I consider that, out of my own love, I delight to take pleasure in certain things that my chosen sometimes cannot appreciate."

5. Again, when she saw one of **her fellow** sisters approaching with great fear to take the life-giving sacrament and turned wearily away in indignation, the Lord gently expostulated, "Do you not consider that I am owed no less the reverence of honor than the sweetness of love? But since the failing of human weakness cannot accomplish both equally in one emotion, since you are *members one of another,*[4] it is right that what someone[5] lacks inwardly himself should be recovered through another. For instance, someone who with too much sweet love yields to less feeling of reverence should rejoice that

---

[1] See Song 5:14.

[2] *Inpediti* L, i.e., masculine gender: *impeditae*, i.e., feminine gender LDP.

[3] Ps 18:11.

[4] Rom 12:5.

[5] *quilibet* L, i.e., masculine gender; *quaelibet*, i.e., feminine gender LDP.

another, who extends greater reverence **for majesty**, makes up for her. She should in return long for that other one to receive the comfort of divine unction."

6. Again, another time, when she saw **a certain woman** trembling with fear for the same reason and was praying for her, the Lord replied, "I wish that my chosen did not think me so cruel, but would believe that **I** receive it as good, or rather as excellent, if they show me some service at great cost. For instance, someone offers **service** to God at great cost when he has no taste for devotion but still serves God in prayers, genuflections, and the like, and on this trusts in the benign **and merciful** loving-kindness of God, that he will nonetheless accept it with pleasure."

7. Again, she was praying for someone who was complaining that the infusions of the grace of devotion took place less often on the day she was to receive communion than on certain other, even ordinary days. **The Lord instructed her with these words**: "This does not happen by chance but providentially. For when I infuse the grace of devotion on ordinary days and also at unexpected times, I strive through this to raise the human heart to me, which would [otherwise] perhaps remain in its sluggish state. But when I withdraw my grace on feast days or at the time of communion, the hearts of my chosen are greatly aroused by the will of their desires or by humility. Hence such eagerness and such contrition profits more for their salvation than the occasional grace of devotion."

8. Again, another time, during the distribution of the sacrament, she strongly desired to see the Host and was prevented from doing so by the crowds of those approaching the altar. She understood that the Lord was gently inviting her: "The sweet secret that concerns us must be unknown to those who are far from me. But you—if it pleases you to know—draw near and experience the taste of that *hidden manna*,[6] not by seeing but by eating."

---

[6] Rev 2:17.

1. **Again,** on one occasion when she was lamenting in her heart that she could not have as great a desire as was expedient for God's praise, she was divinely taught that it is quite sufficient for God, when he can have no more, that a person should freely and willingly have a great desire, and in the eyes of God he has as great a desire as he would wish to have. And because that heart contains such a desire—that is, the will to have a desire—here especially does God more delight to dwell than ever a human being could **delight in** flowers of springtime loveliness.

2. After receiving communion one day, while she was meditating with what care one should guard the mouth, as it in particular among the other parts of the body is the receptacle of the precious mysteries of Christ, she was instructed by this analogy: if someone does not guard [it] from idle, untruthful, ugly, and slanderous words and so on, she comes impenitent to holy communion and in such fashion receives Christ like someone who buries a visitor on his arrival by piling up stones on the doorstep, or hits him on the head with a hard crowbar! Anyone who reads this should consider with a deep sob of compassion what congruity there is of such great savagery with such great goodness, that he who came for human salvation with such great mildness is so cruelly persecuted by those who were to be saved. It is possible to have similar thoughts about any other sin.

1. One day when, about to receive communion, she thought she was not prepared **for such lofty sacraments** and the time was already at hand, she said to her soul, "Here is the bridegroom already calling you, and how can you go to meet him, not prepared with any adornment of suitable merits?" Then pondering again much more on her own unworthiness, completely distrusting herself, and putting her hope in God's loving-kindness, she said to herself, "What **would be** the use of putting it off? Even if **it** were left to my own efforts for a thousand years, I would not prepare myself suitably, since I can have nothing of myself that can in any way lead to such a costly preparation. But I shall go to meet him with humility and trust, and when he sees me from afar, prompted by his own love, he has the power to send to meet me so that, worthily prepared, I shall be able to be brought into his presence." Going forward with this intention, she kept the eyes of her heart fixed on her ugliness and unkempt state.

2. And when she had come a little closer, the Lord appeared, looking on her with a glance of mercy, or rather of love, and sent to meet her, suitably to prepare her, his own Innocence, **[who]**[1] dressed her in a soft white shift. He sent his own Humility, by which he deigned to be associated with such **an** unworthy being, to dress her in a violet-**colored** tunic. He sent his own Hope, by which he pants and burns for the embraces of the soul, to adorn her in **a** green **surcoat**. He sent his own Love, by which he is swayed **towards a** soul, to envelop her

---

[1] *qua* L, emended to *que.*

in a golden cloak; he sent his own Joy, with which he delighted in her soul, to crown her with a jeweled crown. Finally, he sent his own Trust, by which he deigned to **rest upon** a lowly creation of frail human nature when *his delights were to be with the children of men,*[2] to provide her with shoes. And thus he brought her worthily into his presence.

3. Again, one time when about to receive communion, compelled by natural modesty she said to the Lord, "Lord, if I did not have to receive you in this sacrament in that place,[3] it seems to me that I would not want to come near it for any earthly riches." The Lord replied, "Having therefore become greatly pleasing to me because of that virginal modesty, you will be so much the more welcome to me and will experience my clemency so much the more sweetly, as can be noted through what James says in his epistle: how much more reverence is shown the man who is *dressed in fine apparel*, than the one who is dressed *in mean attire*,[4] for virginal modesty is a special adornment for the soul, inflaming my love to desire her."

---

[2] Prov 8:31.

[3] The monastery church seems to have been a public space, also used by the local parishioners.

[4] See Jas 2:2.

1. Once at the time of prayer, when presenting herself **to the Lord,** she asked what he would most like her to meditate on at that time; the Lord replied, "Stand beside my mother who sits at my side, and strive to praise her." Then she, devoutly **complying,** greeted the Queen of Heaven, **the Mother of God,** with this verse, *Paradise of pleasure*[1] and so on, praising her as the most delightful dwelling-place in which the unsearchable Wisdom of God, to whom every creature is **made known**, chose to dwell in among the pleasures of his fatherly delights. She prayed her to win for her **that** her **own** heart might **also** be made **so** charming by the variety of its virtues that God would take pleasure in dwelling in her too. At this the blessed Virgin seemed to bend down as if to plant in the heart **of the one who was making these prayers** the varied flowers of virtues: the rose of charity, the lily of chastity, the violet of humility, the heliotrope of obedience, and the like. By this she intimated how ready she is to hear the prayers of those who call upon her.

2. And when, following up **those requests**, she again greeted her with the verse, "Rejoice, model of virtue" and so on, praising in her that, more than all [other] human beings, she had ruled her household of affections, moral dispositions, senses, and all other impulses with such great care that she rendered most fitting service to the Lord who was lodging in her, so much so that she never did anything unfitting in thought, words, or deed. She prayed that she too might win the

---

[1] See Gen 2:8.

same for herself. At this the Virgin Mother seemed to dispatch her own affections in the guise of tender young girls, as if she were instructing them that they should all join the affections of the woman who was praying and should **employ** themselves in serving the Lord with them and be eager to make up for them, in case those were accomplishing less. Through this she gave her to understand how ready she is to help those who call upon her.

When this interlude had come to an end she said to the Lord, "Since you, my **sweetest** brother, became human to make up for all human shortcomings, **now recompense your most kindly Mother for me** if I have in any way performed her praises unworthily." At these words the Son of God rose up with deepest reverence, and coming before his mother he knelt and bowing his head greeted her most fittingly and most lovingly. **For she ought** to welcome the service <of one> whose imperfection was so fully recompensed by her most loving son.

1. The next day, when she was praying in similar terms, the Virgin Mother appeared to her in the presence of the Trinity, ever to be worshiped, in the likeness of a white lily with, as is usual, three petals—one upright, two drooping. By this she was given to understand that the blessed Mother of God herself is thus worthily called "the white lily of the Trinity," because above every creature she most fully and worthily received in herself the virtues of the honored Trinity, virtues that not even the least speck of venial sin had ever stained. For by the upright petal was denoted the omnipotence of God the Father, by the two drooping petals, the wisdom and goodness of the Son and the Holy Spirit, <all three of> whom she is most like. Thence also she understood from the blessed Virgin that if anyone greeting her devoutly called her "white lily of the Trinity and brightest rose of heavenly loveliness," she would manifest in him most strikingly what power she holds from the omnipotence of the Father, and what great knowledge she has for the salvation of humankind from the wisdom of the Son, and how immeasurably fertile she is in the bowels of loving-kindness from the goodness of the Holy Spirit. **And** the blessed Virgin added, "I shall also appear to anyone who greets me in this way at the moment of death in the full bloom of such great beauty that for his wonderful consolation I shall provide him with heavenly loveliness." From then onwards she decided to greet the blessed Virgin, or her image, with the words, "Hail, white lily of the shining, ever tranquil Trinity, and brightest rose of heavenly loveliness; from you the King of Heaven willed to be born, and of your milk he willed to be fed. Feed our souls **unceasingly** with divine infusions."

<CHAPTER ONE HUNDRED AND THIRTY-SIX =
LDP III.30.40; LDP III.30.34; LDP III.30.16–17>

1. Again at the time of prayer, when she once more asked the Lord what he would like her to concentrate on at that moment, the Lord replied, "I want you to learn patience." For she was strongly disturbed **at that time** for a particular reason. At this she said, "How or by what means could I learn it?" Then the Lord, taking her up to himself like a kindly teacher holding a little pupil in his lap, put before her, as if in the form of three letters, three things that ought to stimulate her to patience. At the first he said, "Ponder with what great friendliness a person is **marked out** by a king who resembles him more than all others in every way. Thence think how much my fondness towards you increases because you *suffer reproach*[1] like mine on my account." At the second he said, "Again, ponder what respect the king's greatest friend, who is most like him in every way, obtains from the household. And from this think what glory is prepared for you in heaven in return for your patience." At the third he said, "**Again, ponder** what solace comes to a friend from his most faithful friend's caressing sympathy, and from this think of the most pleasant caress with which I shall soothe you in heaven in return for the least thoughts that trouble you here."

2. Again, prevented by physical weakness, she had been for some days somewhat sluggish in concentrating **on spiritual things**. Recovering at last with heavily laden conscience, she was eager to confess this failing of hers to the Lord with humble devotion. And although she was afraid that she would have to struggle through a

[1] Acts 5:41.

lengthy period of delay before she would recover the delight of divine grace, suddenly in an instant she sensed that the goodness of God was bending over her in a most alluring embrace and saying, *Son, you are always with me and all I have is yours.*[2] In these words she understood that, although **one** sometimes fails out of human frailty to direct one's attention to God, nonetheless the loving mercy of God does not fail to count all our works as worthy of eternal reward, if only the will is not turned away from God, and a person is often sorry for all those things that gnaw the conscience.

3. From the verse "Grant, O Lord, this day **to keep us without sin,**"[3] she understood that in whatever a person entrusts himself to God, praying that he guard him from sin, even if in the hidden judgment of God it should seem to that person that he has transgressed gravely in something, nonetheless he never does transgress to such an extent that the grace of God does not sustain him like a staff, because he will always return the more easily to **pardon.**

4. While they were chanting the response "In blessing <God said to Noah>,"[4] as if in the person of Noah she stood by the Lord, demanding a blessing. When this had been obtained the Lord in his turn seemed to ask a blessing from her. From this she understood that a person blesses the Lord when in his thought he says that he is sorry that he ever offended his Creator, and demands his help to avoid it in the future. At this blessing the Lord of heaven bowed deeply with joy and showed her that she was as acceptable to him as if his entire well-being were perfected through her.

[2] Luke 15:31.

[3] From the *Te Deum laudamus.*

[4] Response for Sexagesima Sunday.

1. Again, when at the hour of prayer she commended to God all those who had entrusted themselves to her, saying, "Lord, I entrust to your divine heart all those entrusted to me, praying that out of the overflowing depths of your loving-kindness you may be present to each one according to the needs of each, and according to the extent of all their affections by which each one strives to beseech your favor through me, unworthy as I am, even though it had slipped my memory and I could not lay before you the prayers of them all." The Lord appeared, as if accepting from her very many gifts, tied up into a single bundle with a cloth. Undoing this bundle, he seemed to set out the presents on his lap and handling each of them one by one he removed any unsightliness and increased any beauty. Then taking a little from each one he handed it to the person we have mentioned. From this she perceived that the gifts just described symbolized the hearts of those who had entrusted themselves to her, in whom he had emended some shortcomings and increased their progress with her help, and then he gave her a share of all the good things that she had won for them.

1. Again, from the verse *Where is your brother Abel?*[1] she understood that the Lord requires from every religious anything done by a neighbor against religion, whose prevention he could somehow have effected, either by advising the person or by alerting his superiors. That excuse some people make—"It is not my job to correct others" and "I myself am worse than he"—does as little good before God as it did Cain, **because he** said, *Am I my brother's keeper?*[2] For everyone is bound in the eyes of God to restrain his brother from evil and urge him on to good. As often as he neglects this against **his own** conscience, he transgresses against God. Nor does it do any good that he claims it has not been entrusted to him, for this has indeed been entrusted to him by God; on that, his own conscience shows him, and if he is negligent, God will require this from his soul, sometimes even more than from the soul of the superior, who was not there or perhaps, if he was, did not notice. Thence Scripture threatens, "Woe to the one who acts; woe, woe to the one who consents."[3] He who keeps it secret incurs guilt by consenting since by exposure he could promote the praise of God.

2. From the response *The Lord has clothed me,*[4] she understood that he who **goes out to promote** religion in word or deed and rationally to defend righteousness clothes as it were the Lord in a garment

---

[1] Gen 4:9; response for Septuagesima.

[2] Gen 4:9.

[3] See Rom 1:32.

[4] See Isa 61:10; common of Virgins.

at once serviceable and richly ornamented; the Lord will reward him in the life eternal according to the generosity of his royal munificence by wrapping him in garments of joyfulness, and for increase of his reward will adorn him with a *crown*[5] of spiritual glory. But **separately** she understood that he who, in promoting religion, suffers setbacks is so much the more acceptable to God, just as a garment that warms and also covers his nakedness is the more welcome to a poor man. Even if he who promotes religion has made no progress, others putting obstacles in his way, nonetheless his reward is not diminished in the least in the eyes of God.

3. While the response *An angel of the Lord called,*[6] was being chanted, she understood how the hosts of angels, whose help can be more than sufficient, surround the chosen to protect them. But the Lord in his fatherly foresight sometimes suspends that protection to allow the chosen to be tempted in something. By this means they would be rewarded the more gloriously the more they triumph through their own strength, as the angelic guard and **God's** protection has been withdrawn.

4. Again, **from the following words, where they chant** *An angel of the Lord called to Abraham,*[7] she understood that just as holy Abraham, having extended his arm to carry out obedience, deserved to be called by an angel, so when a chosen person applies his mind because of God to some task difficult for him and brings to bear his whole will, in an instant the delight of divine grace smiles on him, and he deserves to be consoled by the testimony of his own conscience. And this is a bonus by which the totally unbounded generosity of God forestalls the eternal reward by which *everyone will receive his own reward according to his own labor.*[8]

[5] See Isa 61:10.

[6] See Gen 22:11; response for Quinquagesima.

[7] See Gen 22:15; response for Quinquagesima.

[8] 1 Cor 3:8.

1. On the Sunday on which Quinquagesima begins, while she was praying around Terce, the Lord Jesus appeared to her as he **is seen** when scourged at the pillar, standing bound between two **men,** of whom the one seemed to strike him with thorns and the other with a knotted scourge, but each was striking him in the face. As a result his face appeared so wretched that, with melted heart, all her inner organs were moved to compassion as she gazed on him, so much so that throughout that day, as often as that picture came to her mind, she could not restrain her tears; for she had never considered in her heart that one would see on earth someone of such wretched appearance as was the Lord's at that moment. For that part of his face that she saw struck with thorns appeared so lacerated that even the pupil of his inner eye was wounded, black and blue from the swelling caused by the knotted scourge. Also from the bitterness of his suffering he seemed to turn his face away, and when he turned away from one, the other assaulted him the more keenly.

2. Then turning to **the woman who saw these things,** he said, "Have you not read what is written of me: *We saw him as it were a leper*[1] and so on?" Then she replied, "Ah, Lord, how can the pain, so **wretched and** sharp, of your most tender face now be relieved?" Then the Lord said, "If anyone meditating on my passion with devout heart were pierced through love **of compassion** and in such charity prayed for sinners, that person's heart would be a gentlest dressing

---

[1] Isa 53:4.

for me, by which all that pain would be relieved." Also she understood that the two who were striking him symbolized **those who at that time were devoted to the attractions of gluttony, that is**, laypeople who openly <strike the Lord> as if with thorns, and some religious who, the more greatly they offend against their religious state, the more they <strike him> as if with knotted scourges. **And this** <they do> in the face: for as far as they can they do not [fear][2] to dishonor the sight of him who reigns in heaven. From this she understood that this is why **the account of** the Lord's passion is recited in the gospel **on this very day**, that that passion may be more devoutly honored by the special <friends> of Christ, both to the honor of the Lord and to the amendment of the church. But in particular **she understood that there is good reason that** there are two mentions of the flagellation **in the same gospel,**[3] **the manner of** which was shown her on that very day so wretchedly.

3. Then she also understood that love is so greatly commended in <the epistle> because, as the proverb says, the love of friends is proved in dire necessity. Hence on those days the Lord's special friends ought particularly to exert themselves in the love of both God and neighbor, that is, by whole-heartedly feeling compassion for God, because the little son of the gentle Virgin, so lovable and delicate, is suffering so innocently and undeservedly at the hands of those for whom he died. Also we should have compassion on our neighbors as if they were our brothers, because they are provoking so stern a judge against themselves. Hence for the amendment of both let us be particularly mindful of the benefit of the Lord's passion, for which let us devoutly give praise to the Lord, and let us pray that he may have mercy and spare those for whom he suffered.

[2] *verentur* LDP; *uiderentur* L.
[3] Luke 18:32 and 33.

1. One night she was asleep and was being delightfully visited by the Lord through a dream, so much so that it seemed to her that she was **refreshed** with more exquisite banquets from her fellowship with the presence of the Lord. Waking from this she thanked the Lord, saying, "Why, Lord, have I who am utterly unworthy deserved this more than **those** who are quite often so troubled through dreams that sometimes they even strike terror into others through their screams?" The Lord replied, "My fatherly foresight **has planned that these people should be sanctified** through suffering; if while awake they are eager to obtain ease for their bodies, and consequently deprive themselves of opportunities for reward, out of my divine loving-kindness I inflict trouble on them through their dreams so that at least in this way they may merit something." She replied, "Surely, Lord, it would not be possible for them to win this merit because they suffer unintentionally and, as it were, against their will?" The Lord then replied, "My kindness accomplishes this. For as it is seen among the worldly, people who deck themselves with glass and copper are perceived as adorned, but those who are crowned with gold and precious stones are considered much richer. So it is with them."

2. Once when she was reading the canonical hours with less concentration, she realized that the ancient enemy of the human race was there. As if in mockery he was completing the rest of the psalm, *Your testimonies are wonderful*,[1] skipping the syllables as if in a hurry. When he had finished the verse, he added, "Your Savior made

---

[1] Ps 118:129.

a good investment in giving you such quick speech that you are able to form any word you like so nicely to **anyone** you like, when in speaking to him you utter so hastily that in that psalm just now you left out so many sounds, syllables, and words!" She understood from this that **if** the cunning enemy had so carefully counted up the individual sounds and syllables in that psalm, he could bring a serious charge after death against those who are in the habit of saying the hours hastily and without concentration.

<CHAPTER ONE HUNDRED AND FORTY-ONE = LDP V.26>

1. Once in her prayer she was beseeching the Lord's mercy for the hour of her soul's passing when she received this answer from the Lord: "It would be quite inappropriate for me not to complete with a most excellent ending what I have begun well in you!" And she said, "If you had brought about my passing, Lord, at the time that, from your answers, I thought I was about to die,[1] then I believe that your grace would have found me the more ready, but as a result of the delay I am afraid that I shall be found extremely negligent because of my inertia and idleness." The Lord replied, "All things have their time in the foresight of my wisdom. Hence, whatever you did at any time, my loving-kindness would keep it safe for you, and whatever you did in addition, it would not be lost to you."

2. In these words of the Lord she understood **this comparison**: for just as it was the practice among the worldly that when some nobleman **decides** to celebrate a wedding, beforehand, while he is collecting wheat for the coming feast at harvest time the rumor spreads everywhere that a wedding is to be celebrated (so, too, when **wines are** collected at the time of the grape harvest): even though the rumor dies down among the people, these reserves, stored in a barn or wine-cellar, do not dwindle but are served up in abundance at the time of the wedding. It happens in the same way when **someone is** told by inspiration to prepare for death **and yet** it is delayed.

---

[1] See L 120 above.

<CHAPTER ONE HUNDRED AND FORTY-TWO = LDP III.30.35>

1. When she had a presentiment of weakness **before a certain feast,** she desired the Lord to **postpone** it until after the feast, or at least temper it in such a way that she should not be hindered from **the celebration of** that feast. Nonetheless, she entrusted herself completely to the divine will. On this she received the following reply from the Lord: "In that you seek this gift from me and in addition entrust yourself to my will, you lead me to a garden of delights, set with flower beds and very lovely to me. But know that if I hear you in this, that you should not be hindered from my service, then I follow you to the flower bed in which [you take greater pleasure. But if I do not hear you, and you persevere in patience, then you follow me to the flower bed in which][1] I take greater pleasure. For **now** I **seek** more loveliness in you if you have desire with suffering than if you have devotion with pleasure."

---

[1] Supplied from LDP, omitted in L through eyeskip.

1. Once when she was pondering by what rationale some abound in such richness of spirit in the service of God while others remain so dry, she **was divinely instructed by this insight, that** the heart was created by God to hold pleasures just as a pot holds water, but if the pot holding water pours it out through tiny holes, eventually it can become so empty that **it** too remains dry. So if the human heart holding pleasure pours it out through **a** physical **sense**, that is, in seeing and hearing and also doing what it wants through the other senses, it can pour out so much that the heart will remain empty of pleasure in God. Anyone could experience this in themselves, when one wants to see something, or speak a single word in which there is little or no profit: if one does it at once one thinks nothing of it, for it slips out like water. But if one determines to hold it back for God's sake, it grows in one's heart so much that one can hardly control it. Thence when a person has learned to control themselves in such matters, they become accustomed to delighting in God, and the harder the effort to do this, the more fruitfully they begin to take pleasure in God.

2. One time she was praying for those entrusted to her **and for her special friends,** and remembering one person before others with greater affection, she said to the Lord, "Hear me, kindest Lord, according to the sweetness of your fatherly affection, when I pray for her." The Lord replied, "I do hear you often, whenever you pray for her." She said, "Why then does she call on me so many times with such hesitant words, as if she never receives any comfort from you but is always conscious of her own worthlessness?" The Lord replied,

"This is my bride's most fastidious demeanor, with which most of all she provokes my affection towards **you**, and her most elegant apparel, in which she is pleasing to me, that she should be so dissatisfied with her own state. And the more you pray for her, the more this increases in her."

3. Again, another time when she was praying for her together with another, the Lord replied, "I have drawn them closer to me; hence it is very necessary that they should be purified by troubles, like a favorite daughter who, because of her tender love for her mother, wants to sit **only** on a seat as high as her mother but must sit less comfortably than the other daughters, who choose their own seats near their mother. Nor could the mother's fond glance be aimed at her as directly as at those who sit opposite her."

4. Once when she had been most unbearably oppressed about some **very** trivial matter, **just as the Lord best knows to inflict an enormous burden on his chosen, sometimes about a very small matter,** she offered up **this** desolation of hers to God to his eternal praise at the elevation of the Host. Thence the Lord seemed to draw **that very** soul to him through that sacred Host, as if *through a lattice,*[1] and she seemed to be reclining sweetly on the Lord's breast, and he courteously spoke these words: "In this reclining you shall breathe free from every annoyance. But whenever you go away, bitterness of heart will seize you again as a healthy antidote."

---

[1] See Song 2:9.

<CHAPTER ONE HUNDRED AND FORTY-FOUR =
LDP III.23>

1. One day when she was taking part in the Mass as devoutly as she could and it had reached the *Kyrie eleison*, it seemed to her that the angel appointed her guardian by God caught her up in her arms like a little child and presented her to God the Father to be blessed, saying, "Bless your little daughter, Lord God the Father." At this, when God the Father said nothing for a while as if he considered it beneath him to bless such a little thing, she examined herself and began with shame to turn over in her mind her worthlessness and unworthiness. Then the Son of God rose up and handed over as recompense the totality of his own most holy way of life. Then it seemed to her as if she were decked out in splendid, elaborate garments and thus had grown up *to the measure of the fullness of Christ.*[1] Then God the Father, too, bent down with most kindly readiness to be appeased and gave her a threefold blessing with threefold remission of all her sins of thought, word, and deed that she had committed against his omnipotence. Then in thanksgiving she offered God the Father all the most holy way of life of his Only-begotten, **and** then every single jewel with which her clothes **appeared** to be adorned, combining together, seemed to make resound a most pleasing and delightful melody in everlasting praise of God the Father. By this she was given to understand **that it is** most welcome to God the Father when someone offers him the most perfect way of life of his **Only-begotten**. After this the angel mentioned above presented her in the

---

[1] See Eph 4:13.

same way to the Son of God, saying, "Son of God, bless your **little** sister." From him too she received a threefold blessing in remission of all that she had committed against the wisdom of God. Finally he presented her to the Holy Spirit, saying, "Lover [of humankind],[2] bless your betrothed." By him too she was given a threefold blessing in remission of all the **things** by which she had offended against the goodness of God. Therefore anyone **to whom it was pleasing to be blessed** can concentrate on these nine blessings at the *Kyrie eleison.*

[2] LDP, not in L.

<CHAPTER ONE HUNDRED AND FORTY-FIVE =
LDP III.30.38>

1. Once when exhausted, her powers failing, she said to the Lord, "What must be done about me, Lord, or what do you intend to do with me?" The Lord replied, "Just as a *mother comforts*[1] her sons, so shall I comfort you." And the Lord added, "Have you not seen a mother caressing her son?" When she **remained silent**, failing to remember, the Lord reminded her that about six months before she had seen a mother caressing her **son**. He particularly **caused her to remember** three things that she had not noticed at the time she saw them. First, the mother often asked the little boy for a kiss, at which **with a great effort** the little boy tried to stand up in spite of the feebleness of his limbs; He added that she should raise herself, with an effort, through contemplation of his most delightful love. Second, the mother tested the little boy's will, saying, "Is this what you want? and is that what you want?" but doing neither! So God tests a person, sometimes allowing him to anticipate troubles that never actually happen. That the person consents **with** his will, however, is quite sufficient for God and makes him worthy of eternal reward. Third, of all those present no one understood the babbling of the boy, who could not yet form words, except for the mother. So God alone understands a person's intention and judges **him** according to that—far differently than human beings, who only pay attention to outer things.

---

[1] See Isa 66:13.

1. Again, while she was praying for someone who had omitted to receive the sacrament of the Lord's Body for a trivial reason, that is, in case some people seeing her might be scandalized, she received an answer in the form of this analogy: "Just as a person who detects **some** obvious stain on the hand immediately washes the hands, but after **cleansing** not only are they **cleaned** from the obvious stain but also the hands as a whole are rendered cleaner, so it happens sometimes to my chosen. I allow them to fall into some trivial fault so that, penitent because of that, they become more pleasing[1] to me from humility. But some frustrate my kindly purpose when they neglect beauty **within**, which I shall make evident after penitence, and are eager for <beauty> without, which depends on human judgment—that is, when they do not care that they are losing my grace, which they could obtain from receiving the sacrament, just in case they should be thought rather disreputable before humans, because they seem to prepare themselves less carefully to receive the sacrament."

---

[1] *placite* L, i.e., feminine gender L; *placiti* LDP, i.e., masculine gender.

1. Again, another day when she was about to receive communion **and** in her inmost being was being invited to this by the Lord, as if she were in the heavenly palace, about to take her seat by God the Father in the kingdom of glory and eat at his table with him, she saw herself as totally unprepared for this and not at all composed and, anxious, was trying to retreat. The Son of God seemed to come to meet her, to prepare her and **lead** her to his secret mysteries. First, as if washing her hands in the forgiveness of sins, he handed over to her the cleansing power of his passion. Then he unclasped his own jewels—necklaces, bracelets, and rings—with which he appeared adorned, and hung them on her, reminding her that with them she would go forward properly and not like a foolish woman who, out of impropriety and awkwardness, does not know how to step forward and acquires contemptuous ridicule rather than respect for her modesty. By these words she understood that those with the Lord's jewels approach like fools who, while **concentrating** on their own imperfections, pray the Son of God to make it good for them, but after receiving his blessing they still remain as timid as before, because they do not have complete trust in the Lord's most sufficient and complete power to make up their deficiencies.

1. Before the feast of the Assumption, **while she had been confined to her bed for more than fourteen days through sickness, she had spent the night of that glorious solemnity completely without sleep because of her weakness. Finally, with the help of others, she got up at the time of Matins and made her way with difficulty to a place where she could hear the chanting of the choir nuns** and sat down there, **or rather lay, completely** exhausted; **nonetheless** *the dayspring from on high* visited her *in the bowels of his loving-kindness.*[1] He appeared to her during the sixth response, as if he were present in spirit at that most **sweet and** joyful festival on which the virginal Mother of God, having died, **flying up joyfully into the arms of her son,** sought the heavenly realms. Therefore from the sixth response already mentioned, that is, "Above health <and all beauty>,"[2] until the end of the *Te Deum*, when she came to herself, **as she ventured to assert with complete certainty**, in every **phrase** that was chanted she received a special insight of wonderful delight. Let me expound a few from among many, as far as they can be expounded to others' understanding **in the words of others**. For that response "Above health" seemed to be chanted by the combined

[1] Luke 1:78.

[2] See Wis 7:10: *Super salutem et omnem pulchritudinem dilecta es a domino, et regina caelorum vocari digna es; gaudent chori angelorum consortes et concives tui,* "Above health and all beauty you are beloved by the Lord, and you are worthy to be called the Queen of Heaven; choirs of angels rejoice with you as your companions and fellow-citizens."

forces of angels and apostles, **and other saints**, rejoicing with their lady for such unique privilege of rewards. During this the **noble** Virgin, drawn by inconceivable delight, left the confines of her body and was welcomed into the sweetest embraces of her son. That most kindly *father of orphans*,[3] taking on the role of his **chosen** bride, the church, and as if wishing to entrust <Gertrud's> neediness, so deeply hidden in his heart, to <the Virgin's> maternal tenderness as well, intoned on her behalf the seventh response, "Saint beloved to God." **This can be confirmed by the fact that on that feast the church repeats these words, "Whom you have taken away from this life, so that she may faithfully intercede for our sins."**[4] Then, as if **they were** preparing to process, the Son, who was swayed by more tender love towards his mother, seemed also to extol her with more frequent praise. And so he greeted her with the eighth response, "Hail, Mary, **jewel of purity**." Following him the company of saints added, "Hail, merciful mother of Christians" and so on. Then Jesus **once again**, as if **concerned for** his bride the church, added in a clear voice, "Virgin, consolation of the desolate," and so on.

2. Next when at the canticle[5] *Hear me, you divine offspring*[6] the blessed Virgin seemed to enter heaven with indescribable jubilation, all the court of heaven seemed so moved at the unparalleled nature of such wonderful exultation that human language could not describe it. For she appeared to enter a meadow, most delightful beyond all human comprehension, full of all kinds of flowers, **so much so that there seemed to be no place, however small, that was not sending out the new growth of a special flower**. Then when that verse was being chanted, "And bring forth leaves in grace" and so on, to welcome their one and only queen, all those flowers sent out from each and every petal a specially delightful splendor and pleasure of sweetest **perfume**, and also so bright and joyful a sound, as if **all the**

---

[3] See Ps 67:6.

[4] From the Secret for the vigil of the Assumption.

[5] Sir 39:17-21, sung as a canticle at Matins on feasts of the Virgin. See LDP IV.48.10, n. 18.

[6] Sir 39:17.

sounds of organs, trumpets, and every musical instrument, together with all the bells, seemed to be making sweetest melody together. Then the blessed Virgin, as if rejoicing and exulting in her unmatched blessedness, sang, *I shall greatly rejoice in the Lord*[7] and so on. **Celestial joy completely enveloped her <in that blessedness> and, as if** *pouring over her head*[8] *torrents of divine pleasure,*[9] **totally permeated and immersed her.** Then God the Father, as if well pleased in the many-faceted perfection of the graceful Virgin, **who, having been fostered on earth, had reached the heavens in such surpassing beauty of virtues,** blessed the church on earth with **the superabundant** sweetness **of his kindliness** through the third canticle,[10] *You shall no more be called forsaken*[11] and so on.

3. After this, in praise of the Virgin Mother the whole **company** of angels burst out, singing loudly, "There are three score queens,"[12] indicating that the Virgin Mary was **chosen** above their ranks. Then the choir of the saints added, "And four score concubines," also proclaiming that the **glorious** Virgin was privileged above **all women.** Then both **companies**, that is of angels and saints, representing the church on earth, chanted, "And young maidens without number," through this too extolling **her** above themselves, as is most fitting. Then the Holy Spirit, the Paraclete, added with sweetest melody, "One is my dove," as if to say, "I have found this woman uniquely like myself, in whom I could be pleased to rest." Then the Son added, "My perfect one," as if to say, "Everything that I hoped to find in both my human and divine nature have I found most perfectly in her." To this God the Father added, "She is the only one of her mother, the chosen of her that bore her"; as if unwilling from excess of love to conceal what he himself felt for her, he revealed that she is the **uniquely** chosen of her mother, that is, of the church.

[7] Isa 61:10; another canticle. See LDP IV.48.10, n. 20.

[8] See Lam 3:54.

[9] See Ps 35:9.

[10] As above. See LDP IV.48.10, n. 21.

[11] Isa 62:4-8.

[12] This and the five chants that follow make up the antiphon for Lauds of the octave of the feast of the Assumption: see LDP IV.48.11, n. 22. See also Song 6:7-8.

4. Then with the melodious praise of the whole court of heaven, at the response, "Hail, noble <rod of Jesse>," she was **placed** on the throne of glory **at** the right hand of the Son with fitting honor. And after this all the citizens of heaven, fittingly united before the throne of the kingdom, from an outpouring of most abundant acclamation extolling her praiseworthy life, were chanting with indescribable jubilation the response, "You are blessed, Virgin Mary." To this the **blessed** Trinity added **a little verse, that is**, "Hail, Mary," renewing in her the sweetness of that angelic greeting that was the most saving prologue to all its work of salvation. Again the choir added, "Behold, you are raised up," praying that she should intercede for the church on earth. After this **the Lord** God the Father, delighting to extol her with more specific praise because she was **uniquely** pleasing to him in her beauty, was chanting **with sweetest melody**, "Hail, bride." To this the Son added: "Sunamite <bride>, after the heart of the supreme King," and the Spirit added, "Hail, **Virgin Mother**." The Son added, "the Holy Spirit bearing witness." Then all the company of the saints added, "You once <saved> Mary,[13] made loathsome by a thousand Egyptian vices." Then the choir of angels added, "You reconciled the despairing apostate Theophilus[14] to your son [and][15] to grace." Then **they all** at once in the name of the church on earth knelt before the blessed Virgin and chanted **the verse**, "O holy, O lofty," and so on. After this, the whole Trinity, bursting out of the profound superabundance of favorable joy and **moving all heaven** to astonishment, was chanting most clearly the twelfth response, "Who is this?" making known all the merits of the **glorious** Virgin.

5. Finally she perceived that in return for her beatification the most blessed Virgin herself was chanting with all the host of heaven, *We praise you, God,* to the glory of the ever-worshipful Trinity. The first verse, "We praise you, God," extolled the whole Trinity all at once;

---

[13] Saint Mary of Egypt, a penitent courtesan.

[14] Saint Theophilus the Penitent, who traditionally made a pact with the Devil but repented: the Virgin appeared to him and returned the pact, which was then torn up and publicly burnt.

[15] LDP; *om.* L.

the second verse, "You, the eternal Father," particularly extolled God the Father; the third, "To you all angels <cry aloud>," the Son; the verse, "To you the Cherubim," the Holy Spirit. And in this way each Person [was extolled][16] by a particular verse, with the exception of those seven verses, "You are the King of Glory" and so on, which **she** specifically **applied** to the Son of God, praising him for each of her affections[17] because, with his help, she always directed them to divine praise and never diverted them to transitory things. The following verses, that is, "Make <them to be numbered with your saints in glory> everlasting," once again extolled each Person in turn. Through all this, such insight was granted **to that sick woman** that each verse attributed to the Father was so peculiarly appropriate to him that it could not possibly seem to be otherwise. It was the same with those attributed to the Son and also to the Holy Spirit. After this, when she returned to herself, she also sensed that her body was so refreshed **and strengthened** from this most joyful solemnity in which she had participated in spirit with wonderful delight that, **casting aside the stick on which she had earlier relied, which had not been enough unless she was in addition supported by the hands of those who were caring for her,** she outstripped all those who were helping her so quickly that she was completely unaware of any weakness. **Rather, it seemed to her that no labor was so difficult that she could not overcome it at that moment.** And this good health lasted until she was refreshed with physical food after Mass. **After this, wishing to get up and leave, she fell to the ground as if lifeless, where she lay for some time while her strength could not be restored by any physical refreshment. At last she was carried to her little bed more like someone about to die than to live, and was subsequently confined to bed for some days, and was also unable to lift her head from the pillow.**

6. In the power of the Godhead, from the innermost depths of my soul, most loving God, I praise the incomprehensible immensity of your inestimably sweet divine plan for the salvation of the

---

[16] LDP; *om.* L.

[17] *affectiones*: see LDP IV.2.6, n. 6, on the seven "affections" of the soul.

human race. For to increase the reward of your chosen ones, during the foretastes of contemplation, so much to be honored and worshiped, by which the loving soul delights to be united to you, you allow it, although guiltless, to be subject to human judgment. I experienced this on that occasion in that woman who, when the force of your unconquerable love drew her sweetly to you, did not in the least escape the slander of others. Humbled by this, she was immediately rendered more fit for your gifts.[18]

[18] This cryptic paragraph by Sister N, writing in the first person, perhaps hints that some of Gertrud's sisters were suspicious of these sudden and dramatic changes in her physical health.

<CHAPTER ONE HUNDRED AND FORTY-NINE
Not in LDP>

1. While she was turning to prayer in her usual way after a minor disturbance, she found her soul like a snow-white dove, resting in the Lord's bosom. The Lord said to her, "Why did you disturb your wings, my dove, ruffling them within my bosom?" She said, "Because, my Lord, I desire to experience only you in that matter,[1] and it is forbidden me." The Lord replied, "Also, my beloved, you were wishing that that book, placed directly against the wound in my side, would receive more forcefully the turbulent flow from my divine heart, from whose drops as they spurt out your soul only too often produces weeds! But let it not perturb you that you are not allowed your own way; rather, come nearer and rest between that book and my divine heart, from which you will receive abundantly as you wish whatsoever you desire from me, both for that book and for other things, nor could you be prevented by anyone." She said, *"If I have found this favor in your sight,*[2] Lord, may it enlighten me, I pray, with the understanding of what I heard just now concerning that book but did not understand: that is, 'In herself she is blind and in this blindness she sees most clearly.'" The Lord said, "That means, the more the soul is blinded in what it finds pleasing, the more it is enlightened in what I find pleasing." Greatly comforted by this, she gave thanks to the divine condescension.

---

[1] That is, the recording of her revelations.
[2] See Esth 7:3.

<CHAPTER ONE HUNDRED AND FIFTY **Not in LDP**>

1. Once, sick in body, she was passing a cross, before which she was accustomed to kneel. On this occasion she thought she would omit this to God's praise, lest by tiring herself out beyond her strength she would be prevented for too long from other things. She perceived that the Lord was saying to her from the cross, "Do not kneel, for I shall kneel in your place before God the Father with all the power and profit of my passion."

<CHAPTER ONE HUNDRED AND FIFTY-ONE =
LDP IV.48.14–18>

1. Three years later, when she was once again sick and confined to bed, she was eager to apply her mind to devotion on the **awe-inspiring** vigil of the Assumption of the glorious Virgin, early in the morning at first light. **By this she could in a small way honor that feast to the praise of God and the reverence of his unspotted Mother.** She saw in spirit, as if in a most delightful garden with flowers of varied colors and pleasantly planted with fragrant spring-tide beauty, the most blessed Virgin now entering her death agony in most tranquil joy of sweetest contemplation; by the serenity of her most lovable countenance and benign bearing she showed herself **to abound most fully in** grace. In the garden **could be seen in particular** most beautiful roses without thorns, dazzlingly white lilies, fragrant violets, and other flowers of every kind, **as described earlier,**[1] but no weeds. Wonderful to relate, the further each flower was from the Virgin, the greater **and more worthy** seemed to be its beauty, **shape, loveliness**, fragrance, vigor, **verdure, and greenness.** As if breathing in the scent from each, one by one, the noble Virgin breathed in completely **the verdure, fragrance, and vigor** of each flower with an **indescribable** heavenly desire. Inhaling **what she had breathed in from those flowers** with inconceivable pleasure, she was eagerly exhaling into the heart of her most loving son, which seemed to be opened towards her.

2. There also appeared a countless multitude of **blessed spirits, each of whom from each choir,** between the blessed Virgin's mouth

---

[1] See L 148.

and **all** the flowers **whose powers** she inhaled, were detailed to serve so great an empress while they joined in praising the Lord. **And the more distant the flowers were from the blessed Virgin, the more noble the heavenly princes that supported them**. <Gertrud> saw there too blessed John the Evangelist,[2] devoutly prostrate in prayer by the head of the Virgin, **whom the Lord had entrusted to him in the confidence of mutual love**. From him, too, the **untouched** Mother seemed to breathe in a sort of wonderful exhalation, **together with all the essences of the flowers, as said before**. Although that **sick woman** certainly took very great delight in all this, she also began to wonder what **everything that she saw** meant. Then the Lord taught her that the garden shown earlier symbolized **that *garden enclosed*,**[3] **that is**, the Virgin's **spotless body, the *gate* of which is perpetually *shut and* is not opened *for the prince*,**[4] **because the Virgin remained ever inviolate. For when the prince entered, I mean the son of the highest King, he blessed her, sanctifying her as a garden of divine delights with the power of his virtues.**

3. **Also she understood to be symbolized by** the flowers the various virtues with which the blessed Virgin was fittingly adorned **through the exertions of her human body**. By the roses, which seemed further away than **all the flowers**, more beautiful, and culti-vated with greater **care and** reverence by **the citizens of heaven, she understood were signified** acts of charity towards both God and her neighbor. The more widely <the Virgin> strove to spread them abroad, the more worthy the fruit she brought to God. The lilies that were sending out a more powerful scent and more lovely whiteness, **she perceived** signified the **fervor** of her holy way of life, **for the greater the number of religious edified by her example, the more fully she prompts the heart of the highest King to do her will.** From the fact that the blessed Virgin seemed to breathe in **through each of her inhalations** a **breath** from the heart of blessed John, she understood that, on Saint John's behalf, the royal Virgin had **brought**

---

[2] On Gertrud and Saint John the Evangelist, see LDP IV.4 and IV.16.

[3] Song 4:12.

[4] See Ezek 44:2-3.

to God a **singular** glory for each good deed to which throughout her life she was the more free to devote herself, thanks to his foresight **and protection**. And when <Gertrud> asked **the Lord** what benefit blessed John had from such <good deeds>, the Lord replied, "My heart is the more sweetly inclined to him by as many degrees of love as my mother possesses virtues that I perceived were assisted by his loving care." **She also understood through this that as often as some devout person increases his reward in spiritual zeal, his superior's reward is also somewhat increased.**

4. Then she understood that the figure of the blessed Virgin seen **lying** in the garden symbolized **that most holy** soul of the **gracious** Virgin, who, **rejoicing with every kind of delight** in the fruit of each of **her deeds and** her virtues **in which she had exerted herself**, as if drawing <it> into herself from the body with the greatest thankfulness, poured it all back into **the very source of all good things, by whom she knew that everything had been freely conferred on her**. And so throughout that day <the Virgin> seemed to lie in such **tranquil repose**, until that **sick woman** again fell into ecstasy during the first response at Matins and saw that mother, most blessed above all creation, leaning on the breast of her beloved son in that same most tranquil repose. With inconceivable delight the Son poured back again to her from his own sweetest heart, **the treasure-chest of Godhead,**[5] every fruit of the virtues that she had earlier directed at him in thanksgiving, so much the more worthy as it had been ennobled **from the power of his own divine virtue** in his divine heart. **They** [i.e., the virtues] **surrounded** her like roses and lilies of the valley, which made her **inestimably** beautiful with gracious springtide loveliness. God the Father Almighty himself seemed to **chant in heaven with sublime voice to the Virgin Mother's praise** that first response with sweetest song, saying, "I have seen her beautiful" and so on, as if making known to **all the saints** through those words how he himself knew her on earth, as a beautiful dove without stain through innocence, ascending **through humility** above brooks of waters through desire, whose indescribable perfume of sanctity was

[5] See also L 27, 51, 108, 153, and LDP III.25.

in her garments **beyond measure**, that is, in her way of life, and, like the days of the spring, flowers of roses and lilies of the valley, that is, various virtues, surrounded her.[6]

5. The Holy Spirit, adding **to this** the second response [in the name of the blessed Virgin and explaining the dignity of her most holy life, was sweetly singing, "Like a cedar."[7] Then all the saints, quickened by the impulse of such great praise, were chanting in wonder the third response,][8] "Who is she **that comes forth as the sun**?"[9] and so on; **in the same way** at each word the sick woman, **just as during the two previous responses,** received a **sweet and wondrous** insight, but **hindered by sickness, she was unable to explain it to human understanding**. And so all the saints, solemnly gathering together in reverend procession before the virginal throne of the glorious mother, extolled her in sweetest harmony with the fourth response, that is, "Rejoice, **Mary all-powerful**," because she was that "**most** powerful queen through whom the brightness of eternal light was already shining" upon them,[10] **adding that she was the one** who was about to become worthy ruler not only of earth but also of heaven,

---

[6] *Vidi speciosam sicut columbam ascendentem desuper rivos aquarum, cujus inaestimabilis odor erat nimis in vestimentis ejus, et sicut dies verni circumdabant eam flores rosarum et lilia convallium*, "I have seen her beautiful as a dove ascending above brooks of waters, whose indescribable perfume is in her garments beyond measure, and like the days of the spring, flowers of roses and lilies of the valley surrounded her": response for Matins of the feast of the Assumption; see Song 5:12, Song 4:11, and Sir 50:8.

[7] *Sicut cedrus exaltata sum in Libano et sicut cypressus in monte Sion quasi myrrha electa dedi suavitatem odoris*, "I was exalted like a cedar in Lebanon and like a cypress on Mount Sion; like choicest myrrh I yielded a sweet odor": response at Matins for the feast of the Assumption; see Sir 24:17 and 20.

[8] LDP IV.48.15, lines 56–48.16, line 3, accidentally omitted by L's scribe because of eyeskip.

[9] *Quae est ista quae processit sicut sol et formosa tamquam Jerusalem? Viderunt eam filiae Sion et beatam dixerunt et reginae laudaverunt eam*, "Who is she that comes forth as the sun, and fair as Jerusalem? The daughters of Sion saw her, and declared her most blessed, and the queens praised her": see Song 6:8-9.

[10] *Gaude, regina prepotens, / eterna luce prenitens*, "Rejoice, all-powerful queen, / shining forth with eternal light," *Analecta Hymnica Medii Aevi*, ed. C. Blume and G. M. Dreves (Leipzig: R. Reisland, 1886), 24:44–46.

because she was indeed the most lovely of all virgins in every beauty of virtues and perfection of graces. **They praised her also for** the fullness of her mercy, **with which** she comes to the aid of the helpless **and wretched** with her maternal loving-kindness. **They were also venerating her because she herself was** the everlasting glory **of all the saints**, while **she increased** inexpressibly the joy and glory of all by her merits. Then, reverently processing, **all** the choirs of **holy** angels [made resound][11] **with most joyful exultation** the verse "Make us joyful"[12] and so on with clear voices, as if with those words summoning her to her death.

6. After this, all the saints, **rejoicing together, chanted**, "Glory be to the Father," **to the praise and glory of the shining and ever-tranquil Trinity,** for every grace **with which it had so abundantly sanctified the most blessed Virgin in this life and was now hastening to raise her inestimably higher in heavenly delights by making her blessed.** Then **all the heavenly host** sang together **with sweetest harmony** all the antiphons and the subsequent psalms to the praise of **the Lord and the same blessed** Mother, **as far as the fifth response, that is, "They shall call me blessed."**[13] During **this**, the **worshipful** Virgin herself rose up with the greatest gratitude, **as if from the bosom of her son, on which up until then she seemed to be reclining and resting in most peaceful security, and chanted the same response with unimaginably sweet melody.** And in this way, **in such sweet rejoicing of praise and jubilation of thanksgiving**, that most holy soul, inconceivably blessed above all creation, released from the **prison house**[14] **of** flesh, amid the embraces of her spouse, leaning most gently on the arms of her son, was plunged into the very fount of all blessedness in an **incomprehensibly and** incomparably happy union, never to come out of it. Then all the court

---

[11] LDP; *om.* L.

[12] *Fac nos lætari faciemque tuam speculari plenam virtutis et dulcedinis,* "Make us rejoice and reflect your face, full of virtue and sweetness."

[13] Luke 1:48-49: *Beatam me dicent omnes generationes, quia fecit mihi dominus magna, quia potens est et sanctum nomen,* "All generations shall call me blessed. Because he that is mighty has done great things to me, and holy is his name."

[14] Cf. LDP V.1.23.

of heaven was made bright and joyful by the most welcome presence of so **indescribably** super-excellent a queen; gazing upon the soul of the tiny little Virgin enfolded with such **most** intimate audacity by the joyous embraces of **her** King **and Lord** and exalted above all the choirs of angels and saints and placed next to the ever-worshipful Trinity, they rejoiced together with a wonderful dance of **exultation. Bursting out** in her praise, **in rejoicing at her great felicity, they sang together the sixth response, reciting,** *Above health and all beauty,*[15] and so on.[16] And thus that vision disappeared.

7. From what has been written earlier, it is very clear with what care kindly God intended the gifts of grace that he generously [bestowed][17] on one person to further the salvation of **all.** For on this occasion he completed the vision where he had begun **on the same night** three years before, **making known by what courteous loving-kindness he condescended to me and others like me**[18] **who, because of our own negligence, did not deserve to be nourished by such spiritual delights.**[19] **However, lest we remain completely desolate, for us he depicted a lovely garden for contemplation of perfect things, from which we are prompted to gather at least some grain of devotion.**

[15] See Wis 7:10.
[16] See p. 291, n. 2, above.
[17] LDP; *om.* L.
[18] This is presumably Sister N speaking once more. Significantly, LDP omits.
[19] That is, by the more intellectual vision in L 148.

1. While the antiphon "In my bed"[1] was being sung, including the phrase that is repeated four times in that antiphon, that is, "whom my soul loves," she understood that there are, as it were, four ways in which God may be sought by the faithful soul. By the first, that is, *In my bed by night I sought him whom my soul loves*, she understood the first route by which God is sought, on the bed of contemplation through the extolling of praise. Then follows, *I have sought him and have not found him*, for the soul, enveloped by mortal flesh, can never be fully expanded to the praise of God.

By the second verse that follows, *I will rise, and will go about the city, in the streets and the broad ways; I **have sought** him whom my soul loves*,[2] she understood zeal for thanksgiving, by which the soul seeks "through the streets and the broad ways," that is, the various ways in which God does good to his creation, while thinking herself totally unable to render suitable praise. Hence this follows: *I sought him and did not find him.*

By the third, **in which there follows**, *The watchmen who keep the city found me*,[3] she understood God's justice and mercy, by which the recollected soul comes to herself and, considering her own unworthiness in the light of God's blessings, begins to seek the Lord's mercy through lamenting and repenting her own evil deeds while she says, *Have you seen him whom my soul loves?*[4] In this way, distrustful

---

[1] See Song 3:1; antiphon for the week following the feast of the Assumption.
[2] Song 3:2.
[3] Song 3:3.
[4] Song 3:3.

of her own merits, she turned in humble trust to the divine loving-kindness through devout prayer, and sometimes through the inspiration of grace she found him whom the faithful soul loves.

2. When the antiphon was over, as a result of this and other things that it would be impossible to commit to writing, which the divine **kindliness** granted her the grace of perceiving through the antiphon, she was aware that her heart was moved by such a powerful force that every limb was **being so greatly** moved that she seemed to have lost the strength of all her limbs. She then said to the Lord, "Now it seems to me I can truly say, 'Beloved, my beloved, not only my inward parts but all my limbs are moved on your account.'" The Lord replied, "I best perceive and know what flows from me and flows back into me. But you, still enveloped by mortal flesh, will never be able to know how, **on the other hand**, all the sweetness of my **divine nature** is moved on your account." And he added, "**I know** this, however, that from the movement of this grace you have **received** a splendor in my sight such as that which my body received on Mount Thabor before my three disciples. And so I too, moved by the sweetness of charity, may fitly say of you, '*This is my beloved son, in whom I am well pleased.*'[5] For it is always the proper accompaniment of such grace that through its workings both body and soul are miraculously illuminated with brilliant shining splendor."

---

[5] Matt 17:5.

<CHAPTER ONE HUNDRED AND FIFTY-THREE
Not in LDP>

1. One Friday, in her usual way she was concentrating on the Lord's passion and, kissing each one of the Lord's five wounds during Mass, was greeting the glorious stigmata. When at last she reached the wound in the side, to which she was praying with these words, "In this cleft me safely hide, Let my heart therein abide, Where resting it will quicken, And by anguish never stricken, Henceforth will it fear nothing,"[1] she was promptly introduced into that divine treasure-chest[2] that contains all delight. Having entered there, she immediately greeted its delightful beauty, saying, "Hail, throne of the Trinity, Ark of great charity, Prop and stay for the weak, Peace and rest for the weary, Couch for the lowly. Hail, heart of the highest King, With joyful heart I greet you; I rejoice to embrace you, And it is my heart's desire That you should let me speak to you."[3] Then the Lord said to her, "Behold, I shall make you rest in my heart in the greatest tranquility, as people customarily rest after blood-letting." She replied, "Why, sweetest?" The Lord said, "Because by sighing so often you have shed blood from your heart, drop by drop, in memory of my passion." Well! At that moment she was given five tender and most beautiful maidens, whose company she enjoyed in that repose: Love, Hope, Patience, Humility, and Peace.

[1] From *Salve, latus salvatoris*, a hymn composed by Arnulf of Louvain (ca.1200–1250) but often attributed to Bernard of Clairvaux (here trans. by Sigfrid Estborn).

[2] That is, the divine heart: see above, L 51, n. 3.

[3] Two more stanzas from *Salve, latus salvatoris* (my own translation).

2. They said to her, "We shall sing you sweetest songs, with which we will invite you to greater delight in spiritual things." Then, chanting first, with most charming melody Love sang, "Sweetest is the love of Jesus, truly the most charming, a thousand times more welcome than we can ever say."[4] To this Hope added, "Jesus has returned to the Father, my heart has gone from me, straightway it followed after Jesus, it entered the King's chamber."[5] To this Patience contributed, "I shall seek Jesus in the bed of my heart in my locked room, in private and in public I shall seek him with diligent love."[6] Then Humility chanted with a clear voice, "Jesu, flower of the Virgin Mother, love of our sweetness, to you be praise, the honor owed divinity, and the kingdom of blessedness."[7]

3. Meanwhile Peace, holding her in her arms, gently made her rest in her bosom. Then from that royal table[8] before which she had sung Vespers on the preceding day[9] in reverence for the worshipful institution of the life-giving sacrament that the Lord had bequeathed to his spouse, the church, at the Last Supper as a sign of his love, saying, *Do this in remembrance of me*,[10] Love served her for her refreshment most delicious dishes: mindfulness of that most abundant healing power with which the divine heart overflowed when at that most holy supper the bread[11] of angels[12] himself, having become food for our salvation and feeding us in wonderful fashion, uttered these sweet words from out of the depths of the treasures of his divine nature, saying, *With desire*

---

[4] *Dulcis Jesu memoria*, also often attributed to Bernard of Clairvaux, lines 41–44.

[5] *Dulcis Jesu memoria*, lines 161–64.

[6] *Dulcis Jesu memoria*, lines 21–24.

[7] *Dulcis Jesu memoria*, lines 121–24.

[8] That is, the altar.

[9] That is, on a Thursday, the day on which the Last Supper was celebrated.

[10] Luke 22:19.

[11] See L 71.1.

[12] From the hymn *Ecce panis angelorum*, composed by Saint Thomas Aquinas.

I have desired to eat this pasch with you,[13] and a little later, *Take and eat: this is my body. This is my blood which is shed for*[14] you.

4. Then Hope, wishing to ravish the ears of her soul, as if instead of entertaining tales[15] interposed what had taken place on the mount[16] where she had sung Compline the previous day in reverence for the Lord's agony: that is, how the Lord of majesty himself poured out the extravagance of his love for us, about which he could no longer remain silent, with such extraordinary words, demanding from us among other things clarity, sanctity, and perfection in union with his divinity, and how, while strength of that love struggled with the anguish of his human nature, a bloody sweat flowed from all the limbs of the Lord's body.

5. After this Patience made known to her most confident freedom, from that garden[17] in which she had celebrated Matins, for reverence of that astonishing condescension by which, for the freedom of his unworthy servants, the Lord of all was betrayed by a disciple's kiss, abandoned by all his friends, bound by terrible chains, captured by the savage hands of Jews, led to the house of Annas and from there taken to Caiphas, and suffered there so many great indignities.

6. Finally Humility brought her, as it were, a diadem of eternal honor from that place where she had sung Prime, in reverence for that awe-inspiring condescension with which the Lord himself, judge of the living and dead, was brought before the vilest of men to be judged. Hence she understood that it pleased the divine will that she should make these things known to others in praise of his name. Then she said to the Lord, "If it pleases your will, most kindly God, that I should reveal these things for the benefit of my neighbors, grant to all those who honor your passion with

---

[13] Luke 22:15.

[14] Matt 26:26, 28.

[15] That is, of the type that minstrels might tell at banquets.

[16] Presumably a representation of the Mount of Olives. It would seem that the convent church contained various "stations" representing the sites of events in the story of Christ's passion.

[17] Presumably a representation in the church of the Garden of Gethsemane.

devout sighs the promise of your special grace." The Lord kindly answered, "To anyone who has sighed devoutly with compunction from mindfulness of my passion or in some other way, I intend to grant special rest in life eternal, for there is no room in the hearts of everyone for me to grant them in the present such a reward as I have bestowed on you for your service. However, in any in whom I have found some room, I shall repay them in the present with incomparably sweet delight in return for each and every groan, and in addition I shall repay them in the future with an incalculable reward."

<CHAPTER ONE HUNDRED AND FIFTY-FOUR =
LDP IV.52.1 >

1. On **the holy day on which** the Exaltation of the Holy Cross **was celebrated**,[1] while she was bowing **with the others** to show reverence to the tree, the Lord said to her, "Consider that **although** I hung upon the cross no longer than from Sext until Vespers, **I** have exalted it with such great honor, and from that reckon up the blessings with which **I am** determined to reward **your heart,** in which **I have already reposed for fifteen** years **with more special grace.**"[2] When she replied, "Alas, Lord**,** that **my worthlessness and negligence** have allowed you to have such little pleasure **in it!**" the Lord answered, "What pleasure did I have on that cross? But my generous loving-kindness, by which I chose it above others, led me to honor it. And so in the same way I shall reward **this too, which** I have chosen **in you before others,** with generous loving-kindness."

[1] 14 September.

[2] If the figure of fifteen years is to be taken literally, and not just as indicating "a long time," this remark should date this vision to 1296.

<CHAPTER ONE HUNDRED AND FIFTY-FIVE =
LDP III.72.1–2>

1. One time, when about to pray for many people and for various concerns entrusted to her, she flung herself devoutly at the feet of the Lord Jesus and with burning desire pressed most potent kisses on those most saving wounds as devoutly as she could, while she commended to the Lord the people and concerns entrusted to her. While she was doing this she saw what looked like a little stream springing from the heart of the Son of God himself and copiously overflowing *wholly round about.*[1] From this she understood that through that little stream the Lord poured out to her all the results of the petitions that she had entrusted to him at his feet. She said to the Lord, "My Lord, what good does it **now** do those for whom I have prayed, since they themselves are not aware of the result of my requests, and so do not believe or **have** any comfort from it?"

The Lord provided this comparison: "When a king declares peace after a lengthy war, this cannot be known immediately by those who are distant, until it is announced to them at the appropriate time. In the same way those who are rather distant from me through lack of faith or other failings cannot **immediately** be aware when someone is praying for them."

2. **Then** she said, "Lord, there are others among those **women**[2] for whom I prayed just now who I know on your authority are not distant from you." The Lord replied, "You are right. But all the same

---

[1] Job 10:8.

[2] *alique inter istas* L, i.e., feminine gender; *aliqui inter istos* LDP, i.e., masculine gender.

if there were someone to whom the king wished to make his decisions known, not through a messenger but in person, he would have to wait until the time seemed opportune to the king. Thus I plan to make known in person the result of your prayers, at the time most opportune for them."

<CHAPTER ONE HUNDRED AND FIFTY-SIX = LDP V.12>

1. Once she was praying for the soul of **someone**[1] who had recently died, and when she asked the Lord where he was, the Lord replied, "Here he is. Because of the **offerings** devoutly **made** for **him**[2] at this moment, we have invited him to feast with us, to some extent, **as best he can**." Then the Lord appeared as the head of a family, sitting at a table on which there seemed to be laid out all the prayers, offerings, desires, and the like that were being made for that soul. The soul just mentioned appeared, too, sitting at the end of the table, sorrowful at heart and with downcast expression, as if not yet purified, for then he would deserve to be consoled by joyous contemplation of God's lovable countenance. But he seemed to become a little brighter because he was wonderfully refreshed from the offerings described above by something like steam coming off hot dishes that was wafted towards him.

2. **The woman who saw these things** also realized that in this there was a serious shortcoming: that soul was receiving the effect of the offerings as if indirectly and not in the way that the Lord, after having taken them into himself, would **serve** up with them perfect joy to the perfectly blessed from himself. However, the Lord, drawn by his own kindliness and by the love of the intercessors, constantly made additions of his own, **like an open-handed king who would always add some most excellent seasoning of his own to whatever his servants had prepared and placed before him,** the result of

---

[1] LDP specifies a lay brother.

[2] *ea* L, i.e., feminine. The soul is traditionally gendered feminine in Latin, but in this translation the soul is given the same gender as the living person.

which made that soul supremely joyful. Similarly, the blessed Virgin, too, sitting beside her son in imperial glory, was seen to place her own contribution on the table, and that soul received great consolation from this because he had honored her with special devotion when still living on earth. Similarly, some of the saints to whom he had shown some special respect on earth contributed from their own, according to what that soul had deserved while alive with greater or lesser labors or devotions. From all of these, but especially from the love of those praying, he grew brighter and brighter from one hour to the next and began more and more to turn his eyes and raise them towards the most joyful light of the beatifying Godhead, because to have once contemplated this with unwavering gaze is truly to have laid aside the memory of all sorrows and to have put on the abundant good things of eternal blessedness that will never fade.

3. When she saw the soul remaining in such a condition, she who was praying for him asked, "For what fault are you now most burdened?" The soul replied, "My own will and my own judgment! For when I did good, I used to take greater pleasure in carrying out my own will than another's counsel. Hence I now bear so great a burden on my conscience for this that if the burdens of all human **beings** were gathered into one, it would not seem to me like what I am experiencing." Then she said, "How could you be helped?" The soul replied, "If someone thought about me, burdened for these reasons, and was alert to similar faults in themselves, it would greatly lighten my burden." Then she said, "In the meantime, what gives you the greatest consolation?" The soul replied, "Loyalty, for on earth I was greatly intent on it. For the prayer that the faithful are offering for me is relieving my burdens from one hour to the next; <I am like> someone who is consoled by very good news. And each and every note that is sung for me during Mass or Vigils is like most delicious refreshment for me. Moreover, the divine clemency has added for me from the merits of my intercessors, so that all that they do that is directed to God's praise through virtuous intention, such as working and even eating and sleeping and so on, is also directed to my relief and continual advancement, because I was always lovingly intent on their profit with sincere loyalty."

4. Then she said, "What benefit do you gain because we have asked God that you should be granted whatever good he has performed in us?" The soul replied, "A very great benefit indeed. For where my own merits are lacking, I am adorned from yours, **like one who does not have a starched garment**[3] **but is adorned as best he may in a green or brown one**." **Then** she said, "Since you asked to be promptly assisted by the proper prayers, does it hold you back if someone who is sick puts it off until they are better?" The soul said, "**From** whatever is postponed through discretion **there** breathes on me fragrance of such wonderful sweetness that I greatly rejoice that it is deferred, as long as neither laziness nor negligence is involved." Then she said, "When you were sick unto death, and we wanted you to recover and prayed for that rather than that you should be prepared for death as to your soul, did it harm you at all?" The soul replied, "It did not harm me in the least. Rather, it brought the benefit that the more the vast kindliness of God, whose *tender mercies are over all his works*,[4] beheld you so affected through human weakness by your love for me, the more he was moved by mercy to benefit me." She said, "Do tears shed for you from human affection harm you?" The soul replied, "They do no more harm than <they would to> a friend affected by compassion for his friends whom he saw mourning for him. Indeed, when I have obtained perfect blessedness, I shall delight in <your tears>, just as a tender youth delights to see very many people congratulating him with love and friendship. And all this I deserve because that loyalty for which I earned your love was fully directed towards God."

5. After this, praying for that <soul> once again, **while** she was reciting the Lord's Prayer and was saying these words, *Forgive us our debts, as we also forgive our debtors*,[5] she observed that soul

---

[3] *starrochium* L: this appears to be a vernacular word, otherwise unevidenced, the exact meaning of which is uncertain. *Roch* means "garment or dress" (cf. modern German *rock*) and *starr* means "rigid," i.e., "starched": colored starch was used in the Middle Ages to color clothing. My thanks to Professor Racha Kirakosian for this information.

[4] Ps 144:9.

[5] Matt 6:12.

make **such** an anxious gesture **that she was greatly astonished**. When she asked what the reason was, she received this response: "When I was in the world, I transgressed greatly in that I did not easily forgive those who opposed me, but treated them sternly for too long. And so to emend this, when I hear these words I am **perturbed** by the anguish of unbearable shame." And when she asked how long this would continue, **the soul** replied, "When my fault has been purified, because of the love with which you all pray so devoutly for me, the divine loving-kindness will be at hand, and thenceforth I shall be the more thankful at those words because God's mercy has forgiven me that fault."

6. Now when the sacrament of the Body of Christ was being offered for **him** at Mass, the soul itself appeared, made wonderfully radiant and joyful. **When she saw this** she said to the Lord, "Lord, has that soul now triumphed over all that it was obliged to suffer?" The Lord replied, "He has triumphed over more than you or any human **could** imagine, even if you saw him fly up to heaven from the fires of hell. Nonetheless, he is not yet so completely purified as to be worthy to be consoled by my joyful presence. However, from one hour to the next he is consoled more and more and relieved by all the prayers poured out for him." And the Lord added, "Your prayers **are not able fully to** help him as quickly as they would do if he did not have this fault: in the world he showed himself so obstinate and unyielding when it came to submitting his will to the will of those who for some reason were asking him for something that he himself did not want."

<CHAPTER ONE HUNDRED AND FIFTY-SEVEN =
LDP V.13>

1. Although it is right that souls leaving the body should be purified from stains they acquired that they neglected to amend here, and
afterwards should be rewarded for their good deeds, nonetheless
God's merciful clemency, as so often, has now revealed its unrestrained loving-kindness. For when **someone**[1] had died who with
great daily labors had had charge of the community, all his laborious
deeds appeared in the likeness of a flight of stairs. On this his soul,
having left the body and still to be purified for some negligence, as if
climbing from one step to the next, rose higher and higher as its suffering seemed to lessen. But since it is difficult to avoid negligence
in the midst of many cares, and **since** the Lord's justice does not allow
even the least fault to remain unpunished, while he was climbing
some of the steps on that stair he trembled as if stunned, just as if
the step beneath him were giving way and threatening to collapse.

From this she realized that these were those deeds in which he
had committed some wrong, and that that fault was being purified
through the insensibility just mentioned. But when one of the community would pray for that soul in word or thought, immediately a
hand, as it were, seemed to be stretched out from above to help, and
then that soul was greatly raised up. After this she perceived that by
his loving-kindness the Lord had conferred on that community this
special privilege: as soon as those who had in life **conferred** any
benefit on it by their labors **died**, they earned the right to be consoled,

---

[1] Identified in LDP as "brother John, the convent steward."

even while their faults were being purified, for **those things**, and the community itself would retain this privilege as long as it did not deteriorate.

1. When she was offering to God every good work that the kindly Lord himself had deigned to perform through her for a dead man's soul, she saw this set out before the throne of the divine majesty in the form of very beautiful and varied **colors**. Both the Lord and all the saints seemed to rejoice wonderfully in this. And the Lord **drew it to himself** very kindly, as if delighted to have something with which he could benefit the needy who had not **deserved** their own blessings by their own actions. Then she saw the most kindly Lord add something from his most generous loving-kindness to each of the works **that she had** offered him, and thus return them to her that she might receive them doubled, in return for her good will, and keep them as an eternal reward. **From this** she perceived that a person loses nothing by helping others in charity but is richly rewarded.

1. **While** she was praying for someone who was depressed she received this answer: "Do not lose faith: I do not allow my chosen to be burdened in any way *above that which they are able*,[1] and I am also with them, weighing due measure. Just as a mother, when she wants to warm her child at the fire, always holds her hand between the fire and the child, so I who know what is suitable to purge my chosen through tribulation do not do this to burn them up but rather to test them and save them."

[1] See 1 Cor 10:13.

1. Again, when she was praying for someone whom she saw **suffering from a serious deficiency and** said among other things **with desire**, "Lord, since I, the least [of your creatures],[1] pray for that person to your praise, and since you are so all powerful that you can do everything, why do you not hear me?" The Lord replied, "Just as I have the power to do all things from my omnipotence, so I discern all things from my unsearchable wisdom. Nor do I do anything that is not fitting. Just as an earthly king who has a force of willing troops, when he wants to have his stable **cleaned** nonetheless does not by any means do it with his own hands, as it would not be fitting, so I turn no one from the evil into which he has fallen voluntarily unless he himself forces himself, changes his will, and shows himself to me as fit and proper."

2. If anyone wants to enjoy good health or be free from responsibilities solely in order to be more available to God and serve him more devoutly, and, when their wish is granted, they are eager to exert themselves in these ways as devoutly as they can, they lead the Lord into a lovely garden, as it were, in which he takes pleasure. But if anyone wholeheartedly commits their will to God and is very willing to be healthy or free to serve God if it pleases him, but if it pleases God more that they should be sick or busy, in this too they conform their will to the divine will; they follow the Lord into an even more lovely garden, in that divine Wisdom herself has chosen it, according to her pleasure. In this the soul's profit is so much the more, as God knows more than a human being how to choose what is good.

[1] LDP; L *om.*

<CHAPTER ONE HUNDRED AND SIXTY-ONE =
LDP III.87[1]; **not in LDP**>

1. A person who is stubbornly attached to his own opinion is himself a barrier that cannot admit the sweetness of **divine** grace. For when **God attracts his** chosen ones by the faint whiff of the taste of intimate love, a person stubbornly attached to his own opinion creates a barrier like that a man creates who buries his nose in a cloak so as not to catch the sweet fragrance of exotic scents. But if anyone by renouncing his own opinion for **God's** love follows another's opinion, the more difficulty he has in denying himself, the more greatly his reward is increased. For there is in this not only humility but also the power of victory. And so the apostle says, *He shall not be crowned unless he has striven lawfully.*[2]

2. The Lord himself bore witness that the highest perfection lies in this, that one should accept with equanimity everything that happens to one, whether good or bad, as ordained by God.

---

[1] In LDP the Lord himself speaks almost all of this chapter in the first person.
[2] 2 Tim 2:5.

<CHAPTER ONE HUNDRED AND SIXTY-TWO = LDP I.17;
I.11.1, lines 24–40; **not in LDP**; LDP I.10.1, line 15– I.10.2,
line 8; **not in LDP;** LDP I.10.4; LDP I.10.3; **not in LDP**>

<LDP I.17> 1. At one time the Lord had not visited her for some time. She felt no distress at this, but on one occasion when she had the chance she asked the Lord **why this had happened**. The Lord replied, "Too great a closeness sometimes hinders friends, so that they see one another less clearly. For instance, when someone is **very closely joined to** another, as usually happens with kissing and embracing, the pleasure of seeing one another is impeded for a while." She understood from these words that sometimes the withdrawal of grace increases merit **when** a person does not, through **that** withdrawal, act more sluggishly, even though burdened.

2. While she was turning over in her mind how the Lord was now visiting her with his grace in a different way from before, the Lord added, "**In earlier times** I quite often enlightened you by means of replies with which you could make known to others my good pleasure, but now when you pray it is only in your spirit that I make you feel my inspiration, which it would sometimes be very difficult to put into words; in your understanding, as if in my treasure chest, I am heaping up the riches of my **glory**, intending that anyone may find what they seek for in you; **for I would like anyone who wants to discover my good pleasure through you to be intent at all times and in all places on your words, like those of a bride who has her spouse always present** and from living with him over a long period **best** knows his wishes in all that has to be done. It would not be fitting, however, for her to reveal her spouse's secrets, **or for her to disclose to anyone the secret things done to her by her spouse,** thanks to their mutual intimacy."

3. And so she herself experienced this a little, when she realized that when she prayed for some intention, **however carefully** entrusted to her, she was quite unable to wish to **request** an answer from the Lord, as she had done earlier. It was now quite enough for her when she was **merely** aware of the grace of praying for some intention, for out of her confidence in divine inspiration she held this impulse to be as authentic as she had before held the divine answer to be. Similarly, whenever anyone sought advice or encouragement from her, she instantly felt the grace to answer flooding into her at that moment, with such great confidence that she would dare to endure death fearlessly to assert the truth of her words, although she had never before understood anything about the subject from her reading, from conversation, or even from her own thoughts. **Also,** when she prayed for some intention on which she received no revelation from the Lord, she took deep pleasure in the fact that the divine wisdom is so unsearchable and so inseparably united with kindly love that the safest thing of all is to entrust all things to it. At such times this pleased her more than if she had been able to fathom all God's profoundest secrets.

<LDP I.11.1, lines 24–40> 4. **Since she inwardly knew these things and others like them**, nonetheless in the light of **divine** truth she **judged** herself as the lowest among those of whom the prophet says, *All nations are as nothing in his sight,*[1] and earlier, *<behold the islands are> as a little dust.*[2] For just as a speck of dust lying under a twig or some such thing is hidden from the sun's rays by a sliver of shadow, so she by effacing herself did all that she could to deflect the excellence of such noble gifts of God, and to accept those gifts only because he who offered them precedes by his inspiration those whom he calls, and follows with his help those whom he justifies. For herself she retained only the guilt that, she thought, she revealed in being so ungrateful for, and so unworthy of, such freely given gifts. But with his glory in mind she could not keep silent about God's loving-kindness toward her. She was careful to bring it to the notice

---

[1] Isa 40:17.
[2] Isa 40:15.

of others with this intention in her heart: "It is quite wrong for God's goodness toward me not to produce better fruit than it can produce in **you**,[3] an abandoned and utterly worthless creature. **Thence if, in accordance with what you have deserved, as yet you should be committed to the prison of hell, God's praise and glory could nonetheless increase from this, since others who possess a similar gift and from humility consider themselves unworthy can take heart because they know that you, less worthy than all others in life and morals, have received such freely given and undeserved gifts from the overflow of the divine loving-kindness."**

<LDP I.10.1, line 15> 5. **But even though she thought of herself in this way, she nonetheless possessed such unshakable trust in God's sweetest goodness that** she never seemed so oppressed or demoralized by her own weakness as not to be encouraged by the presence of divine grace to receive whatever gifts of God for which she was rendered most ready. **For** when she seemed to herself, **from her own merits,** as dark as a dead coal, she would suddenly take on new life with the help of God's grace; when she struggled to rise up to the Lord by concentration, she would soon receive the likeness of God in herself as if in this very act of **introspection**, like someone who steps out of darkness into sunlight and is instantly flooded with light; in this way she felt herself to be flooded with the light of the **Lord's** presence. She also sensed that she had received all the lovely clothes and ornaments that befit a *queen surrounded with variety*[4] who stands before the immortal King of the ages, thus made worthy and fit for intimate union with God, **so that earth is rightly astonished and heaven wonders at God's inestimable courtesy.**

<LDP I.10.2> 6. She had nevertheless decided that it was right for her, spattered as she was with the stains that are an unavoidable part of human existence, to run frequently to the feet of the Lord Jesus to be washed. But, as we said earlier, when she was aware of a more generous influx of divine mercy, she then gave her willing consent to God's good pleasure in all things and gave herself up as

---

[3] Here Gertrud begins to address herself.
[4] Ps 44:10.

an instrument to display all the workings of love in her and with her, to such an extent that she did not hesitate to play with the Lord God of all the world as his equal.

7. **And when this happened, she discarded beforehand the thought of her shortcomings and unworthiness, like a person who puts dirty clothes just outside the door or in a corner of the house, with the intention, if the Lord allowed it, of going back and cleansing them through penitence, but [she did this] only if confident of forgiveness through God's mercy. But truly, whenever she was left to herself, she was always eager to plunge into the valley of humility and to reverence the Lord of majesty above her in highest excellence, as was fitting. However great the divine favor she experienced in this eagerness, she was unable to describe it in words, except that sometimes, sweetly swayed by its memory, she would say, "O how easily my Lord is attracted by the lowliness of humility, and how gentle the sweetness that inclines him towards it!"**

<LDP I.10.4> 8. Because of **this** trust, hour by hour **she possessed such great confidence that** she longed for death, **nor did she ever find herself so negligent or weighed down by sin that she feared to die, but always running to God's mercy and loving-kindness, she would confess her guilt. Nor did she hope to postpone her death at any time, but entrusting herself completely to divine Providence, she was convinced that,** whatever death she was to die, she would never lack God's mercy, without which she knew she could not be saved by any means, **as much in a** death long foreseen **as** sudden.[5]

<LDP I.10.3> 9. Again, from the trust we mentioned above she possessed such grace concerning the reception of communion, that reading in Scripture or hearing from anyone about the danger run by those who receive communion unworthily **did not prevent her from always saying in her heart with steadfast hope, "Lord, whenever it is possible for me to partake, I will certainly not forgo communion, but will always approach your most kindly loving-**

---

[5] In LDP I.10.4 Gertrud speaks this sentence in the first person.

kindness with confidence." She considered her own efforts so virtually null that she never **shrank from** receiving communion if she had neglected the prayers and the like with which people usually prepare themselves, judging that all human **preparation**, compared to this supremely excellent free gift, is like tiny drops compared to the vast expanse of the ocean. And although she could settle on no way of preparing worthily for communion, nonetheless she placed her trust in the [unchanging nature][6] of divine generosity as better than any preparation, and did her utmost to receive the sacrament with a pure heart and devoted love. She also used **quite often** to attribute every blessing of **special** grace that she received **so often from the divine generosity** to her trust **in the Lord**. She considered that gift to be the more freely given in that she recognized that she had truly received that noble gift of trust, freely and without any merit on her part, from the Giver of every grace.

10. Hence she cherished in her heart that trust in God's goodness, always feeling it to be from the Lord, and if from human weakness she sometimes trembled at some example of the severity of divine justice, she always attributed this to human deserts, which should by no means escape the vengeance of divine justice. As a result of this oft-mentioned trust she also possessed this gift: she did not grow sad when she lost the grace of devotion, but confident in God's most kindly plan, as if hoping for its even more fruitful return, she would exult, saying in her heart, "O Lord, what will that consolation be like for which you are preparing me through this present desolation?"

---

[6] *incommutabilitate* LDP, *commutabilitate* L.

1. While she was wondering why the Lord was **so strongly** urging her, through his Spirit, to make public what **had been** written **previously, that is, concerning trust and similar things**,[1] since she knew that some people are so poor spirited that, greatly undervaluing such experiences, they often denigrate them rather than draw any sort of enlightenment from them, the Lord taught her by these words, "I have so invested my grace in you that I demand a **greater** return from it! So I will that those who possess similar gifts, and through negligence do not realize their great value, should grow in gratitude when they hear **these things** about you. Achieving a true recognition of their own gifts, they may grow in thankfulness, and my grace may in this way increase in them. But if any, out of malice, decide to denigrate these things, let their sin be upon them while you remain untouched, for the prophet has said on my behalf, *I shall set a stumbling block in their way.*"[2]

This verse led her to understand that the Lord often prompts those whom he has chosen to do things that shock others. However, his chosen are not to refrain from acting out of a hope of keeping peace with the wicked, for the best sort of peace is **where** good overcomes evil, that is, when someone, not refraining from **something in which he knows there to be** God's praise, overcomes the wicked by winning

---

[1] The preceding chapter, L 162, on "trust and similar things," was written, or at least written down, by Sister N, not by Gertrud herself. So at least some of what later became LDP I was written down while Gertrud was still alive and with her knowledge.

[2] Ezek 3:20.

them over with pliancy and good will, for **in this way one's neighbor is enriched**. But if it does no good, these still do not lose their own reward.

1. Again, another time she understood that God in his hidden judgment sometimes allows that, when some corrupted person seeks by cunning temptation the knowledge of some secret from the chosen, he should sometimes receive an answer by which he becomes even more obstinate in the corruption of his error. This is to his disadvantage, but acts as test **and purification** of the chosen. And so **Ezechiel witnesses, where we read**, He *that has placed his uncleannesses in his heart, and set up the stumbling block of his iniquity before his face, and shall come to the prophet, inquiring of me by him, I the Lord will answer him according to the multitude of his uncleannesses, that* he *may be caught in* his *own heart.*[1]

[1] Ezek 14:4-5.

<CHAPTER ONE HUNDRED AND SIXTY-FIVE =
LDP III.18.24>

1. **One time**, when she **had received** communion, while she was offering the Lord the sacrifice of the Lord's Body for the relief of all in purgatory, she perceived thereafter that a great alleviation for the souls of the faithful had resulted. Then in great astonishment she said to the Lord, "My most kindly Lord—I call you this by reason of your grace—although, alas, I am unworthy, nonetheless you always deign to visit me with your presence, or rather to dwell within me. [Whence comes it that you do not always bring about such an effect through me as I am now experiencing after the reception of your most holy Body?"[1]]

The Lord replied, "Just as when a king lives in his palace, access is not readily granted to everyone, but when, vanquished by love for the queen who lives nearby, he deigns to descend from his palace into the city in order to visit her, all the citizens and inhabitants of that city, by reason of the queen, **experience** more easily and freely the generosity of his regal magnificence and rejoice in his riches; so when, vanquished by the goodness and sweetness of my **loving** heart, I bend down through the life-giving sacrament of the altar to any of the faithful who is without mortal sin, to all who dwell in heaven, on earth, and in purgatory is granted the increase of an inestimable blessing."

[1] LDP; *om.* L.

1. Many people quite often asked her advice on certain doubtful points, and in particular whether they should, for one reason or another, refrain from receiving communion. She would advise those who seemed reasonably fit and ready to approach the Lord's sacrament with confidence, as God is gracious and merciful. Sometimes she almost forced them. On one occasion, however, she began to worry, as is the habit of the sincere and honest mind, that she was taking on herself more than she should by giving such replies. And so running to the clemency of the divine loving-kindness, so familiar to her, and trustingly confiding in it her fear, she was comforted **by it** with this answer: **"Why are you in doubt, daughter? Is it not appropriate that I, the almighty Lord, God supremely wise and good, I who am infallible Truth itself, should rightly be questioned by means of those in whom I have lived for so many years with my divine virtue and grace, as I have lived in you, and that I should be heard beyond all doubt? But sometimes a person possessed by the devil, who has been a liar since the beginning, is also asked about certain hidden things, and credence given to the answers they have given. Therefore** do not be afraid, but **rather** be strong and confident, for I, the Lord God and your Lover, who by my freely given love created you and chose you in whom to dwell and take delightful pleasure, I give a definite answer, beyond all doubt, to all who ask me this question with devotion and humility through you. You shall hold this sure promise from me, that I will never allow anyone whom I judge to be unworthy of the life-giving sacrament of my Body and Blood to seek out **an answer** on this **from**

you. So if I chose to send you for assurance anyone who is weary or oppressed, you shall declare to that person that it is safe to approach me, for because of your grace and love, I will never bar them from my fatherly heart, but I shall gladly open my arms to them, to embrace them in dearest love; nor shall I deny them the delectable kiss of peace."

1. After this, while one day she was praying more especially for those women who were going to communion under her guidance, the Lord of infinite loving-kindness and sweetness gave her this reply: "If someone consents to your exhortations, and in trembling at their own unworthiness and trusting in my loving-kindness humbly approaches that most magnificent sacrament, I look upon them, or rather welcome them, as lovingly as some courtly noble receives his beloved. He does so the more gladly when she is dressed *in purple and fine linen,*[1] **wondrously crowned with gold and sparkling jewels,**[2] **coming to meet him with a numberless multitude of servants, than if he saw her running to meet him, all alone and dressed in threadbare garments."**

[1] Luke 16:19.
[2] Cf. LDP III.32.3, lines 17–18.

<CHAPTER ONE HUNDRED AND SIXTY-EIGHT =
LDP I.14.3–4>

1. Hence, when she was praying for someone with more fervor, fearing that that person might be hoping to be able to receive more through <Gertrud> than she could gain for herself, the Lord replied very kindly, "As much as anyone hopes to be able to gain through you, she will certainly receive from me. Moreover, **every** promise you make anyone **on my behalf**, I shall certainly keep. Even if the person concerned is prevented by human weakness from being aware of the effect, nonetheless I shall carry out in her soul the **perpetual** improvement you promised."

2. Some days later, remembering the promise the Lord had made and not forgetting her own unworthiness, she asked the Lord how it could come about that he condescended to perform such **magnificent things** through her, totally worthless as she was. The Lord replied, "Does not the church's faith rest universally on the promise I once made to Peter alone when I said, '*Whatever you shall bind on earth*'[1] **and so on?** And does not the church firmly believe that this has been accomplished to the present day through all the ministers of the church? Therefore why do you not equally believe that I am able and willing to do anything, prompted by love, that I promise you with my divine mouth?" And touching her tongue he said, "There! *I have given my words in your mouth*,[2] and I confirm in my truth every single word that you will speak to anyone on my behalf, at the prompting of my Spirit. And if you make a promise to anyone on earth on behalf

[1] Matt 16:19.
[2] Jer 1:9.

of my goodness, **I shall keep** it in heaven as a promise that has been irrevocably validated." She said in answer to this, "Lord, I would not rejoice if anyone should suffer condemnation as a result of this—if I, impelled by **vehemence of spirit,** told someone that some guilty act could not remain unpunished, or something like that." The Lord replied, "Every time that you are impelled by justice or by your passion for souls to say such things, I shall surround the person with my loving-kindness, moving her to compunction so that she will not deserve my vengeance."

Then she asked the Lord, "Lord, if you are truly speaking through my mouth, as your loving-kindness deigns to assert, how is it that my words sometimes have so little effect on people—words that I offer up for the salvation of souls with such **vehement** longing for your praise?" The Lord replied, "Do not be surprised that your words sometimes labor in vain. I myself, during my earthly life, preached many times **with** the ardor of my divine Spirit, and nonetheless **with** some people my words brought about no improvement. For **in accordance with** my divine plan, all things have their time."

<CHAPTER ONE HUNDRED AND SIXTY-NINE =
LDP I.14.5>

1. In addition, when she had criticized **a person's** deficiency **rather harshly**, she took refuge in the Lord, praying devoutly that he would condescend so to enlighten her understanding with the light of his divine knowledge that in no case would she give anyone an answer other than that pleasing to his divine will. The Lord replied, "Do not be afraid, my daughter, but have faith **in my grace,** for I am **giving you** a special privilege: when anyone asks your advice in humility and faith on any matter whatsoever, in the light of my divine truth you will discern that case just as I judge it, in respect to its fundamental nature and that of the person concerned, **as more or less serious.** If I **have judged** someone's case to be more serious, your answer on my behalf will be **the more terrible**, and if I **have reckoned** someone's case to be less serious, I shall make you answer in gentler terms." Then recognizing in the spirit of humility her own unworthiness, she said to the Lord, "O Ruler of heaven and earth, now take back, and hold back, the extravagant profusion of your generosity, for I, since I am *dust and ashes,*[1] am totally unworthy of so great a gift." The Lord replied, soothing her kindly, "Why is it such a great thing for me to grant you to discern the reasons for my enmity when I have allowed you again and again to experience the secrets of my friendship?" And the Lord added, "Any who are oppressed or sad, who humbly and honestly seek consolation in your words, will never be deprived of [their][2] desire. For I, God, dwelling

[1] Gen 18:27.
[2] *suo* LDP; *tuo* L.

in you, at the prompting of the **freely given** loving-kindness of my **unrestrained** love, long to bring blessings on many people through you. The joy that your heart feels at this, it draws up from the brimming well of my heart."

<CHAPTER ONE HUNDRED AND SEVENTY= LDP III.33>

1. **Another time**, when she was burning for the Lord with greater desire, she said to the Lord, "Ah, my Lord, could I pray to you now?" The most kindly Lord gently replied to her, "Indeed, lady and queen, best of all you could command me; for I shall obey your will and desire in all things more readily than ever any servant can serve his mistress." She said, "The word of your most loving condescension is in all things inviolate, most kindly God. And yet since you condescend to show yourself so **infinitely** attentive to me, most unworthy, please tell me why my prayer is so **many times** ineffectual?" The Lord replied, "Suppose a queen says to her servant, 'Give me the thread that is hanging down back there, over my left shoulder,' thinking it is indeed there, although she cannot see behind her. The servant seeks to do what he has been ordered and when he sees the thread is not hanging over her left shoulder but above her right he at once picks up **what** he finds and gives it to his lady, **judging** it more sensible than if he pulled a thread out of her tunic on the left side, to carry out her order! Similarly if at times I who am unsearchable wisdom do not hear your prayers in the way you wish, there is no doubt that I always **dispense more beneficial** things, although you, hindered by human frailty, cannot discern that they are **more useful**."

1. She was acknowledging the worthlessness of her life and the multiplicity of her shortcomings, while simultaneously pondering the virtues of others; like a weaned child in its mother's bosom she fled to the protection of the divine loving-kindness, groaning plaintively, "Alas! Lord God, *father of mercies*,[1] when various people diligently please you with their various virtues, and exert themselves in good works to your praise, I, *the offscouring of all*,[2] alas! bring you no fruit of virtues or good deeds, but I am a useless branch[3] that boys cut up for fun to make a little knife, which is good for nothing except to be used by that childish folly." To this the Lord replied, "So if you are good for nothing else, except that my *hands have handled*[4] you in delight, it is highly appropriate that I should adorn you so properly with my grace, that my divine will may sufficiently delight in you!"

---

[1] 2 Cor 1:3.

[2] 1 Cor 4:13.

[3] *truncus inutilis* L; compare Horace, Satires I, 8, line 1, *Olim truncus eram ficulnus, inutile lignum*; "I was once a fig-tree's trunk, a lump of useless wood."

[4] 1 John 1:1.

<CHAPTER ONE HUNDRED AND SEVENTY-TWO
Not in LDP>

1. Again, another time, pondering her unworthiness, she turned to the Lord, in whose kindliness she always found safe refuge, and said, "Whatever I am, I am belong to you, my sweetness, my God." To this the Lord, the overflowing abyss[1] of loving-kindness, replied, "Therefore since you declare yourself to be mine, I shall make from my own something that can enhance my royal magnificence." To this she replied, "And how, my Lord, could you do this from me? For I, alas! have reached such ignominy through my own sins and negligences that I am completely unworthy of every grace of yours." Then the Lord reminded her of a childish deed that she once had done, saying, "What did you once select on that little branch[2] among the apple trees, which you wrapped so carefully in a silken cloth?[3] If you could accomplish this as a child, be sure that the power of my insuperable love can accomplish far more, so that I can also by my own efforts perfect with my grace the one whom I have chosen by my freely given loving-kindness, and *in him I* could be perfectly *well-pleased*[4] according to the pleasure of my deified heart."

[1] Cf. LDP III.65.3.

[2] *trunco* L; see L 171 above.

[3] Possibly to protect the fruit from frost.

[4] Matt 3:17.

<CHAPTER ONE HUNDRED AND SEVENTY-THREE =
LDP III.18.1–2>

1. **Once** when she was coming forward to receive the life-giving sacrament, while the phrase "Holy, holy, holy" in the antiphon "**The Lord shall come**"[1] was being sung, she fell to the ground in humility of heart and prayed the Lord that he would condescend to prepare her so that she might participate worthily in the heavenly banquets, to his praise and the profit of **all the** world. **The King of Glory,** the Son of God, like a **bridegroom captivated by love,** quickly leaned towards her and imprinted a most delightful kiss, **surpassing a draught of honey,**[2] on her soul; while the second "Holy" was being sung, **he said,** "Behold, in this kiss, with that 'Holy' that is addressed to me, I give you all the holiness of my divine and human natures, so that you may come to communion worthily prepared by it."

2. On the Sunday following, while she was **devoutly** thanking God for that gift, there was the Son of God, more beautiful in form than thousands of angels, taking her up in his arms as if he were glorying in her. He joyfully presented her to God the Father in the perfection of that holiness that he had given her in his own person. Then God the Father too, through his Only-begotten, took such pleasure with her in her soul that, as if unable to contain himself, he too

---

[1] *Dominus veniet, occurrite illi dicentes magnum principium et regni ejus non erit finis; deus fortis dominator, princeps pacis, alleluia*: antiphon for many feasts, including the fourth Sunday in Advent, the Nativity, and the Annunciation. It does not contain the phrase *sanctus, sanctus, sanctus.* LDP III.18.1 names a different antiphon, *Gaude et laetare.*

[2] Cf. LDP IV.5.1 and LDP V.4.5.

with the Holy Spirit bestowed upon her their own "Holy," so that she might gain the full **perfection** of complete holiness, that of Omnipotence, of Wisdom, and of Goodness.

1. Another time, when she was about to receive communion, she saw that very many women were kept from communion for various reasons. Rejoicing in spirit, she said to the Lord out of the deepest affection of her heart, "I give you thanks, my **sweetest** lover, because you have brought me to such a condition that neither my relatives nor any other reasons can prevent me from sharing in your most joyful feast." The Lord, according to the usual sweetness of his goodness, replied, "Just as you declare that there is nothing to **keep** you **from me, in the same way** you should know that absolutely nothing, in heaven or earth, or rather neither judgment nor **my** justice, is strong enough to keep me from blessing you according to the high pleasure of my divine heart."

1. Similarly, another time when she was approaching communion, **since** she greatly desired to be worthily prepared by the Lord, the sweet and loving Lord *caressed her with these words*:[1] "Look, I am now donning you like a garment so that I can stretch out my tender hand unharmed among rough sinners, to bless them, and I am clothing you with myself so that you may draw all those whom you bring before my presence in your mindfulness, or rather all those who are like you in nature, to that honor so that I can bless them in accordance with my royal generosity."

[1] Esth 15:11.

1. On another day, when she was about to take part in the divine mysteries, while she was recalling God's **limitless** blessings towards her, that verse from the book of Kings came into her mind: *Who am I, or what is my father's family?*[1] She rejected that phrase, *what is my father's family?* as if they had been people who in their day had lived according to God's ordinance, but thought of herself as a little offshoot that, receiving blessings from the proximity of the unquenchable fire of the divine heart, naturally catching fire in herself but growing steadily weaker **as if burnt to ashes** because of her faults of negligence, was now, as if *brought to nothing*,[2] lying there like a tiny burnt-out coal. When she turned to the most kindly intercessor, Jesus the Son of God, praying that he would deign to present her, such as she was, to be reconciled to God the Father, Jesus himself, most loving, through the warm breath of the love of his wounded heart, seemed to draw her to himself and wash her in the water flowing from it, then wash her in the life-giving blood of his heart. At this she grew in strength from a minuscule coal to a vigorous green tree whose branches **seemed to be** divided into three, like those of a lily. The Son of God took the tree and presented it with gratitude and glory to the Trinity, ever to be adored. When it was presented, the wholly blessed Trinity inclined towards her with such great courtesy that God the Father, out of his divine omnipotence, hung on its upper branches every fruit that soul could have produced if she had conformed as

[1] 1 Sam 18:18.
[2] Job 30:15.

she should to the divine omnipotence. Similarly the Son of God and the Holy Spirit seemed to hang the fruits of wisdom and goodness on the other two branches.

2. After this, when she had received the Body of Christ, she saw that her soul, in the likeness of a tree as has been said above, had its root fixed in the wounded side of Jesus Christ. Through that wound, as if through the root, she felt in a new and wonderful way as if she were penetrated by the power of the **human and divine** natures together through each branch, fruit, and leaf simultaneously. As a result the fruit of all his way of life on earth gained a new splendor through her, as gold shines through crystal. Thence not only the Trinity but also all the saints received the delight of a wonderful joy. In their honor all rose up and as it were bent the knee; one by one they offered their own merits in the shape of crowns, hanging them on the branches of that tree, to the praise and glory of him who, shining through it with new delight, deigned that they should feel joy. But when she prayed the Lord that at least he would now give to those in heaven, on earth, and in purgatory (who would all by rights have had the benefits from the **fruits** of her works if she had not neglected them) the benefit of the fruits bestowed on her by the divine goodness, each **apple** in whose form the fruit of the tree appeared began to exude a most potent liquor. Part, flowing onto those in heaven, increased their joy; part, flowing into purgatory, lessened their pains; part, flowing to the earth, increased sweetness of grace for the righteous and bitterness of penitence for sinners.

1. One day during Mass at the elevation of the Host, while she was offering that most sacred Host to God the Father as worthy reparation for all sinners and as compensation for all her own acts of neglect, she perceived that her soul was brought before the gaze of the divine majesty in that *good pleasure*[1] in which Christ Jesus, *splendor and image of the glory*[2] of his Father, spotless lamb, offered himself at the same time on the altar to God the Father for the salvation of the world. For through the most blameless human nature of Jesus Christ, God the Father saw her as purified from all sin and unspotted, and through his most excellent divine nature saw her as enriched and adorned with every sort of virtue with which the glorious divine nature flowered through his most holy human nature.

2. While to the best of her ability she was **rendering thanks to the Lord**, delighting in such wonderful regard of the divine lovingkindness, she gained this insight from him: as often as someone attends Mass with devotion, concentrating on God, who there offers himself in the sacraments for the common salvation of the whole world, he is truly seen by God the Father **in** the same *good pleasure*[3] as God looks on the sacred Host that is offered to him. It is like someone who steps from darkness into the radiance of the sunlight and is at once completely flooded with light. Then she asked the Lord, "My Lord, does someone who falls into sin immediately lose

---

[1] Eph 1:9.
[2] See Col 1:15; Heb 1:3.
[3] Eph 1:9.

this blessedness, just as someone who retreats from the light of the sun into the dark loses the welcome brightness of light?" The Lord replied, "No; for although, in sinning, to a certain extent he obscures the light of the divine favor from himself, nonetheless my loving-kindness always preserves a vestige of that blessedness in that person for eternal life: he multiplies this blessedness as often as he strives with devotion to take part in the **divine** sacraments."

<CHAPTER ONE HUNDRED AND SEVENTY-EIGHT =
LDP IV.2.6, line 9–2.7, line 15; **not in LDP**>

1. On the vigil of our Lord Jesu's honey-sweet Nativity, she stretched out her desire **to** God that **she might be worthy to celebrate that sweetest feast with such devotion** that **everything** that she **performed**, both in body and soul, should resound highest praise of the ever-worshipful Trinity. While the bell for **matutinal** Lauds was being struck, the Lord, **most kindly assenting to her desire,** said to her, **"Listen! At the sound of those three bells whose chimes begin the feast of my Nativity,** I grant you that in all that you perform on that feast, in singing, reading, praying, meditating, or even in physical labor, eating, sleeping, and such like, **the desire of my divine heart that I possessed to the praise and glory of God the Father, and that love in which all my works were performed, and the delight of that union** by which I have never been at odds with the will of God the Father, shall resound **in highest perfection** to the holy Trinity." When seven candles were being lit **at Lauds,** the Lord bestowed on her soul the adornment of the seven gifts of the Holy Spirit, insofar as she could receive them, in the same dignity as the Lord Jesus was himself adorned with them **in his human nature.**

2. After this she was praying **the Lord** that, by the condescension with which he **condescended to be** born in an inn, he would also condescend **so to prepare her heart by his grace that he could worthily dwell in her.** Again, the most merciful Lord, **kindly consenting to her desires,** disposed **the** omnipotence, wisdom, and kindness **of the shining and ever-tranquil Trinity** in her as if they were the roof and **two** walls **of the inn. Enclosed by them in the depths of her being,** as if in the inn, she rejoiced wonderfully, since

she saw that over the whole roof and walls were hanging in the manner of delightful little bells all the works that by the help of the omnipotence, wisdom, and goodness of God were ever accomplished in anyone. It was as if they had been granted her as a means of assistance by which she might celebrate the feast more praiseworthily to God. And when she was enjoying such a choice experience, as if in heavenly **joys**, the Lord Jesus appeared **with a new and more loving condescension, as if with inestimable delight setting himself on one side as the third wall and setting a countless multitude of heavenly princes opposite as the fourth wall to serve him. Therefore as she lingered in this palace, while she was reciting to the glory of the feast of the Nativity three hundred and fifty short prayers on behalf of all the parts of her body,[1] it seemed to her as if along with every single prayer she brought the service of the parts of her body[2] and offered them to God to his eternal praise. To the giver be praise and thanksgiving for this gift of his loving-kindness!**

---

[1] Possibly a scribal error: in LDP there are several references to Gertrud's belief that the human body has 225 parts. See LDP V.30.6, n. 2.

[2] Cf. LDP IV.2.7, lines 18–20.

<CHAPTER ONE HUNDRED AND SEVENTY-NINE =
LDP III.67>

1. One day she was praying for certain persons who had damaged the monastery by despoiling it and were in addition oppressing it excessively.[1] The kind and merciful Lord showed himself to her as if he were suffering from one arm so far bent back that it was almost torn out of its socket. The Lord said, "Consider what pain would torment me if someone were now to punch me on that arm. Judge that I am burdened with a similar pain by all those who, with no pity for the damnation of souls risked by those who attack **them,** wickedly proclaim over and over again those people's failings and the injuries inflicted on themselves, not remembering that those people too are my members. Indeed, all those who, moved by compassionate mercy, beg for my clemency, that I should mercifully turn them from their error to a better life, soothe my arm as with most gentle ointments. But those who kindly guide them to reconciliation and amendment by counsel and advice are like thoroughly experienced doctors who gently re-set my arm into its proper place by manipulation."

2. Then, astonished at the Lord's indescribable kindness, she said, "By what judgment, most merciful God, can people who are so unworthy be called your 'arm'?" The Lord said, "Because they are from the body of the church, whose Head I am proud to be." But she said, "Right now, my Lord, see how they are unfortunately cut off from the body of the church by an interdict, for they have been excommunicated and publicly denounced because of the damage they inflicted on

---

[1] Probably a reference to the depredations of Adolph of Nassau (King of the Romans 1292–1298) in the summer of 1294.

our monastery." The Lord replied, "All the same, as they can still **be reconciled through absolution and returned to the church,** caring for them and **overcome** by my own loving-kindness, I long with incredible desire that they should turn to me through penitence."

Then she prayed that he would condescend to guard the community with his fatherly protection from their assaults. The Lord replied, "If you all are *humbled under my mighty hand,*[2] acknowledging before me in your hearts that you deserve to be punished as your **sins and** negligences **rightly** demand, my fatherly mercy will keep you unscathed[3] from every attack of your enemies. But if through pride you all become wickedly arrogant towards those who besiege you, hoping or praying that they will receive evil in return for evil, my justice and my just judgment will allow them to prevail against you, harming you and troubling you in very many ways."

---

[2] See 1 Pet 5:6.
[3] *illesos* L, i.e., masculine gender.

<CHAPTER ONE HUNDRED AND EIGHTY =
LDP III.68.1–3 >

1. One year the community was in great distress because of a debt,[1] and this woman was devoutly intent on praying the Lord in his loving-kindness to move the stewards of the convent to pay off what they owed. The Lord, gently soothing her, replied, "What profit would I gain from it if I helped them in this?" She replied, "They would have time to engage more zealously and devoutly **for you** in spiritual exercises." The Lord said, "And what good does that do me? I *have no need of your goods*,[2] and it makes no difference to me whether you have time for spiritual concerns or are sweating away at exterior works, as long as your will is directed at me with free intention. For if I took pleasure in spiritual exercises only, I would have immediately reconstructed human nature after the Fall **as I had created it** so that from then on it would not need food or clothing or the other things for which human industry **now** sweats, in seeking out and putting together the necessities of life. But just as a powerful emperor not only takes pleasure in having refined and elegant girls in his palace, but also appoints princes, dukes, knights, and other servants fit for various tasks, each one of whom he has available in his palace for his varied affairs, so I too take pleasure not only in the interior delights of contemplatives, but also in the varied tasks of practical business that are done for the sake of my honor and love. I am drawn to linger and dwell delightfully among the sons of men, for they labor

---

[1] This probably refers to the events preceding the interdict: see L 94, 96–103.
[2] See Ps 15:2.

greatly in such works, in love, patience, humility, and the other virtues."

2. Then she saw the man on whom the greater responsibility lay, sitting in the presence of the Lord, as it were leaning **to the** left side. Raising himself awkwardly over and over again, he offered the Lord with his left hand, on which he was leaning, a gold coin distinguished with a precious stone. The Lord said to her, "Look! If I were to lighten the burden on him for whom you pray, then I would lose that noble jewel that pleases me in **those coins**. He too would be cheated of his reward, for then he would only offer me with his right hand [a coin][3] without the jewel. For he offers simply a coin if, without adversity, he is intent on God in all his deeds. But he offers God a gold coin with a most excellent stone if he is dogged by adversity in all that he does, and still does not quarrel with the divine **goodness**."

3. When she did not give up, but prayed the Lord more urgently to lighten that burden on the convent's stewards, the Lord replied, "Why does it seem hard to you if someone endures burdens for my sake, since I am that one true friend in whom faithfulness never grows old? For when a person draws near the end, bereft of all human help and comfort, if someone then remembers some faithfulness shown him, he does so with great bitterness. But I, the one true friend, come to the comfortless soul at that time of anxious need with a bouquet of all the good works that person ever **carried out** in thought, word, or deed in this life. They are all flourishing in my garments like roses and lilies. And from that the flourishing vigor of my divine presence revives the soul *unto the hope of life everlasting*,[4] for it realizes that it is summoned to it and is rewarded for each separate deed. And then the soul, through its pleasure, assumes the ability by which it can, once released from the flesh, receive eternal happiness so that truly rejoicing and breaking out into praise it can say that verse from Genesis, *Behold the smell of my beloved is as the smell of a plentiful field*.[5] For just as the body consists of various limbs joined together,

---

[3] LDP; *manum* L.

[4] Titus 1:2.

[5] See Gen 27:27.

so the soul consists of emotions, which are fear, sorrow, joy, love, hope, hate, and shame. Insofar as a **soul** has exerted itself to my praise in each of these, he finds in me the pleasure of a joy that cannot be **described, or rather fathomed**, and of security by which he is prepared and fitted for eternal blessedness. For in the resurrection to come, when *this mortal body will put on incorruption,*[6] then every individual human limb will receive the individual reward of its deserts, for every single labor and exertion carried out in my name and for love of me. But the soul will receive the nobility of an incomparably more worthy excellence for every single exertion of the holy emotions by which the soul was ever moved for love of me, or pierced with compunction, or that invigorated the body."

[6] See 1 Cor 15:53.

<CHAPTER ONE HUNDRED AND EIGHTY-ONE =
LDP III.68.4>

1. Then, again feeling **great** compassion for a faithful steward of the convent, she **besought** the Lord that he would mercifully make up to him for the difficult labors he often performed in the community's affairs. The Lord replied, "The body of that man, which is so often battered **because of me** by such labors, is to me like a treasure chest in which I place as many silver coins as the number of times he has moved a limb to obtain necessities for those in his charge. His heart is to me like an ark, in which I rejoice at having as many gold coins hidden as the number of times he made careful provision, motivated by his thoughts, to my praise, for his subordinates." Then she said to the Lord in astonishment, "Lord, that man does not seem to me so perfect that all his acts have been undertaken purely for your praise. But I believe that often other reasons motivate him, such as worldly profit, and consequently physical comfort. And how then could you, my God of unadulterated sweetness, have such delight as you claim in his heart and body?" The Lord replied very courteously, "Because his will is so [conformed][1] to my divine will that I am always the supreme cause for all his actions. Therefore in each one of his thoughts, words, and deeds he reaps a priceless harvest. But if he concentrated on each of his affairs with a purer and more devout intention, then all his deeds would be as much the more noble as gold is worth more than silver. Similarly if he concentrated with purer and more devout intention in directing each of his thoughts and preoc-

---

[1] *adaptata* LDP, *adoptata* L.

cupations at me, then they would be as much the more noble as *the finest **tested** gold*[2] and most highly refined is better than old and tarnished gold."

[2] Song 5:11; Rev 3:18.

1. It happened on one occasion that a person was accidentally injured while working and was suffering great pain. Feeling compassion for her, this woman was praying to the Lord for her, that he would not allow a member, injured in a righteous work, to be endangered. The Lord kindly replied, "She will certainly not be endangered, but will purchase a matchless reward for this suffering, **for that member that is suffering was in the inmost depths of my divine heart when injured in this way, and all my mercy had tightly surrounded it, and thence eternal salvation will come to it**. Also all the members that are moved to serve that member to relieve its pain and cure it will similarly gain an eternal reward from this, just as when one piece of cloth is dyed with saffron, if something else falls in, it is dyed the same. And so when *one member suffers anything, all the other members*[1] that serve it will be rewarded together with it by eternal glory."

2. Then she said, "My Lord, how can members deserve so great a reward for serving each other, since they do this not so that the wounded member may suffer more extensively or patiently for your love, but only for this, to relieve their suffering?" The Lord gave her a reply of inestimable consolation, saying, "I have sanctified that suffering that a person bears patiently for love of me that, after **every kind of remedy** for the pain **has been tried**, she cannot assuage by her own effort, in those words with which I prayed to the Father in the moment of my **extreme** need, saying, *Father, if it be possible, let*

[1] 1 Cor 12:26.

this chalice pass from me,[2] that a person may garner incomparable merit through it."

3. She replied, "Does it not please you more, my **sweetest** God, that someone should patiently suffer for your love **whatsoever** will befall him than what he is suffering at this moment, since they can by no means avoid it?" The Lord replied, "This lies hidden in the abyss of my divine judgments and transcends human understanding, but according to what can be discerned by human judgment, the difference between the two is like that between two exquisite colors, both of which **would be** judged by people to be of such great beauty that it is difficult to discern which **of them** should rightly be preferred to the other." Then she desired of the Lord that he should give that person powerful consolation in these words, as they had been unfolded to her. The Lord replied, "I will not. But you should know that I disregard this by the hidden dispensation of my divine wisdom: that is, so that the person herself may be tested further and particularly may be commended in three virtues, that is, patience, faith, and humility. In patience, for if she felt such power of consolation from these words as you now experience, every burden of hers would be lightened, so much so that the reward of her patience would also be lessened. In faith, so that she may trust more in another for what she herself does not experience, for, according to Gregory, faith has no reward if human reason offers proof.[3] In humility, so that she may trust that another is superior because **that one** knows through divine inspiration what she is not worthy to know."

---

[2] See Matt 26:39.

[3] Gregory the Great, Hom in Ev 26 (PL 76:1197), as quoted in the twelfth lection at Matins for the octave of Easter.

1. On the feast of Saint John the Evangelist, she was taking much pleasure in hearing extolled so often on that day in ambrosial words the virginal integrity in blessed John. Finally, having turned to that special friend of God, she prayed that by his prayers he might deign to win for us, insofar as with the help of God's grace we were assiduous in such careful guarding of chastity, that in the life eternal, in God's glory, we might also in our own measure share the proclamations of such sweet-sounding praises with him. At this she received this reply from Saint John: "If anyone longs to share with me in blessedness the prize of victory, let him be assiduous in keeping to my way of running the race."[1] And he added, "Throughout my entire life, I recalled quite often with what sweet and intimate friendship my most loving Lord and **kindest** master Jesus **had** looked on me, or rather he **had** rewarded me with that continence that enabled me to abandon my bride and follow him away from the wedding.[2] Afterwards I always manifested, in all my words and deeds, this eagerness to take greater care lest I might furnish an opportunity, either in myself or in others, to sully in any way that virtue that my master **approves**: chastity."

[1] See 1 Cor 9:24.

[2] Saint John traditionally "had thought of marrying but instead was called by the Lord" (*Jacobus de Voragine: The Golden Legend*, trans. William Grainger Ryan, 2 vols. [Princeton, NJ: Princeton University Press, 1993], 1:55).

2. And he added,

For the other apostles were in every respect wary of what was suspect but allowed more freely what was not suspect: as we read in Acts, "They were *with the women and Mary, mother of Jesus*"[3] and so on. But I always conducted myself warily among them so that when some bodily necessity or the salvation of a soul demanded it, I was never seen to flee the sex, but neither did I ever omit to show caution in guarding chastity. For it was my custom, whenever any opportunity of human kindliness presented itself, always to **invoke** the aid of the divine loving-kindness. And this is what is sung of me: *In affliction have you called upon me, and I have heard you, **and I delivered you**,*[4] for the Lord never allowed anyone to be sullied in any way at all by love for me. As a result I received this too **in** reward from my most beloved master, that chastity is praised in me more than in all the other chosen. And this is not all: I have also received a place in heaven pre-eminent in special dignity, where sitting in glory and resplendent brightness I receive more directly, with sweet delight, the rays of that love that *is the unspotted mirror and brightness of eternal light.*[5] For as often as the church commemorates my chastity in any text, the Lord himself, my lover, greets me with a most delicately tender gesture and fills all my inner parts with an **inestimably** sweet joy that, like a most potent drink, penetrates all the innermost recesses of my soul. And this is why they sing in my praise, "I shall place you as a seal in my sight,"[6] that is, like a vessel to catch all the emissions of **his** most burning—or rather, most delightful—love.

[3] Acts 1:14.

[4] See Ps 80:8.

[5] Wis 7:26.

[6] Ninth response for Matins of the feast of Saint John; see Hag 2:24.

<CHAPTER ONE HUNDRED AND EIGHTY-FOUR =
LDP IV.4.8>

1. After **those words, therefore**, led to higher knowledge, she understood that, according to what the Lord said in the gospel, *"In my father's house there are many dwelling-places,"*[1] there were in particular three dwelling places in which in a threefold way followers of the integrity of virginal modesty enjoy blessedness. The first dwelling place belongs to those who, as was said before of the apostles, completely flee anything suspect, and allow within reason what is not suspect. And if anything has assaulted their mind with temptation, they struggle courageously to defeat it. But if at times they succumb a little from human weakness, they expunge this with *worthy fruits of penance.*[2]

The second dwelling place belongs to those who act quite cautiously both in what is not suspect and in what is, and who completely distance themselves from everything that could be an opportunity for temptation. They *chastise their body and bring it into subjection,*[3] so much so that it is impossible for it to rebel against the spirit. Among their number we see blessed John the Baptist and other spiritual men, who are all made happy in that second dwelling place, both because God's loving-kindness has freely sanctified them and because they themselves particularly cooperated with God's grace by withdrawing from evil and exerting themselves in good.

[1] John 14:2.
[2] See Luke 3:8.
[3] 1 Cor 9:27.

The third dwelling place belongs to those who, *preceded by the Lord in the blessings of sweetness*,[4] abhor all evil as if innately: however, among various accidents they sometimes have dealings with the wicked and sometimes with the good, **now among the spiritual, now among the carnal**, for various reasons **experiencing various things**, but nonetheless *hating evil and cleaving to the good*[5] with immutable purpose; it **is not enough for them to keep their own conscience unscathed but rather, as much as they can, they eagerly desire** to keep **everyone** unsullied. And since **from time to time there is no lack of human affection among such people living among men and women, they** profit wonderfully from it when, fearing the disturbance of that same love, they are brought low and thence alerted more carefully to their own protection. As Gregory says, "It is the mark of virtuous minds to **fear** a fault where there is no fault."[6] **For in this way those tested in this state and found perfect in the divine scrutiny are granted a singular glory.** Among these **it should be known that** blessed John the Evangelist gained the privilege of principal victory. Thence on his feast is **rightly** chanted **in his praise by the church this verse from the Apocalypse:** *He who has overcome I shall make a pillar in my temple.*[7] **This can be understood in this way:** "He who has overcome human affection **with spiritual charity, so that although my love impelled him to show brotherly charity, he values human affection so little, not only in others but also in himself, that, after demonstrating self-control, in other respects he entrusts to God what should become of him, at least so that he might carry out God's will according to his most praiseworthy good pleasure**, *I shall make him a pillar in my temple*, that is, like a strong vessel on which I may rest to support the overflow of divine delight. *And I shall write my name above him*,[8] that is, I shall clearly imprint on him the pleasure

---

[4] Ps 20:4.

[5] Rom 12:9.

[6] Gregory the Great, Ep XI.64 (PL 77:1195B).

[7] Rev 3:12.

[8] See Rev 3:12.

of my divine intimacy (**and thence although he has a well-deserved special glory, no one knows what that sweetness is accomplishing in his innermost being except the recipient, for it is** *hidden manna*[9] **that he** *that eats shall yet hunger, and he who drinks shall yet thirst*),[10] and <I shall imprint> the name of the new city of Jerusalem,[11] that is, both inwardly and outwardly he shall receive a unique reward **for all those collectively and individually** whose salvation he sought on earth, **and who could have been a hindrance to him if God's grace and his own self-control had not intervened. For** *he that could have transgressed and has not transgressed, and could do evil things and has not done them* **will have greater glory; for** *his goods are established in the Lord,*[12] **and all the church militant declares his victories with praise and thanksgiving in heaven."**

[9] Rev 2:17.

[10] See Sir 24:29 and LDP II. 24.1, lines 15–17.

[11] A much elaborated version of *Qui vicerit, faciam illum columnam meam in templo meo, dicit dominus; et scribam super eum nomen meum et nomen civitatis novae Jerusalem*; fifth response at Matins of the feast of Saint John; see Rev 3:12.

[12] Sir 31:10-11.

1. This agrees with another occasion, on which she was considering why blessed John the Evangelist was praised **with such joyful commendations** for his virginal integrity, **although he seems to have leaned a little towards corruption** when summoned by the Lord **when he was attending a wedding**, while the blessed Baptist, completely untouched by any **corruption**, is less praised **by the church** for such a virtue. The Lord, who is *the discerner of thoughts*[1] and distributor of rewards, showed her both in a vision. The Baptist was sitting on a throne raised up and completely removed from everything, above the sea. But the Evangelist was seen **sitting** in the middle of a path that was burning so terrifyingly that the flame completely engulfed him above, below, and around. When she saw this and was **amazed** at it, the Lord instructed her, saying, "Which seems to you more praiseworthy, that the Evangelist is not on fire, or that the Baptist is not **consumed**?" From this she realized that the rewards for virtue that is attacked and for virtue preserved in peace are very different.

[1] Heb 4:12.

1. Similarly, **on the same feast** when she was constant in prayer and **eager to come to** the Lord with special devotion, **and thought she had already entered his presence,** she saw blessed John leaning on him, holding him tight with sweetest embraces and sweetly caressing him in various ways. **When she saw this, withdrawing, she considered that it was indeed most worthy that that chosen one should more freely enjoy such delights than other disciples, and judging herself completely unworthy of such things,** she humbly flung herself at the Lord's feet so that she might mourn her own shortcomings. Blessed John, gently speaking to her, said, "Do not flee my company! Here is the neck that is sufficient for the embrace of a thousand lovers, and the mouth that offers sweetness to the kisses of many, and the ears that keep secrets safe from the whispers of all."

<CHAPTER ONE HUNDRED AND EIGHTY-SEVEN =
LDP IV.4.10, line 11–4.11>

1. **When at** Matins, *Mother, behold your son*[1] was being sung, she saw a wonderful **divine** splendor coming forth from the heart of **the Lord** over blessed John, which prompted the gaze of all the saints toward him with reverent wonder, **because he alone was that charming <youth> who, after the Son of God, had deserved to be called the little son of the unspotted Virgin in the place of his master. Blessed John was moved by unspeakable delight from this.** The blessed Virgin was also seen to caress him with particular alacrity, since she was called his mother. Thence also that chosen disciple, moved by a special caress of sweeter love, greeted her in return. Similarly, when the individual privileges of the special **love** bestowed on him by the Lord were being recited **in the church services,** that is, "This is John, who lay on the Lord's breast <at the Last Supper>. This is the disciple who was worthy," and so on,[2] **and** "this is **he whom** Jesus loved,"[3] and so on, with the glory of a splendor, new but ever the same, it was made manifest to all the saints **that he was that chosen one of the Lord who had deserved so singularly to be distinguished by him with such worshipful privileges.** And

[1] *Mulier, ecce filius tuus; ad discipulum autem, ecce mater tua*; verse at Matins of the feast of Saint John; John 19:26.

[2] *Iste est Joannes qui supra pectus domini in cena recubuit, beatus apostolus cui revelata sunt secreta caelestia*; response at Matins of the feast of Saint John; see John 13:25.

[3] *Iste est Joannes qui supra pectus domini in cena recubuit quem diligebat Jesus*; antiphon at Vespers of the feast of Saint John; see John 13:23 and 21:7.

from this all the saints were prompted to the praise of God by the **inestimable** joy **and delight** of so beloved a disciple.

2. At that sentence **in which they chant about the summoning of blessed John**, "<The Lord Jesus Christ> appeared to his beloved John,"[4] and so on, she perceived that the form in which the Lord then visited John renewed in him all the sweetness of the shared intimacy that ever he had experienced **in any friendship** all his life. As a result blessed John, as if transformed into another man, tasted in advance to a degree the delights of eternal banquets,[5] in three things especially for which he gave thanks **when he was preparing to pass to eternal life.** Of the first he said, "I have seen your face, and I am awakened as if from the tomb." Of the second, "Your perfume, Lord Jesus, has awakened longing in me." Of the third, "Your voice is full of sweetness flowing like honey, <and your speech is incomparable>."[6] For from the power of his sweetest presence he had received, as it were, a certain quickening of immortality, and from the power of the divine summons, hope of sweetest consolation, and from the gentleness of his words, the enjoyment of highest delight.

---

[4] *Apparuit caro suo Ioanni Dominus Iesus Christus cum discipulis suis, et ait illi: Veni, dilecte meus, ad me, quia tempus est ut epuleris in convivio meo cum fratribus tuis*, "The Lord Jesus Christ appeared to his beloved John with his disciples and said to him, Come to me, my beloved, for it is time for you to feast at my banquet with your brethren"; antiphon at Matins of the feast of Saint John.

[5] See previous note.

[6] *Vidi faciem tuam, et quasi de sepultura susciturus sum. Odor tuus concupiscentias in me excitavit eternas. Vox tua plena suavitate melliflua, et allocutio tua incomparabilis*; fifth lection at Matins of the feast of Saint John, derived from Odericus Vitalis, *Historia Ecclesiastica*, I.2.11 (PL 188:153).

<CHAPTER ONE HUNDRED AND EIGHTY-EIGHT =
LDP IV.4.12>

1. Hearing it read that, rising up at the Lord's call, he began to go,[1] as if wishing to follow **his** Lord **physically** on foot to heaven, she perceived that blessed John had so great and so firm a trust in the most loving goodness of his Lord and master because he **who, often *going before him in blessings of sweetness and following after*,[2] had distinguished him above others with so many privileges of special love, also** thought <John> worthy to be taken up into heaven, **a stranger to all** pain of death **and corruption of the flesh**.[3] And because he **faithfully assumed** this in the daring of love, he immediately deserved to receive it. **For Bernard[4] says of these words, *Every place that your foot shall tread upon, shall be yours*,[5] that a person will undoubtedly acquire all things whatsoever that anyone can expect from the Lord's sweetest loving-kindness, or rather, the most generous goodness of God is accustomed to lavish things much greater than could ever be anticipated on anyone who trusts in him.**

---

[1] *Surgens autem Johannes cepit ire*; opening of the fifth lection at Matins.

[2] See Ps 20:4.

[3] According to the legend read at Matins and also disseminated in the *Legenda Aurea*, John went down alive into his grave. He was then hidden from sight for an hour by a huge light, and when it dissipated, nothing was found in the grave except manna: see *Golden Legend*, trans. Ryan, I:55, and further Jeffrey Hamburger, *St John the Divine: The Deified Evangelist in Medieval Art and Theology* (Berkeley and Los Angeles: University of California Press, 2002), 147 and 157, fig. 140.

[4] Bernard, *Sermo in Psalmum "Qui habitat"* 15.5 (SBOp 4:479).

[5] Deut 11:24.

Then she began to be astonished **how this could be, that is, that it was for his trust that he was honored by this privilege, since Bede says in a homily that he escaped unscathed from the pain of death because he was a stranger to the corruption of the flesh,**[6] **and also since very many people say that John had not experienced the bitterness of death because he had paid that debt through his most bitter compassion on Good Friday beside the cross of his sweetest lover. The Lord,** *true searcher of the heart*[7] **and** *discerner of the thoughts*,[8] **breaking into her meditation,** replied, "For **those two things, that is,** the integrity of his virginity and his compassion for my **passion and** death, **with which John, my chosen one, who is honored more fittingly than others, greatly pleased me,** I have **repaid him** with pre-excellent glory in eternal life, **because all the court of heaven is not sufficient to wonder at the super-eminence of his dignity.** But as for that **trust** that led him to assume that I could refuse him nothing out of the superabundance of my sweetness, it pleased me to reward it in the present life in such a way that I took him up from the body in jubilation, unharmed by every pain of death, and I elevated his virgin body uncorrupted and already glorified, with special honor."[9]

---

[6] Bede, Hom in Ev 9 (CCSL 122:64).

[7] See Wis 1: 6.

[8] Heb 4:12.

[9] Cf. Mechtild of Hackeborn, LSG I.6.

1. On the feast of blessed Elizabeth,[1] while they were singing "Ah, mother, behold us"[2] in the sequence, <Gertrud> was devoutly greeting that blessed woman and praying that she would **condescend to be mindful of her, unworthy though she was, by beholding her in God's presence** <The saint> replied, "I behold you in the mirror of eternal brightness,[3] in which there clearly shine all your deeds' intentions." And when she said, "Lady, do you not consider it a detraction from your praise that, in singing **your praises**, I am concentrating solely on that One from whom you freely received all those things for which you are praised, as if I were paying no attention to you?" She replied, "Not at all. In fact I find it infinitely **better**; indeed, by this you **delight me so much** the more sweetly, just as **strings or a pipe or a sonorous organ** pleases someone **incomparably** more than the bleating of sheep or lowing of cattle!"

[1] Saint Elizabeth of Hungary (1207–1231), who had been canonized in 1235. In the Middle Ages her feast fell on 19 November: see Ottó Gecser, *The Feast and the Pulpit: Preachers, Sermons and the Cult of St. Elizabeth of Hungary, 1235–ca. 1500* (Spoleto: Fondazione Centro Italiano di Studi sull'Alto Medioevo, 2012), 51.

[2] From the penultimate verse of *Gaude, Sion*, "Rejoice, Sion," a sequence for the feast of Saint Elizabeth widely used in Germany: see *Analecta Hymnica Medii Aevi*, ed. Clemens Blume (Leipzig: O. R. Reisland, 1922), 55:140, Nr. 120.

[3] See LDP IV.55.1, line 8.

<CHAPTER ONE HUNDRED AND NINETY **Not in LDP**>

1. Once, acutely distressed by a swelling on her head, she dreaded falling into impatience out of human weakness only too often and, devoutly trusting that by his loving-kindness the Lord would guard her from this fall into impatience, she was offering that pain in her head to the Lord God, for his eternal praise. The Lord, who by the power of his own love *calls those things that are not as those that are*,[1] seemed to place on her head a diadem distinguished by a most intricate engraved covering[2] of purest gold, with these words: "Look! as often as you would like to lessen your pain by some thought or word, and nonetheless entrust it to my divine will for my praise against your own wishes, so often that diadem of vivid verdure, flourishing in springtide loveliness and bearing sweetest fruit, will wonderfully assuage the thirst that cannot be satisfied[3] of my divine delight."

[1] Rom 4:17. See L 19.
[2] *celatura*, "covering," or more generally, "decoration."
[3] See LDP II.6.2, line 19.

1. On the feast of certain martyrs, while they were chanting those words in the second response at Matins, "They poured forth their glorious blood,"[1] she was taught by the Lord that just as blood, which is a loathsome substance in itself but, because it is shed for Christ, is honored in many different ways in holy Scripture, as it is called "sacred," "precious," "glorious," and so on, so in the same way the negligence of religious that results from obedience or brotherly love pleases God so much that it can rightly be called "glorious." For it is much safer for someone engaged in a duty enjoined on them by obedience or in a work of charity, such as visiting the sick, consoling the sorrowful, and the like, to commit some minor offences or sins of neglect in fear and trembling and wash them away immediately through humble contrition than, by arrogantly relying on their own opinion and despising charity and obedience to others, to please themselves in the strict observance of those duties that they have chosen.

---

[1] From the Common of Martyrs.

1. One day it happened that a Host fell out of the altar-hanging while it was being folded **up**, and there was some doubt as to whether or not it had been consecrated. When she was seeking the Lord's advice on this and, having learned from him, understood that the Host had not been consecrated, she was overjoyed, quite rightly, because such negligence had not been perpetrated. In her eagerness for the gain of God's praise, however, she said to the Lord, "Although your immense loving-kindness forestalled here the **commission** of such an affront towards you in the sacrament of the altar, nevertheless, since you, Lord of all, have so often undeservedly suffered similar affronts, not only from your enemies—that is, pagans and Jews—but also from your dearest friends—that is, the faithful redeemed by your precious blood and, *I tell you weeping*,[1] even on occasions by priests and religious—I shall never reveal that this Host was not consecrated, lest you should be cheated through me of some reparation."

2. She went on, "Grant, Lord God, that I may understand what reparation would be most acceptable for any offense. For even if I have to deploy all my strength, I **would** be eager and willing to **labor at it** for the praise and glory of your love." Then she understood that the Lord would **gladly** accept it if in honor of his most holy members she were to recite two hundred and **fifty** *Our Fathers*, and if the same number of works of charity were shown towards her neighbors, in

---

[1] Phil 3:18.

reverence for him who said, *As long as you did it to one of these my least [brethren], you did it to me,*[2] in union with that love through which God became man for our sakes. He would also accept the same number of rejections of vain and unprofitable pleasures, offered for his divine pleasure. How great and how unspeakable is the mercy and loving-kindness of the Lord our lover, who **in the same way** accepts such gifts so greatly from us, or rather rewards offerings that, if they were not offered, a suitable and painful vengeance would rightly follow!

[2] Matt 25:40.

< CHAPTER ONE HUNDRED AND NINETY-THREE =
LDP III.70 >

1. She was praying for a certain person, sorrowing because she had heard her say something impatiently, that is, why did God send her such troubles, which were inappropriate for her? The Lord said to her, "Ask that person what troubles are appropriate for her and tell her that since it is not possible to win the kingdom of heaven without any trouble, let her now choose for herself **from among troubles** what seems suitable for her and, when **it has** come her way, then let her practice patience!" In these words of the Lord she understood that the most dangerous kind of impatience is this, when it seems to someone that she would be very patient in other circumstances but cannot in those that the Lord sends. On the contrary, a person ought always to have faith that what the Lord sends is more useful, and when she fails to practice patience in that situation she should be humbled by that.

2. The Lord also added, as an endearment, "And what do you **lovingly** think about yourself? I **do not** send you, too, unsuitable burdens, **do I**?" She replied, "Not at all, my Lord. But I confess, and will confess it as long as I **will be** able to draw breath, that both in body and soul, both in good fortune and bad, you have provided for me in the most suitable fashion that no wisdom could ever have exceeded it, from the beginning to the end of the world, except you, sole Wisdom uncreated, my most sweet God, *reaching from end to end mightily and sweetly ordering all things.*"[1]

---

[1] Wis 8:1.

3. Then the Son, catching her up, **brought** her to God the Father, asking what profession she would make to him. Then she said, "I give you thanks, **Lord,** holy Father, as far as I can, through him who sits at your right hand, that I have received such magnificent gifts from your generosity. For I confidently recognize that no power could ever have exceeded this, except only for your divine **omnipotence** that invigorates and rules all created things with strength." From there he led her to the Holy Spirit, that she might make profession to his goodness. Then she said, "I **render** you thanks, dear Spirit Paraclete, through him who became human by your cooperation in the virgin womb, that you have in all things gone so gently before me, unworthy though I am, *in the blessings of* your freely given *sweetness.*[2] For no kindness would ever have done so, except only for your **inestimable** sweetness, in which lies hidden, from which proceeds, and with which at the same moment is received every good thing."

4. Then the Son of God, embracing her most lovingly and kissing her, said, "Therefore after this profession I take you into my special care, above every care that I owe to anyone by right of creation, of redemption, and of special election." From this she understood that when someone makes profession **in a similar way** to the divine goodness, entrusting and committing herself with thankfulness to his providence, then the Lord takes him into his special care, just as a superior is obliged to take greater care of his subject after his profession.

[2] Ps 20:4.

1. Once when interceding with the Lord for the soul of a patron, she saw him, having escaped the other torments that he had undergone, traveling along a pitch-black, very rough road. Whenever he tried to lift his foot to move forward, a sticky mass of melted, burning pitch seemed to pull him down to the ground so violently that only with the greatest difficulty and effort could he go forward a short distance, with lengthy delays. From this she perceived in spirit that that soul was tormented because of this offence: in his position as patron, which is very difficult to handle without deceit, he was found to be very far from above reproach. Further, she perceived that all those who are more eager in some official position to increase their own honor, comfort, and profit than God's praise and the salvation of their neighbors will be weighed down by a similar hindrance on the road to heaven, after the other sufferings that they deserved for their other sins, unless they diligently wipe it away by true penitence and worthy satisfaction in this life.

1. A certain person, informed in <Gertrud's> presence of the death of a **canon**, was so distressed by this that **she testified to the inner sorrow of her mind with bitter tears;** <Gertrud> **was so greatly moved by** compassion that she showed herself the more intent on **supplicating** for the soul of the dead person. **Then when she was praying she was** instructed **that what was said earlier, that is, that that person's death was announced in her presence, had happened by divine dispensation, so that that soul might be helped the more swiftly by such an occurrence.** When she said in response, "Lord, you could well have given me the grace to pray for that soul without that sense of compassion," the Lord replied, "I take special pleasure in this work when a person directs their natural feelings towards me with a good will **in accordance with the way that I have created and ordered human nature** and thus accomplishes a good work."

2. Afterwards, while she was praying **the more devoutly** for the soul we have **frequently** mentioned, he appeared as a toad, black as coal, and contorted from the immensity of its **unbearable** suffering. No torturer **or torment** was visible, but he was being inwardly tortured in each and every limb by those sins that each limb had committed. Then while she caressed her sweetest lover, importunate in the ploys of love, among other things, **as if rushing to the Lord's kisses and embraces**, she said to him, "Ah, my Lord, would you be willing to have mercy on that soul for my sake?" As if caressing her **and holding her chin**, the Lord **kindly** replied, "For love of you I am willing to have mercy not only on that soul, but also on a thousand

thousand souls!"[1] And the Lord added, "How do you wish me to bestow my mercy on him? Would you like me to forgive every sin and free him from every torment?" She replied, "Perhaps that does not advance your justice." The Lord replied: "It advances it very well, just as long as you ask me this with confidence. For as I am God who knows the future, I have made **him** fit for this in his agony with certain <good> intentions." Then she said, "Ah, *health of* my *soul,*[2] carry this out **according to what it could obtain from your mercy**, for thanks to your gift I do indeed have confidence in your loving-kindness." While she was saying this, the dead man's soul **seemed to rise** up promptly and, **as if standing** there in human form, laid aside all its blackness **like a garment**, **displaying** the whiteness of his <still> rough skin with great joy and thanksgiving, as if released from **everything**.

3. Nonetheless she understood that that rough skin still had to be purified to **dazzling** snowy whiteness before the soul would be **deemed** worthy to experience the presence **of the divine.** And that purification was taking place in that soul like this: as if **rust were being purified from iron by blows [and] pressure**. In addition, because of the habit of sinning—for he had persisted in his sins for a long time—his soul found it as hard to achieve whiteness as the human heart would find it hard to bear its body remaining stretched out for a whole year exposed **to** the sun to be bleached. While she was astonished at how that soul could be joyful amid such troubles **that had been kept back until then**, she also learned that souls that die burdened by such great and varied sins cannot be helped by the usual intercessions of the church until, purified **for a while, when God finally has mercy they can** put off that **weight** of guilt that prevents them from sharing in the **usual** intercessions of the church, which continually rain down on those being purified like most saving dew and salve of delight, or draught of sweetest refreshment.

---

[1] Possibly this is the origin of the story about the prayer associated with Gertrud that is said to release a thousand souls from purgatory every time it is recited.

[2] See Sir 30:15.

4. Then giving thanks **to the Lord for the mercy shown that soul,** she asked the Lord, "Make known to me, most loving Lord, by what labors or prayers a person could win from your mercy the release of the soul **of their dead friend** from this terrible burden that obstructs intercessions; for I saw this soul **as joyful** as if it had been moved from the depths of hell to the throne of glory, in the heights of joy, just because this <burden> had been laid aside. Indeed, I am now to see him benefiting from the church's intercessions that make him unceasingly joyful." The Lord replied: "Only through **the effect** of love such as you felt at the time[3] can **you [perform]**[4] any labors or recite any prayers to afford **any** soul such great assistance. And just as no one can do this by themselves, except by my gift, so such help cannot be rendered souls after death unless they have deserved it by **my** special grace in this life **by special good works**. Nonetheless, you should know that with the passage of time this unbearable burden is alleviated by friends' prayers or labors, if performed with loyal intention, and <souls> are released the more quickly or the more slowly depending on how persistent are the efforts of the faithful **laboring for their release**, by more loving devotion, on their behalf, and also on what they earned in this life **by certain good works**."

5. When the soul felt relief from the prayer **of the faithful**, he stretched out his hands to God and prayed that **he** would accept **this** in the power of that love because of which he had come down from heaven **for him** and undergone death, and, in accordance with that, he would reward those <benefactors> when **it would be most profitable**. Then the Lord, as a sign that he had heard this prayer, seemed to accept a single penny from the hands of the soul, and put it aside to be paid back as a reward to those who were praying.

---

[3] That is, the impulse of compassion recorded in para. 1 above.
[4] LDP; *om.* L.

<CHAPTER ONE HUNDRED AND NINETY-SIX =
LDP V.9.1–2>

1. Since, as Scripture witnesses, *by what things* someone *sins, by the same also*[1] they are punished, and conversely in what things someone does good **or endures something**, in the same also they are rewarded, we shall add this account for the profit of our readers. For there were two women sick at the same time; **the first** of them was **so obviously** consumptive **that there was no hope at all of her recovering.** Because of this she was treated by those who served her with more tender **love**, as seemed appropriate. **But** because the nature of the **second woman's** sickness was unknown, and so she seemed less needy, she was not given the same loving care. But as human judgments are so often fallible, the one who was expected to recover died more than a month before the other. She had **come to** her final days sanctified, rather than purified, by much patience and devotion. But the benign loving-kindness of our lover, not allowing even the smallest speck of a stain in the bride so [dear][2] to him, purified in her an unwillingness from time to time to make her confession. Although her conscience was not troubled by any sin, she neglected to seek absolution through the priest's words, at least from specks of venial sin, without which human life is impossible: sometimes she pretended to be asleep when **he** was there, so as not to speak to him.

And so, **as I said before,** when the time had come that she was about to enter the marriage chamber of her heavenly bridegroom with joy and exultation, her faithful lover first washed away that stain of

[1] See Wis 11:17.
[2] *dilecta* LDP; *electa* L.

hers in this way. For she anxiously asked that a confessor should be **summoned** to her, and then she immediately **gave up** the power of speech. Thence she was seized by **a certain** fear that she would have to be purified after death for her neglect of confession, and thus through that same fear she was purified. Hence the beloved of the heavenly bridegroom arrived at the celestial marriage chamber with inestimable glory **and jubilation**, *all lovely, with not a spot*[3] clinging to her: on this subject **the Lord in his most merciful lovingkindness revealed to his servants certain things that should be recalled with devout wonder**, one of which I shall expound here for the edification of our readers.

When she had been brought before the throne of the King of Glory, he endowed her with this special privilege: he coaxed her with most delightful gentleness to take each of those rewards that he bestowed on her, just as a most sweet mother **might** coax her only child who is sick to take the medicine by which he would recover **complete** health. He did this because she had been afflicted with sorrow from time to time from hearing her fellow invalid being coaxed, although to her they spoke more sternly.

2. After this, the Lord added, speaking to that soul, "Tell me, my daughter, what would you like me to do with the soul of your companion **on her death**, and what kind of consolation do you wish me to bestow on her? For just as on earth **it was left for her to decide** what refreshment she **could have**, and you sometimes had to share it with her even though you would have chosen something else, so now it will depend on you what kind of blessing I bestow on her." She replied, "Ah, sweetest **one**, bless her in every way just as you have blessed me, for I cannot think of any way that would please me **more greatly.**" The Lord most kindly assented to these words and declared that he would **carry this out**.

---

[3] See Song 4:7.

1. Now **some days** later, when the other woman had also died, she too appeared on the day following her death, wonderfully adorned, as was appropriate, because during her entire life she had possessed a most innocent simplicity, and in addition **had been** very devout and attentive to the strict observance of the Order. Nonetheless it was understood that there was still a stain that had to be purified in her: in her sickness, as was **said** earlier, she used to enjoy certain things that she did not need, that is, gifts and consolation from her friends. And so **the problem of** this stain was shown being purified in this way: she was as it were standing in a doorway facing the throne of the King of Glory, who appeared *beautiful* in form[1] **above the countenance of angels**[2] and most sweet and lovable beyond all human understanding. **And because that most kindly king so sweetly** caressed the aforesaid soul, **she seemed to be, as it were,** almost fainting with desire, **since she so ardently desired to be united with him**; but there was no way that she could come any closer, as if a nail in that doorway were catching on some of her clothing, from which she could not **free** herself. And when <Gertrud> saw this and prayed for her out of compassion, the divine mercy released her from this problem.

2. Then **by God's mercy** she asked the Lord, "Since that soul has friends among us who are particularly close to you, I am astonished that **it seems to me** it was only **through** my prayers that you set this

---

[1] See Ps 44:3.
[2] See LSG IV.35.1, lines 8–9, and Bernard, SC 28.2 (CF 7:89; SBOp 1:193).

problem aside, although I would be quite sure that they too would have poured out devout prayers for her and would also have been sure to be heard by your loving-kindness." The Lord replied, "I have most certainly heard the prayers of my intimate friends for that soul, and have done so more kindly and blessed that soul more greatly than they could believe, even if they had seen me conveying this soul from purgatory to heaven at their prayers with their own eyes. But I did not make that problem known to them because I wanted to dispel it at your prayers. And so they did not pray for her in the way that you did."

Then she said, "How could this be done, as you assured me that you wished to bless that soul in all respects as the one who died before her, even though the latter had served **you** longer in the habit of religion, and in addition had **abounded** in certain virtues **that the former seemed not yet to have achieved**, and moreover was brought before you with greater glory without any problem?" The Lord replied, "My justice always remains constant, because *every person receives their own reward according to their own labor*.[3] Nor can it ever come about that he who has deserved less should receive more than he who has deserved more, unless certain circumstances, such as superior intention, more strenuous struggle, more fervent love, or the like have enhanced their work. But my generous loving-kindness adds to the reward that is deserved, and also sometimes because of the prayers of the faithful or other meritorious circumstances. Consequently I have blessed them both alike in this way, for I have given both of them more than they deserve."

3. Since **love of earthly things** is indeed a problem that should be avoided, after this she saw that same blessed soul again, not yet completely released from her problem. For she appeared standing before the **King of celestial glory's** throne, and she now desired, with the same desire with which she had earlier desired to reach **him** when she seemed to be caught in the doorway, to rush into his embraces and be satisfied by the kisses of the one who is *beautiful above*

---

[3] See 1 Cor 3:8.

the sons of men,[4] *on whom the angels desire to look.*[5] But she was held fast by the same problem, as if unable to bend or turn. When she was again released **by prayers** after a while, she finally appeared, having not **yet** received perfect glory, but the Lord seemed to be holding a crown wonderfully embellished in his hands, and when he placed it on her, she would receive with it perfect glory.

4. She who saw this asked the Lord, "Surely, Lord, it cannot be that a soul is tormented in your kingdom by such anticipation?" The Lord replied, "She is not tormented, but she anticipates the consummation with joy, just as a girl who sees in her mother's hands pieces of jewelry with which she **is to** be adorned the next day at a feast anticipates that day with joy."

5. After this, that soul was gazing upon that person who had poured out prayers for her, and thanked her with great affection. To this <Gertrud> replied, "Although you had always been quite close to me, nonetheless when you were sick you seemed to me to **welcome it the less** if I sometimes reproved you." The soul responded, "For that reason your prayer has greatly benefited me, for it was poured out more disinterestedly in love for God's sake."

[4] Ps 44:3.
[5] 1 Pet 1:12.

Scriptural Index

Citations are identified by Prol[ogue], Pref[ace], or chapter and note number.

Gen

1:1	48, n. 4
1:26	Prol., n. 75
2:8	134, n. 1
2:23	6, n. 6
4:9	138, nn. 1, 2
9:12	72, n. 1
18:27	Prol., n. 98; 169, n. 1
22:11	138, n. 6
22:15	138, n. 7
27:27	180, n. 5
43:30	Prol., n. 227
49:21	Prol., n. 124

Exod

1:14	115, n. 6
33:20	Prol., n. 155

Deut

4:24	Prol., n. 119; 20, n. 2
11:24	188, n. 5
32:42	46, n. 2

1 Sam

2:3	Prol., n. 146
14:27	Prol., n. 121
18:18	176, n. 1

1 Kgs

8:44	108, n. 2
10:1-2	108, n. 1
19:7	Prol., n. 26

Neh

8:10	79, n. 2

Esth

1:6	Prol., nn. 18, 19
2:12	85, n. 2
7:3	149, n. 2
15:11	175, n. 1

Job

4:12	Prol., n. 108
4:16	Prol., n. 109
9:3	7, n. 3
10:3	106, n. 3
10:8	155, n. 1
13:15	110, n. 8
17:3	76, n. 2
30:15	176, n. 2

Pss

1:3	Prol., n. 13
2:7	15, n. 1